The Society of Terror

The Society of Terror

Inside the Dachau and Buchenwald Concentration Camps

Paul Martin Neurath

edited by
Christian Fleck and Nico Stehr

with an afterword by Christian Fleck, Albert Müller, and Nico Stehr

Paradigm Publishers
Boulder • London

Copyright © 2005 by Paradigm Publishers

Published in the United States by Paradigm Publishers, 3360 Mitchell Lane, Suite E, Boulder, Colorado 80301 USA.

Paradigm Publishers is the trade name of Birkenkamp & Company, LLC, Dean Birkenkamp, President and Publisher.

Library of Congress Cataloging-in-Publication Data

Neurath, Paul Martin, 1911–
The society of terror : inside the Dachau and Buchenwald concentration camps / Paul Martin Neurath ; edited by Christian Fleck and Nico Stehr ; with an afterword by Christian Fleck, Albert Müller, and Nico Stehr. — 1st ed.
p. cm.
Includes bibliographical references and index.
ISBN 1-59451-094-6 (hc : alk. paper) — ISBN 1-59451-095-4 (pb : alk. paper)
1. Dachau (Concentration camp) 2. Buchenwald (Concentration camp)
3. Germany—Social conditions—1933–1945. 4. Holocaust, Jewish (1939–1945)—Germany—Dachau—Personal narratives. 5. Concentration camps.
I. Fleck, Christian, 1954– II. Stehr, Nico. III. Title.
D805.5.D33N49 2005
940.53'1853224—dc22

2005004916

Designed and Typeset by Straight Creek Bookmakers.

09 08 07 06 05
1 2 3 4 5

Contents

Part Two: The Society

To Lucie
To Oswald
To Franz

Lucie helped me through and out of hell. She did everything an outsider could do for a prisoner. She carried on the enervating negotiations over visas and ships' passages, tax declarations and exit visas, and went through all the chicaneries that were connected with emigration from a Nazi country. She undertook all the humiliating trips to Gestapo and other Nazi offices that were necessary to gain the release of a prisoner. And all this she did with such care and with such spirit that I, in my utterly helpless position, never lost confidence that if anything could be done at all, she would certainly do it. I could hardly have come through without her.

Oswald Richter was one of the leading lawyers of the Social Democratic Party in Vienna. He was an old friend of my family, and during the Dollfuss era from 1934 to 1938, when I lived alone in Vienna, he opened his house to me and treated me like a son. He fought fascism from its very beginning. When Dollfuss destroyed Austrian democracy in 1934 and the workers took up the underground struggle for freedom, Oswald Richter kept defending them before the fascist courts. When the Nazis conquered Austria, he was immediately put into a concentration camp. We were there together from the first day until he died on January 2, 1939.

Franz Steinberg was an unknown student from Berlin—a tall young man with the innocent face of a baby, a dreamer who belonged more to heaven than to earth, but certainly not to hell. He liked to talk to me about Virgil and Catullus and to meditate about God and the good in man. One day, his dreamy eyes and his thoughts far, far away, he asked all of a sudden, "Say, do you believe in eternal justice?" I shrugged my shoulders— "Look around you. Maybe you will find it." "But it is just because of all this that I am asking. Somebody has to avenge all this sometime." "Listen boy, if you won't avenge it yourself, nobody is going to do it for you." "Maybe you are right. But a man can die before that." "Now don't be silly. You are not going to die tomorrow. And if you should die tomorrow, I will avenge you." Franz Steinberg died the next day.

And don't be mistaken. This
is not a prison, nor is it a
penitentiary. This is concentration
camp Dachau. That makes
a difference. You will soon see
the difference.

From the speech Baranofsky,
former commander of
concentration camp Dachau,
used to give to newcomers.

Prelude

It was Sunday night, March 13, 1938, forty-eight hours after Chancellor Schuschnigg resigned and gave his farewell speech over the radio, thirty-five hours after the arrival of the first German army detachments in Vienna.[1]

I was busy burning the anti-Nazi part of my library. The stove was glowing deep red. I tore up book after book and threw them into the flames. The room was hot and smoky, and I had nothing on but a dark gym suit and sneakers.

Two men in civilian clothes with rifles on their backs came running across the courtyard. "Let's cover the upper exit too," I heard one of them say. I suspected that they were searching the house for hidden weapons, and I thought I'd better not have them find me amidst my auto-da-fe. I left the room and went out to the door. In the doorway an SS man with a gun in his hand stopped me. "Heil Hitler, where are you going?" "Oh, just next door, to visit a friend." "Hm, you'd better wait a while." "Why, what's the matter?" "Oh, nothing in particular, just a little interlude." He took me to the two SS cars outside the door. He searched my pockets and took away my keys. Otherwise, he was quite friendly and offered me a cigarette. He kept chatting with me, but all the time his gun was pointing at me. He told me how they were out to catch their enemies, one by one. I expressed my admiration and wished him good luck in finding all of them. I tried to appear calm and undisturbed and innocent. Excitement and the cold air made it difficult for me to refrain from shivering.

---

1. Editor's note: On the evening of March 11, 1938, Austrian Chancellor Kurt Schuschnigg announced over the radio that his government would step down and hand over power to a pro-Nazi interim government to avoid violent clashes between members of the two German nations. As a consequence, the German army invaded Austria the following morning and was welcomed by Austrian Nazis and huge crowds.

"And now we are after one whose name is Neuman or something like that." That sounded ominous. I did not know of any Neuman in the house. I was almost certain that his companions inside were looking for me.

On a balcony above appeared Mrs. Merwarth. I hardly knew her; she just happened to live in the same house. "For God's sake, what's the matter? They are shooting in the house!" Well, if they were shooting, they couldn't be after me. There was nobody in my room.

My friend with the gun quieted her, "Take it easy, there won't be any shooting. Must be some sort of mistake." But immediately after that, the whole gang came out of the door, carrying their rifles with the butts up. "Where is that son-of-a-bitch? Where has that damned dog gone to? The light in his room was on a moment ago. We'll dash his brains out when we get him. We'll beat hell out of him. He can't be far away." (I was exactly two yards away from the speaker, and one yard from the gun.) They had smashed my door with the butts of their rifles—that was what had sounded like shooting.

They put their heads together, deliberating. The chieftain called up to Mrs. Merwarth, "Say what do you know about this Neurath?" "Well nothing definite. He is said to be a doctor." (I had received my law degree three months before.) Again they deliberated.

I saw my chance and asked my friend with the gun in a most innocent voice, "Well, what about me now?" "You can go wherever you like." He handed me back my keys, and I went "wherever I liked."

I had taken about ten steps at a moderate speed, when all of a sudden Mrs. Merwarth yelled, "There he is, that's Neurath!"—and with a wild jump I took off. In an instant I had the whole gang after me swinging their guns and rifles. Some of them took the cars, the others ran. I expected them to shoot at any moment. I jumped up and down so as not to offer an easy target. With a mad dash, I swung around the corner; one more dash—and I had vanished. I knew how to get through the backyards and staircases, while the cars had to take the long way around the buildings.

At the next corner we met again. They were scrutinizing passersby with the searchlight of their car. I lounged against a wall, hands in pockets, legs crossed. They turned the light on me, apparently thought that I was just out for a stroll, and drove on.

As soon as they were out of sight, I ran toward the railroad. I climbed a fence, two yards high with barbed wire on top, jumped down on the other side and ran uphill toward the tracks. There I ran into a railroad man. Furiously and in great haste I yelled at him: "Have you seen a man

climbing over this fence?" "No, I haven't seen anybody." "But he must
have come over this fence, there is no other way for him. He just gave us
the slip down the street." "I haven't seen anybody." "But man, in times
like these you've got to watch out!" "I just left my room …" "You are a
damned idiot!" And I raced on searching for the man who had jumped
over the fence.

Across the tracks, over a similar fence on the other side, across courtyards, roofs, a firewall, until all of a sudden I found myself two flights
above the street, with no way down. Now I had to make the whole way
back again—the roofs, the firewall, the courtyards, the fence. Walking
along the tracks I approached a station. There were many lights on, and
I preferred to leave the tracks. I climbed again over the blessed fence
(for the fourth time that evening), passed through gardens and backyards, until I finally found myself on a side street.

I went to an old aunt who lived in the neighborhood. There I got
dressed, after a manner. "After a manner" because the good old uncle,
who had died years ago and whose outfit I was now wearing, was a head
shorter than I. Everything was too short and too small—The jacket, the
pants, the coat, the underwear. Worst of all were the shoes. They were
about an inch and a half too short. I couldn't get my heels into them.

My aunt lived on the outskirts of Vienna, and behind the last houses I
took a right turn across large meadows and into the forests. I wandered
all night. In the morning I took a nap in a ditch, then up again, north-
ward, towards Czechoslovakia. Having no identification papers with me
I did not dare to take a train, because I suspected that the passengers
would be searched (which turned out to be true).

A number of incidents followed. Peasants stopped me and wanted to
turn me over to the police. I talked them out of this notion. An innkeeper
got suspicious and admonished seriously, "If you are fugitive, you'd
better confess it right away. You wouldn't be the first one I handed over to
the police at this place." And I answered sheepishly, "I would be the
damnedest fool if I did."

My feet were worn raw. My heels hurt so much that I had to walk
barefoot. After two days I came to a town where I could buy new shoes.
In this town I bought my first food. From there I took a bus for sixty
miles.

Altogether I spent four days and nights in the open. There was hoar-
frost every night. When I took a nap, the ground around me was white
with frost needles; so was my coat. Only the spot under me was dark.
My hands and face began to swell. But I drew closer to the border.

Thursday night I expected to cross into Czechoslovakia. Before a little frontier village I went into a field, waiting for the cover of darkness. Suddenly a car came out of the village toward my hiding place. I thought that it was running on a road, and figured that in this lonely village a car meant either the Germans or the Austrian Nazis. I was afraid that if they should discover me crouched behind a tree, they would immediately arrest me. I preferred to try my luck with calmness and freshness, by simply asking them for the way. When I stepped toward the "road," they turned their searchlight on me and came straight toward me, so that I was blinded by the glare. Only when they stopped about one yard in front of me did I realize that they were not on a road but had come across the field. It was clear they had come for me. The game was up.

One of them jumped out of the car screaming, "Halt, halt, hands up!" and put a rifle with a mounted bayonet to my chest. I still remember that bayonet, prodding my chest. I remember seeing the hills two miles away, which meant freedom over in Czechoslovakia. And I remember the man at the other end of the rifle, excited, thrilled by the experience, shouting, yelling, asking a lot of unintelligible questions. I told him that I understood the game was up anyway, and he might as well stop asking questions. He kept on. I began to laugh. That almost drove him crazy. I must admit that I did not laugh because I thought it was funny. I laughed because it was the only way to teach them that we are not afraid of them. The man did not have much sense of humor; he yelled and shoved his rifle so that it almost pierced my coat.

The driver of the car came and asked more reasonable questions. I gave short explanations. They took me into the car. On the way back he leaned out of the window and shouted across the field, "Go home, go home, we've got him!"—and the message went from man to man, resounding and re-echoing from all sides, "They have got him ... have got him!" These were Austrian peasants, helping the Nazis catch fugitives. Later on I found that a peasant woman had seen me walking into the field and had notified the storm troopers, who were lying in ambush along the border. "There is a stranger in the fields, perhaps a fugitive." And they had manned their car and come out to chase the game.

First, I was brought before the commander of the storm troopers. After a few minutes, he and I were involved in an excited political dispute. Later in the evening, he took me down to the little town of Raabs-an-der-Thaya. He handed me over to the police.

Next morning the police inspector drew up a short report about my arrest; the commander of the storm troopers came to sign it. As he was about to leave the room, I called him back. "Just a moment please. You have treated me surprisingly decently. What is your name?" "What do you need my name for?" "Well, you see, today *I* am the prisoner, but things might change sometime, and it might be good to remember who has been decent." He gazed at me in surprise, shook his head, muttered, "You begin to hope early!" "When else should I begin?" "All right, my name is Hofstetter." He came back and shook hands with me. Then he left the room.

In Raabs they kept me in solitary confinement for two weeks. I felt lonely in my cell from the very beginning, and on the first morning I drew up a list of 300 songs and kept shouting them cheerfully. The jailer came downstairs. "The judge sends you word not to sing so loudly. He can't conduct his court this way." I was not mistreated in this prison, but they starved me half to death. However, the regular inmates liked me and provided me with food.

One morning I was transported to Vienna. I had a heavy iron chain around my wrists, beautifully polished but otherwise uncomfortable and secured by a big lock. The accompanying police officer was polite and inoffensive. In the railway car he let me have a seat by the window, and I had a last look at spring entering Austria.

At noon we arrived in Vienna, and at police headquarters I was handed over to the Gestapo, on March 30, 1938.

I was put in a cell with about thirty prisoners. Everyone kept continually guessing about the possible reason for his incarceration. The best guess perhaps was that of the 72-year-old owner of a paper mill—"Because I happen to own something." But nobody knew anything and nobody was ever told.

Without any hearing or trial, I was sent to concentration camp Dachau on April 1, 1938. I was one of 150 prisoners, the first batch of Austrians to be sent to a German concentration camp.

Paul Neurath

PART ONE

THE SCENE

Chapter 1

From Civil War to Organized Terror

When the National Socialists came to power in Germany in 1933, there arose a peculiar state of civil war. One side fought furiously, backed by the powerful support of the government, which gave freedom to act and promised legalization of every violation of the law. The other side submitted without any attempt at physical resistance.

Thousands and thousands of people were arrested. Most of them were active Social Democrats or Communists or members of trade unions. Others belonged to various conservative parties that had not yet lined up behind the Nazis. A great many who did not belong to any particular group were arrested for personal reasons.

New laws made it possible to arrest practically anyone on the mere suspicion or assertion that he was "against" the new government. In this way millions of people became liable to persecution. The actual selection of those to be arrested lay in the hands of local party organizations and police departments. Guided by the "revolutionary spirit of the National Socialistic uprising," they translated, by virtue of power, the romantic party slogan of the "Night of the Long Knives" into a bloody reality of imprisonment, torture, and death.

Cruelty and revenge led the field, and the most horrible crimes and atrocities took place in what the Nazis were fond of calling the "most

3

bloodless revolution in history." Reports of the way the Nazis mistreated their victims shook the conscience of men all over the world.

Soon all the prisons were overcrowded, and temporary concentration camps were opened. Most of them were located in abandoned factories, for example, an old brewery in Oranienburg near Berlin and an ammunition factory in Dachau near Munich. But as the stream of new prisoners continued, the temporary camps became too small, and new ones had to be constructed.

The new camps were either erected on the sites of the old ones, as was the case in Dachau, or they were completely new constructions, as was Buchenwald. The work was done by the prisoners, with the most primitive tools and a minimum of mechanical power. It was slave work in the literal meaning of the word, done by emaciated slaves who were driven by slave drivers. The resemblance of these working conditions to the records in the Bible is striking. A fellow prisoner asked me on one of the first days, "Do you remember how we built those pyramids?"

As the camps grew larger and larger, they were combined with military camps of the SS Verfügungstruppe, the elite guard of the National Socialist party. The young recruits underwent regular military training, and serving as guards in the concentration camp was part of their daily routine. Several purposes were thus fulfilled at the same time. The prisoners were kept busy, new camps were erected, and the Reich did not need to employ special guards for these camps, since the SS recruits had to be trained anyway.

One more purpose was also served. The SS Verfügungstruppe were organized primarily for the purpose of providing special military troops able to suppress potential civilian revolts. These troops not only had to form an excellent military body but also had to be possessed by a spirit of utter ruthlessness. Doing duty as a guard in a concentration camp seemed to be the best way of creating this state of mind.

It might be mentioned that whenever a new country was occupied by the German army, the SS Verfügungstruppe were sent there to "restore order." SS Verfügungstruppe from concentration camp Dachau were sent to Austria in March 1938, and troops from concentration camp Buchenwald were sent to Czechoslovakia (Sudeten district) after the Munich agreement of September 1938.

The concentration camp was originally organized as a political institution. As the years passed, its character changed somewhat. The various offices of public safety, such as the Gestapo and the police, began to send their prisoners to the camps without trial or sentence. Later on it became customary that prisoners who had served their time in penitentiaries were not released but were committed to concentration camps instead. This was particularly true of political prisoners, professional criminals, and Jews (regardless of what crime they might have committed). Political and social service institutions added new groups of prisoners. Whenever one of these institutions wanted to get rid of a person without trial in court, whenever they saw fit to arrest people by the hundreds of thousands, they sent them to concentration camps.

Eventually all sorts of prisoners were thrown together: political and nonpolitical, guilty and guiltless, Communists and dissident National Socialists, Jews and Gentiles, ministers and murderers, pimps and secretaries of state, vagabonds and Jehovah's Witnesses, professional criminals and homosexuals, "asocials" and gypsies.

Thus the concentration camp changed from a temporary institution of civil war to an integral part of the internal power apparatus of the Reich. The functions which it fulfilled were as regular as those fulfilled by penitentiaries and prisons. There existed, however, one principal difference between the court-penitentiary and the Gestapo-concentration camp mechanism. The task of the ordinary mechanism of justice is the prosecution of individual violators of the law. The defendant is accused in court by the prosecutor. During the trial, he is sentenced according to rules, which are themselves part of the law, only if it has been established that the law has been broken. Penitentiary and prison are then the executive organs of justice.

The main task of the Gestapo was to watch and prosecute groups that the government considered dangerous and undesirable. The individual was prosecuted not so much for actual crimes committed but for his alleged or real membership in a group. To be a Socialist, a Communist, a Jew, or a Jehovah's Witness made a person liable to prosecution before the question of his personal activity was even raised. The Gestapo, as part of the power apparatus of the Reich, was the representative of political concepts and raison d'etat. The concentration camp was its executive organ.

The Gestapo had other functions too as a participant in the struggle for power going on inside Germany. It represented a certain group within the National Socialist Party, fighting other groups there, and at the same time it represented the power of the party against other forces, especially against the army. There were always a certain number of prisoners in the concentration camps who were there because they happened to stand in the Gestapo's way in the internal struggle for power—members

5

of the Röhm group, high party officials, followers of Otto Strasser, and others.

But the vast majority of all political prisoners in the German concentration camps were there as victims of the battle the Gestapo fought in the name of the Third Reich against its opponents. And the vast majority of all prisoners, irrespective of the "crime" that had brought them there, belonged to groups which the Reich wanted to get rid of—political opponents, professional criminals, so-called "asocials," and Jews.

The difference in function between the court-penitentiary and the Gestapo-concentration camp mechanism also produced a difference in treatment and procedure. To the Gestapo, the person arrested was not a "defendant"; usually he was not even "accused." In most cases he was not even informed of the reason for his incarceration. One morning the Gestapo would bang on his door or come to his place of work, he would be taken away without further explanation, and soon he would find himself in a concentration camp. He could only guess why he was there. And he was never told how long he would stay there or whether or not he would ever be released.

The treatment in penitentiaries and prisons is based upon two fundamental necessities—to enforce the discipline of the institution and to prevent riot and escape. The prisoner who complies with the disciplinary rules and does not plot escape is by and large left alone.

The treatment in concentration camps was also based upon these two fundamental necessities, but in addition to that it served another purpose. The concentration camp as a whole had the function of spreading terror throughout the Reich. The whole German people were to be kept under control by the fear of being put into a concentration camp. Therefore the concentration camp had to be a veritable hell, both in reality and in the imagination of the German people, feared and dreaded by everyone. The SS proved itself extremely able to create this hell and keep it going.

It was forbidden to talk about what one had seen and experienced in a concentration camp. Thus the camp was surrounded with a veil of mystery. On the other hand, enough information leaked out about the tortures the prisoners had to undergo to excite the imagination of the average citizens outside. Only with utmost horror and fear did they think and talk about this place.

In the beginning the treatment of the prisoners was prompted by a situation that was similar to civil war. Personal feelings and personal hatred played a much larger part than they did later on. Every guard knew at least a few prisoners personally or by name and therefore considered every prisoner his personal enemy. The guards had grown up during the Weimar Republic; many of them even before the First World War. Whatever evil had happened to them during the inflation after the war or during the depression up to 1933, they blamed somehow on their prisoners. Were not the prisoners representatives of the hated Weimar Republic? Or even worse, were they not Communists who had prepared a revolution against the Third Reich? Had not thousands of them been arrested because they had burned the Reichstag in Berlin? Each and every mistreatment and abuse was considered a just and insufficient punishment for these criminals.

Later on, when the concentration camp became a regular institution and ordinary recruits were used as guards, this picture changed. The new guards were youngsters who did not know or did not remember the good or evil of the Weimar Republic. Guards in Buchenwald in 1939, by that time 18 years old, had been children of 12 when Hitler came to power. They had no personal knowledge of the political parties of the democratic era. Their noncommissioned officers, who were then 24 to 26 years old, had been young men of 18 or 20 in 1933, and politics to them had been a romantic game.

The young men therefore were taught to hate the prisoners as members of dangerous groups who had set out to imperil the National Socialist state.

The camps grew bigger and bigger, until they actually became small cities. In the summer of 1938, Dachau held 5,500 prisoners; in the fall of 1938 Buchenwald held 10,000, to whom were added another 11,000 during the pogroms of November 1938. Sachsenhausen near Berlin held 18,000 by that time, and there were a great number of smaller camps with 1,000 to 5,000 prisoners each.

The SS camps grew larger too. There were about 6,000 SS men in Dachau in 1938, and about 2,500 in Buchenwald.

All this made for rather impersonal relations between guards and prisoners. The guards no longer knew their charges personally. Their duty had changed from revenge to daily routine. The number of prisoners had become too large to allow for personal treatment or mistreatment. Terror and persecution, therefore, became more organized, more directed against whole groups—either working groups or groups that lived together in one room, or against a whole barrack. Maltreatment assumed the form of punishment for crimes and misdemeanors committed against the disciplinary rules of the camp. The prisoner's previous life or crime no longer played a large role.

The whole system became a mixture of personal and group responsibilities. No prisoner ever knew whether he was going to be punished next because he himself had been loafing or because someone else was "lazy"; perhaps he did not even know that the other man existed.

This created complete insecurity.

Personal maltreatment by the guards became in part replaced by "reports" filed against prisoners for any kind of misdemeanor. The consequent maltreatment was meted out as "punishment" by the commander and executed by the guards.

"Punishment," or organized maltreatment, consisted of a few ordinary and a number of extraordinary punishments, practically all of them corporal ones. The dominating features in this system were the "twenty-five," where the victim was lashed to a stand and given twenty-five heavy blows with sticks, and the "tree," where the victim was hanged by his wrists on a pole or on an actual tree, usually for an hour at a time.

But to a great extent, direct maltreatment by the guards on the spot and without any intermediate "report" and "sentence" remained in existence.

The individual prisoner lost his personality and his importance. He became simply a number. This became especially true from 1938 on, when every prisoner had his prison number sewed on his clothes. This augmented the common insecurity, because now the guard no longer had to ask the prisoner for his name in order to file a report. There were guards who amused themselves by filing reports without informing the prisoners, or by threatening the prisoners, without filing the reports.

As the treatment became more and more impersonal, the differences in the treatment accorded the various groups dwindled. Only a few main groups were distinguishable by color-signs, which the prisoners wore on their jackets and trousers. Red, green, black, yellow, and a few other colors, marked a man as a political prisoner, a professional criminal, an "asocial," a Jew, or something else; the exact meaning of these color-signs changed as time passed. Any differences in treatment usually corresponded to events occurring outside of the camp, as when the waves of political passion rose high against the Jews. Then the Jews in the camps were subjected to more severe treatment. But even then it was directed more against whole groups than against individual Jews. During the pogroms in November 1938, all Jews had their rations cut, all Jews were forbidden treatment in the infirmary, all Jews were deprived of meals on Sunday, and so forth.

Gradually, the administrators of the camps found out that they alone could not master the situation by day and night. Some discipline had to be maintained in the barracks and at work, even if the guards were not present. A system was set up consisting of "seniors" in rooms and barracks, and "capos" (foremen) at work, who were put in charge of work and discipline. They did not work themselves but were held responsible for the efficiency and good behavior of their subordinates. They could report their subordinates for punishment, or they could mistreat them as they pleased in exactly the same manner as the SS guards did.

Work and daily life became more and more routinized, subject to a bewildering complex of regulations and regimentations. The complicated system of dos and don'ts was made the backbone of the system of report and punishment.

More and more functions in the daily routine of the camp administration were carried out by prisoners. Prisoners were put in charge of the clothing department, the barber shop, the infirmary, and many other special jobs, all, of course, under the supervision of SS officers. But this supervision was not always exercised as much as it was intended to be, and a certain degree of autonomy developed that gave strong support to the growth of a sense of community among the prisoners, which developed beneath the surface.

Thus the concentration camp seemed more and more like a hell smoothly organized from top to bottom, where every step the prisoners made, every torture they had to undergo was calculated, and where no man was mistreated and killed without the formal or informal consent of the devils in the higher positions.

But under the surface, the society of the prisoners grew to a life of its own, a life whose frame was set by the natural and administrative conditions of the camp, but whose human and social content was greatly influenced by the social, political, and religious background of the men who were living it.

Chapter 2

First Impressions

When a newcomer first enters a concentration camp, it looks completely different to him from what he had imagined it would be. He may have thought of it as a sort of super-prison, with thick stone walls and a great number of dark cells, where black-clad Gestapo officers would torture him by the most refined third-degree methods to make him confess his secret activities and ideas.

What he actually finds is a sort of military camp. He will usually not be put into a dark cell or solitary confinement, but rather into a light barrack together with hundreds of fellow prisoners. The SS men, who are soldiers in field-grey uniforms with skulls and crossbones on cap and collar, beat him without worrying about refinements of torture, and they do so without asking questions and without caring what his answers might be.

He discovers that life can be made unbearable by regulations and conditions which lack the romanticism that the free world is accustomed to ascribe to the sufferings of its heroes. He finds mistreatment and abuse standardized to such a degree that he comes to look upon it as boring, unless it happens to be he himself or his best friend who is suffering under it.

In the beginning, however, each new experience is an isolated incident, and his new world looks like an amazing kaleidoscope, changing shape and color every minute. The only part of the picture that is stable is its frame—the concrete wall and the barbed wire.

When the prisoner enters the camp, he either has already undergone terrific mistreatment on the train, or he is subjected to violent mistreatment as soon as he leaves the prison van. He is immediately beaten into a state of mind that leaves no chance for systematic observation of his surroundings. Driven by constant bullying and blows, he is rushed through a well-organized routine—undressed, fingerprinted, numbered, registered, given prisoner's clothing, has his hair clipped off, and so forth. After that he and the other newcomers are lined up on the roll-call square where they stand until after evening roll call, when he is taken to the barrack which from then on is to be his "home."

Perhaps the first thing that strikes him when he enters the inner camp of Dachau is the inscription worked into the heavy iron gate, which reads, "Work makes one free" (*Arbeit macht frei*).

In Buchenwald he passes through gates with ponderous wood carvings reading "His share to everybody" (*Jedem das seine*) and "My country right or wrong" (*Recht oder Unrecht, mein Vaterland*), which has an ominous ring at the entrance to an institution of "justice."

From the roll-call square he gets his first impression of the world in which he will live. In Dachau this world surprises him with its gleaming cleanliness—like a doll's house with green strips of grass, and beautiful flower beds with tulips and hyacinths. Buchenwald impresses him with its utter shabbiness and dirt. But doll's house or dirt, he is struck by the large number of machine gun nests towering high above the wall, by signs indicating that the barbed wire is high-voltage, and by other signs with skulls and crossbones telling him that he will be shot on trespassing.

The camp itself is silent. The prisoners are at work, most of them outside the wall. Occasionally, he sees men pushing wheelbarrows or marching in military order with heavy stones on their shoulders, shouted at by a fellow prisoner who is the foreman. He may catch the amazing view of a wagon drawn, not by horses, but by men pulling on long ropes. SS men with revolvers on their hips stroll around, yelling orders or abuse, or beating the men at work.

He does not have much time to think about all of this. He is kept busy. An SS man may stroll by, "Eh, eyes front, dirty swine, dirty!" (The prisoner will soon learn that repeating the first offensive word at the end is a Bavarian way of swearing.) All the prisoners try to look straight ahead. "Yes, you in the second row, you!"—and he belabors the man in the second row with his fists. Then perhaps he picks the next man. "Stand up straight, lazy swine, lazy!"—and he slaps his face. When a friend of mine was hit, my face twitched. Immediately I was rewarded with a blow, "Don't look so sympathetic." Now everyone stands erect, eyes front.

The SS man begins to ask questions. "What is your profession?" "I am a merchant, Herr Wachtmeister." "So, you lousy swindler, lousy! We'll teach you to cheat your customers!"—and it is the merchant's turn to be beaten. Perhaps the next man has a big stomach. "Where did you get that belly, you fat swine, fat? Why are you here anyway?" "Because I am a Jew, Herr Wachtmeister." "So you have been growing your Jewish belly while German children were starving? We'll get you over that, we'll work the fat off you!"—and the man is kicked for his big stomach. Another man wears eyeglasses, or has big ears, or small ears, or a big nose, or a small nose; he is short, or tall, or lean, or heavy—anything may be a reason for blows.

The prisoner learns his first law: To be different is dangerous.

One man is beaten for having been a worker—"So you are a Communist, you criminal you!" Another for not having been a worker—"So you enjoyed life at a desk while others did the hard work!" One is kicked for having been an intellectual—"Perhaps you believe that you're somebody? We'll disillusion you. Here you are nobody." Another receives the same kick for having been nobody—"So you have been loafing around while we were working!" To have been sent as a professional criminal is reason for getting beaten. Not to know why one was sent to camp is also reason for mistreatment. To be rich is bad, but to confess poverty is not good either, because of course that would be a lie.

And the prisoner learns his second law: Common logic does not apply in the camp. They beat you not because of the content of your answer, but merely for the sake of beating.

A frightful slap in my face followed this puzzling question: "Do you believe that your best times are over now?" "Yes, Herr Wachtmeister." "You are right and I will show you!"

Questions and answers, beating and shouting continue throughout the day, interspersed with periods of waiting for the next blow. At night, after roll call, the newcomers are led to their barracks. There they are handed over to the barrack senior (a prisoner in charge of discipline), who shows them their bed, their place at a table, their locker. They receive their first food and make their first acquaintances.

If the newcomer is a Social Democrat, a Communist, a Jehovah's Witness, or a member of another important group, he will immediately find brothers-in-creed who try to take care of him. They will explain the meaning of what he has seen and tell him what is going to happen next. They will prepare him for the ordeal through which he must go during the first days. Perhaps they will give or lend him some money or food from the canteen.

If he does not belong to any of these groups, not many people will pay attention to him. One or two may ask him a question, but by and large he will be left alone.

And he learns a new law: To be a member of a group means to be cared for, to find friends easily, to be trusted, to not be completely lost. Someone is willing to listen to his story. And his new friends will talk about him to his room senior, who is more often than not his brother-in-creed.

To not be a member of a group makes it more difficult to make friends. This is understandable, but difficult to bear.

During the first days and weeks, event after event will happen, and it will take the new man a long time to piece his experiences together. But slowly, and without his completely realizing it, his new world will begin to make "sense" to him. He will develop his own judgment when faced by new situations; he will learn how to get away with the least amount of mistreatment and perhaps also with the least amount of work. After the dizziness and stupor of the initiation have passed, his personal initiative will come back to him to some degree. He begins to live a life of his own, with friendships, enmities, quarrels, feuds, crooked dealings, sacrifices, group relations. He becomes familiar with the prejudices and traditions of the camp. He realizes that he has a certain status among his fellow prisoners. He feels that he is a member of a community.

After a few weeks or months the prisoner is completely adapted to life in the concentration camp. This means, in some cases, that he has regained his spirit as a political fighter, in other cases, that he has regained his private personality. In still other cases it may mean that he has restricted his intellectual life to the petty camp gossip about food, mistreatment, and release, and has limited his personal life to close contact with only one or two men.

But no matter what form the adaptation takes, the new man becomes part of the community of prisoners. He learns to think and evaluate in the same ways that the others do and acquires the distorted logic of the camp. He learns how to master a situation of complete insecurity, in which one can never tell what is going to happen next. Insecurity itself becomes part of his daily life, just as security may have been part of his previous life.

Against the amazing number of surprises that the camp has in store for him, he has only one weapon—not to let himself be surprised by anything. He expects the unusual every moment, and when it comes, he shrugs his shoulders—"Everything is possible in Buchenwald."

We got used to hard work, mistreatment, lack of justice, lack of logic. We got used to being whipped and hanged by our wrists for ridiculous misdemeanors, even if we had not committed them, or if they had not been committed at all. We got used to being driven from our beds at midnight for any reason, and to receiving no food on Sunday for no reason at all. We learned how to watch with outward calm while a man was beaten to death or while he died of a sickness which would not have been fatal if he had been given medical treatment. When one of our fellow prisoners was hanged on the gallows, we registered it in our minds and did not make much fuss about it. When the commander announced that a wolf had been killed by snowballs, we did not quite understand the meaning of it, but we told ourselves, "Why not? Everything is possible in Buchenwald."

Once the prisoner has acquired this calm outlook, he begins to understand the system of the situation. He compares reports of fellow prisoners who have been in other camps before, and he begins to realize that in spite of all the variation between camps, in spite of all the individual incidents that remain unexplained, the concentration camp presents a certain pattern. In some camps, to be sure, wheelbarrows are used, and in others handbarrows; in one camp gravel is dug, in another sand, in a third clay, and in a fourth peat. The whims of commanders and officers vary. One has a cleanliness obsession, another a singing obsession, a third insists on salutes (we once had one who made two thousand men practice putting their caps on and off for four hours straight), a fourth and fifth have still other obsessions. The system of punishment also varies slightly. In one camp the "twenty-five" dominates the penal code, in another the "tree," and in a third the "bunker" of solitary confinement. Yes, there are variations. But throughout Germany and throughout conquered Europe, it is essentially the same carefully designed machinery of terror, planned and standardized to the minutest detail, part and parcel of the Nazi power apparatus.

Chapter 3

The Layout

Both Dachau and Buchenwald (and most of the other German concentration camps up to 1939) were laid out on the same general pattern. There was a prisoners' camp and an SS camp. The prisoners' camp was heavily guarded by walls and ditches, high-voltage barbed wire, and machine guns. Inside the wall and extending completely around the camp was a strip of lawn several yards wide, known as the "neutral zone." To step on the lawn meant to be shot immediately and without warning "on attempt to escape." The entrance from the SS camp to the prisoners' camp led through a heavy iron gate that was part of a hallway through an administrative building—the "door," or "jour-house."[1]

In front of the "door" was the roll-call square, and beyond the square were the prisoners' barracks. These were low structures similar to those in many army camps. Inside the prison camp, separate buildings housed the kitchen, the baths, the supply department, the dungeon, etc. One or two barracks were detached to serve as the infirmary.

Most of the working grounds were either inside or close to the barbed wire, since the work consisted primarily of constructing the camp itself and the roads and military buildings around it. Only occasionally were

---

1. From the French *jour,* or perhaps from "journal," meaning that the journal or dayroll was kept there.

the working grounds farther away—for instance, a police housing project between Buchenwald and Weimar.

Inside the camp all barracks were directly accessible from the main street or the side streets. But there were certain prohibitions that hampered free communication. For example, Jews and non-Jews had to keep within their respective zones of barracks. Theoretically prisoners were not even allowed to enter any barrack except their own. In reality there was always considerable traffic between the barracks, and the administration was usually not too much interested in keeping the groups strictly separated.

Concentration camp Dachau was situated on a plateau near the village of Dachau, a well-known resort of artists, about eight miles from Munich in Bavaria, southern Germany. The summers were very hot, the winters very cold, the climate in general more extreme than in other parts of the country. The soil consisted mainly of gravel, with a thin top layer of humus.

The SS men were housed in part in big stone barracks several stories high, in part in low huts similar to those of the prisoners. Connected with the SS camp were several factories (chinaware, furniture), large fields and woods where military training took place, a park, an herb garden, and several other establishments. Just outside the wall was a modern garden city for SS commissioned and noncommissioned officers and their families. Higher ranking officers lived in nearby villas.

Working grounds were located within the SS camp and outside it. The ordinary prisoner never entered certain parts of the area, but some working groups got about more than others. Including the prison camp proper, the whole world of the prisoner measured about two miles in any direction.

The prison camp was a quadrangle about 350 by 550 yards. One small side was formed by a large building which contained the kitchen, bath, storage rooms, and so forth. Behind this was the dungeon. In front of the large building was the roll-call square. Beyond the square were thirty barracks in two rows, their narrow ends facing the "camp street." Behind the farthest barracks were a greenhouse, vegetable gardens, and flower beds.

The camp was encircled by the "neutral zone." Beyong this was a canal with high concrete walls and filled with water, then a barbed wire entanglement, then a wire fence several yards high, charged with electric current. Outside the fence was a runway for the sentinels, and beyond that a concrete wall about four yards high, topped by high-voltage barbed wire.

Every 200 yards there was a high tower in the wall, manned day and night by four guards and two machine guns. Large searchlights on top of the towers rotated incessantly all night, searching the wide plain and the camp streets for any suspicious movement.

Practically never did anyone escape. Whenever relatives were sent the ashes of a prisoner with the notice, "shot on attempt to escape," it could safely be assumed that he was shot in the "neutral zone." Both suicide and murder were committed in this way. A man either ran or was chased onto the green lawn and was shot to death. Sometimes the same thing happened on the working grounds, where the sentinels themselves formed a kind of "neutral zone" around the prisoners.

The barracks were one-story wooden frame constructions. Each barrack covered an area of about ten by 100 yards. They were made up of four compartments of fifty-two prisoners each. Each compartment consisted of a day and a night room, and two compartments shared a small entrance hall, a washroom, and a toilet with about eight water closets.

In the center of the day room was a big Dutch stove. There were seven tables with fifty-two backless seats and twenty-four lockers (which, however, could not be locked). The senior had one locker and a small table for himself. Usually, two prisoners shared a locker; occasionally three had to use one.

The dormitory contained fifty-two wooden beds in double bunks, and each bed was provided with a straw mattress, a straw pillow, one sheet, one blanket, a checkered pillow case and blanket case, and in winter one additional blanket.

All wooden furniture was manufactured in the camp. The furniture and hygienic accommodations were first class. So were the kitchen and bath. There was plenty of good water. Concentration camp Dachau used to be shown to Nazi officers and functionaries as the "model camp," with due pride in the efficiency of slave labor.

Adjoining the camp on one side was a park that belonged to the SS camp. Here the commander kept deer, foxes (in a concrete pit built by prisoners), and a swan which majestically sailed the canal. This menagerie was completed by the commander's Danish dog and his monkey.

Concentration camp Buchenwald was located on top of a small but rather steep mountain, which rose from the middle of a large plain. It was about five miles from the city of Weimar in Thüringen, in central Germany. The climate was less severe than in Dachau. The soil consisted mainly of clay. There were some quarries on the slope of the mountain. The camp was surrounded by forests—"Buchenwald" means birch forest.

The first prisoners brought there in 1937 erected the first barracks. When new ground for buildings was needed, trees had to be felled to make room. However, when we came from Dachau to Buchenwald in 1938, a considerable part of the work was already finished.

The SS camp and the prison camp were more closely connected in Buchenwald than in Dachau. The whole area on top of the mountain, including the two camps and the main working grounds (garages for a motorized regiment), covered an area perhaps two miles in diameter. There were also some working grounds farther away, for example, filter beds, quarries, a brick factory, and housing projects.

The prison camp was an irregularly shaped quadrangle extending steeply downhill. The shortest side, on top, measured about 800 yards, the others about 1,500 yards each. Only a small part of this area was actually covered by barracks and cleared space. The rest was forest.

On top of the mountain was the "door," one wing of which comprised the dungeon. Below the "door" was the roll-call square, and below the square were the barracks. In the summer of 1939 there were forty-eight barracks, standing eight rows deep, six in each row. Below the last barracks, foundations for new ones had already been laid.

About seventy yards below the last barracks the forest began. Farther down in the forest was the main infirmary, and still farther down the dog kennel, the pigsty, and the riding school. Still within the prison camp, but separated from it by a fence, was a section containing the sawmill, carpenter shop, and other workshops. Furniture for the living and coffins for the dead were the main products.

A high wire fence charged with electric current, a barbed wire entanglement, a "neutral zone," and a number of machine gun towers separated the camp from the rest of the world. Escape over the fence was as impossible as in Dachau. But the lack of a concrete wall and the sight of the forest made imaginative souls think of escape. However, the only two serious attempts to escape undertaken during my time were tried not from inside the camp, but from the less closely guarded working grounds.

A barrack covered an area about twelve by sixty yards. The first six rows of barracks were one-story wooden buildings; the last rows were brick, two stories high. The wooden barracks had two compartments each, the brick ones four. Two compartments shared an entrance hall, washroom, and toilet. The layout was like that in Dachau, but less modern and clean. Originally, each compartment was intended to house seventy-two men, but in September of 1938, when we came to Buchenwald, they were frightfully overcrowded. There were 108 beds in three-layer bunks, in and between which 130 to 170 men had to find a place to sleep. Usually there were three men in two beds, and the others slept on the floor. The day rooms were, of course, equally overcrowded. Only about two-thirds of the men could find a place to sit or stand and eat their meals. The rest had to wait outside or in the dormitory until the first ones had finished. There were no closets, only a few small drawers, each shared by four men. Hundreds of others had no place in which to keep their belongings.

Most of the furniture in Buchenwald was old military stock. Some of it, incidentally, was marked *Wöllersdorf,* indicating that it was taken from the Dollfuss Austrian concentration camp Wöllersdorf, which the Nazis were so proud of having abolished.[2]

There was a severe water shortage in Buchenwald, partly because pipes had not yet been laid, and partly because there was not enough water available. Therefore, the water closets could not be used. Instead, open latrines were used throughout the camp. Pits were dug about four yards deep, a railing was set up around the pit, and a light roof above it. That was the extent of the conveniences.

Water for washing purposes was also at a premium. It was turned on for only a few minutes, usually in the morning and sometimes in the evening. During that period, men fought each other so that they might clean up a little at least once every few days. At times in some of the barracks there was no water for weeks. The water problem was relieved and finally solved long after I had been released.

Buchenwald too had its menageries, actually a little zoo next to the "door," right in front of the roll-call square. There was a big aviary for birds of prey, with a lonesome eagle as the main attraction; a natural enclosure with three or four brown bears; a large run for a herd of wild bear; and a fox pit.

---

2. Shortly after our arrival in Dachau we received a copy of the *Völkischer Beobachter* showing pictures of burning barracks in Wöllersdorf. The caption, surprisingly enough, read: "We National Socialists do not need the barbarism of concentration camps. We burn them."

Chapter 4

A Day in a Concentration Camp

The day in a concentration camp begins long before dawn—in the summer at 3:20 and in the winter at 4:30. First, the room senior wakes up the men who go for the coffee. They get up hurriedly and dress in almost no time. The rest of the men then jump out of bed, grab their blankets and run to the day room. On the tables there they fold their blankets in the complicated way that is required. There are only a few tables, and the grumbling and pushing begins immediately. Meanwhile, others run to the washroom and toilet.

In a few minutes everyone is busy "constructing" his bed. This is one of the most complicated and important activities in the prisoner's life, hallowed by many a thrashing of "twenty-five" awarded to men who failed to grasp the essentials. The bed is expected to look as neat as a box, with the checkers of the blanket-case exactly parallel to the edges. But usually there is too little straw in the bag; it sinks in the middle, the edges sag, and creases are visible. All sorts of tricks are used to make the bed look better. Sticks and so-called "flat irons" (boards with handles) are employed for the purpose, and some of the new men even take to the forbidden practice of threading a cord or wire along the edge inside the bag. This may sound ridiculous to the uninitiated, but not to a man who may be hanged by his wrists for an hour because the checkers were slightly askew.

As soon as the men have washed and dressed, they line up for the "coffee" that has been brought in the meantime. We never found out what they dyed the water with, but it was always welcome, because it was hot. Everyone sits down for a few minutes and gulps the hot water and a few bites of bread. Then there is a rush for the washroom to clean the aluminium dishes, then back to clean the closets and make them ready for inspection. The latter sounds easier than it is. Every object has an exact spot where it must be stood, hung, or arranged, and must be folded, turned, or placed in a particular way. A knife put where the fork should be can bring a man to the "tree." So can a shirt, if it is folded with the sleeves in front of the body instead of behind it.

As soon as the closets are finished, the men are driven out of the barracks, no matter what the weather, no matter whether roll call begins five minutes or an hour later. The barrack detail immediately begins to prepare the room for inspection.

When the whistle blows, the men from each barrack get into military formation and march to roll call. The senior sets the pace—"Left, left, left and left ... close up, line up with your neighbor, keep in step, lines straight ... left, left, left and left ..."

But what of the man who is unable to get up because of sickness, injury, or old age? There is no such man.

If a man cannot get up, his fellow prisoners help him. If nobody else helps him, the senior does. He will drag him out of bed by one foot, or beat him with a broom, or he will be gentle. Which, is a matter of temperament. But whether the man finally gets up is not a matter of temperament. He simply has to. If he can't walk, others will carry him. No one is left behind except those who are already in the infirmary.

I carried Franz Steinberg when he was dying, and Oswald Richter when he fainted from pain. Others have carried their friends. No one is left behind. Not even the dead. If a man has died during the night and has not yet been taken from the barrack roll, the corpse is carried along on a stretcher. The barrack senior then reports, "Barrack six present with 202 men, one in the infirmary, one in arrest, one dead." Nobody is surprised. After all, why not?

Officers of the day count the men, barrack by barrack. Mistakes are frequent, so that roll call is often protracted. If someone is missing, the men's first thought is not "escape," but "suicide." If this happens in Buchenwald, the order is given, "Stubendienst in den Wald, Vogel suchen!" (Barrack detail to the forest, search for the bird!). The woods inside the barbed wire are searched, and usually within twenty minutes the corpse is found, hanging on a tree.

When at last the count is right, the commander comes to receive the report. Commander Rödl in Buchenwald likes to start the day with a song. He orders the conductor, a former singer from the Cologne opera, to mount a high pile of gravel. Waving his arms, the conductor tries his best to lead 10,000 untrained voices singing "The Little Village."

The first verse is over. Will there be an interruption? No, so far everything is all right. The second verse begins—cautiously at first, but then loud and strong, full of hope that we will again get past the dangerous point in the song, where there is a break, and everything depends upon the ability of 10,000 men to stop singing at the same moment. This time we are not so successful. Rödl's angry voice comes over the loudspeaker—"Stop that noise! The first verse was tolerable, but the second verse is shit! All of you, lie down! Up-down-up-down-up-down ..." Ten thousand men wallow in the deep mud, sand, dust, snow, or whatever it happens to be at the moment. The SS officers storm down the hill like mad watchdogs, trampling men because they don't lie down or get up fast enough.

Ten thousand men wallow in mud. Four thousand are only dirty Jews, so what difference does it make? But the other 6,000 are Aryans, Germans, the flower of mankind. If, in any other country in the world, anyone dared to offend one of them, the sacred wrath of the German nation, with the Führer in the lead, would descend upon that unfortunate nation! For the time being, however, they are wallowing in mud, because the second verse of "The Little Village" was shit.

Meanwhile, two companies of SS men march in, with rifles and sidearms. We hear the clatter as they fix their bayonets, but we are so accustomed to it that we are no longer conscious that they are aimed at us.

The order is given, "Newcomers and retransferred step forward!" (The latter are those who have been sent away from the camp temporarily, for example, to a court for a hearing.) They are formed into a special group and especially mistreated for the first few days.

Next order: "Working groups gather!" The rigid lines disperse, and for a few minutes the camp looks like a disturbed anthill. Everyone runs as quickly as he can to his working group. Officers scurry around and shout and beat and kick those who are not fast enough. Finally the working groups are formed. Group after group passes the officer in charge of construction. The capo (that is, the prisoner in charge) reports the number, the officer checks it, the necessary SS men are detached. They take their rifles from their shoulders, form alongside the column of prisoners, and the group moves through the "door" with the iron promise, "Work makes one free."

The prisoners go to work, no matter what the weather may be. We worked when men died like flies from sunstroke, and we worked when men dropped dead from the cold. We worked in snowstorms when we could not see each other and in fog so dense that we could not see our own hands. We worked in hail and thunderstorms and endless pouring rains. The prisoner goes to bed in his wet shirt and dries it with the heat of his body, but the rest of his clothing is still wet in the morning.

As soon as the group has passed the "door," the first guards begin to shout for a song. Again, "The Little Village" is taken up, telling for the hundredth time about the old widow who dreams of her husband who died for the Kaiser. Or perhaps it is the ballad of the "Forester's Daughter," who was in love with the happy hunter. The sentimental "Esterwegen Song" is often sung, and in Buchenwald, the "Buchenwald Song." A few of the songs are not bad, such as the ones the German Youth organizations used to sing when they wandered through the country.

As the men march on, the guards begin to scold them for not keeping step, not singing loud enough, or for speaking to their neighbors. Occasionally, they hit them, but not too often, for that might bring disorder into the ranks.

After marching from ten to thirty minutes (in some cases as long as an hour), the group arrives at its working ground. If they are new at the job, the capo will assign the men to their tasks. If it is an old job, he only shouts, "To the job, double quick!" and everyone runs to his place or to the tool shed. There are squabbles for the good tools, which are few. A bad tool may make a man's day unbearable hell instead of the ordinary hell which every day is.

Men with a mechanical bent soon learn how to distinguish good tools from bad at a glance. They learn how to select a better working place, which perhaps offers shelter from the sun or cover from the guard. There are countless imponderables that a man has to watch out for. The one who is aware of them and takes advantage of them most shrewdly has a better chance for survival.

When I came to Dachau on April 2, 1938, with the first 150 prisoners from Austria, the first job given to us was the destruction of the old dungeon, filling up the foundation, and building a road where the building had been. The morning after our arrival we were organized as a special working group. Guarded by an unusually large number of officers and capos, we were marched to the working place. Someone shouted, "To the job, on the double!" and immediately a storm of beating and kicking began. We were completely confused and did not know what we were supposed to do. Everyone took one of the tools that lay around. Most of us did not have the slightest idea how to handle them. There were shovels used to throw rubbish through nets to get sand, wheelbarrows to carry away the material, sledgehammers for breaking up blocks of concrete, and pickaxes for loosening the earth. The capos began to bring a bit of order into the confusion. They assigned men to carry away bricks, or to pass them along from hand to hand in long chains. Others were ordered to man the tipcarts and get material to fill in the hole. Still others had to carry stones on their shoulders. The yelling and beating continued without interruption for hours.

The first days were the hardest. We were driven harder than the rest of the prisoners, to celebrate our initiation, and we were unused to the tools and did not know how to handle them. The skin on our hands and shoulders was still tender. Unaccustomed to pickaxe, shovel, and wheelbarrow, our hands were covered with blisters within a few hours. Since they were not cared for, the blisters burst and the skin came off. Dust and dirt got into the open wounds. They began to fester and large sores developed. When our hands were so swollen that we could no longer work with them, we dared to go to the infirmary. There a few drops of iodine were applied—and we were sent back to work. After a few minutes the wounds were dirty again. Some of us were lucky, and no serious infections developed. Others, whose wounds grew worse, finally had their hands bandaged, but they had to keep working. Two of our group each lost a hand within the first few weeks.

The stone carriers suffered another kind of sore. The heavy concrete blocks that they carried on their shoulders were jagged, with knife-sharp edges. The men were forced on continuously and were not allowed to put down their stones to rest nor to handle them carefully. Soon the sharp edges cut through their thin clothes and into the skin and flesh of their shoulders. If they tried to use their caps as cushions, they were beaten.

To make things worse, there was still frost every morning at the time of our arrival. We used our fingers to thaw the ice from the tipcarts and tools. This made our fingers less resistant, and within a few days all the men's fingers were swollen to twice their normal size.

One of the main jobs in Dachau is digging gravel. Gravel is needed for almost everything—constructing roads, filling up excavations, making concrete walls, heat shafts, barracks, and for many other purposes. And there is plenty of gravel for all of these needs. Scratch the surface anywhere, and under ten or fifteen inches of humus, you will come to gravel. When more gravel is needed, a certain area is designated. Several hundred men march to it and remove the humus with shovel and pickaxe. Then they simply begin to dig. Just dig, and dig, and go on digging, for days, and weeks, and months, and years. The gravel pits eventually become deep cavities, wounds cut into the face of the earth all around the camp. Deeper and deeper they sink, but there is still more gravel underneath. When the hole is several yards deep, the subsoil water begins to rise into it. Never mind, keep digging. Take off your shoes and stand in the water, but keep digging. If the water continues to rise, you can always roll up your trousers. But keep digging. If it rises still higher, nevermind the trousers, just keep digging. I have worked in water that was over my knees, and others in water much higher than that.

And the men stand in water, for five hours without pause in the morning, and five hours without pause in the afternoon, and five hours the next morning and five hours the next afternoon. They push their shovels deep into the yellow water and fish for gravel. They can't see where they are pushing, and come out with a poor catch. Never mind, keep fishing, there is always some gravel left. All the hopelessness of our existence is condensed into one grim joke, "How long will all this last?" "Buddy, don't you know? 'Til all the gravel is gone!" ("*Mensch! Bis der Kies alle ist!*")

Since the pit is many yards deep, the gravel must be elevated. High terraces are cut into the walls of the pit, and the gravel is thrown up shovelful by shovelful. It is amazing to see hundreds of men dig a hole into the earth and then fish for gravel, and hand it from man to man as if it were the most precious material in the world.

Finally, the gravel is carried away to where it is needed by means of a wheelbarrow, man-drawn wagon, or tipcart. Officers and capos see to it that the carts are loaded full and that they keep rolling fast enough. Sometimes a curse does the trick, sometimes a stone thrown at a head, sometimes a blow or kick from a heavy boot; often fear alone does it. If the man at the gravel pile takes pity on his brother with the wheelbarrow and does not fill it up completely, he himself is assigned to the wheelbarrow and the other man gets his place.

Before the new camp was built in Dachau, the gravel was heaped up until it formed a hill forty to fifty feet high with a base of 150 yards. When we came to Dachau, this gravel was used. A path was cut that wound up the hill in a huge spiral, forming terraces over which men were spread out by the hundred doing exactly the opposite of what the others did in the gravel pits—handing the gravel down from terrace to terrace in thousands of wheelbarrow-loads and millions of shovelfuls. In April the hill had looked as though it were built for eternity, and by August not a single pebble was left.

In Buchenwald there is no gravel, but there is clay. Shafts are dug out where foundations are being laid for buildings. First, there is a tough layer of clay and humus, then comes a layer of dry clay that breaks easily. Below are layers that become progressively thicker and harder. At the bottom of the shaft, the layers are petrified into actual stone, fifteen to twenty inches thick. With big sledgehammers and nothing else, the men smash at the stone—and sooner or later it breaks.

After morning roll call, while the other prisoners are at work, the "barrack detail" is busy making the barrack ready for inspection. They wax the floor, dust the furniture, and polish the washroom and toilet. A good senior will check his men's beds and closets and correct mistakes. A bad senior lets them get caught.

At about eight or nine o'clock, the barrack leader (that is the SS officer in charge of a barrack) comes. All closets are opened for him, and he sees what delights an SS man's heart: fifty plates, fifty dishes, fifty glasses, fifty spoons, knives, forks, underwear, shirts, slippers—all alike, all in exactly the same order. The closets look so much alike that often even the owners can't identify their own. In the bedroom there is the same uniformity—fifty pillows, fifty blankets, all in exactly the same position. Any irregularities are so insignificant as to be almost unnoticeable. It depends entirely upon the momentary mood of the officer, whether he will be satisfied with what he sees or become angry, declare the room a pigsty, pull the beds apart, and report the barrack for disorderly conduct.

This is the time when a good senior is of the greatest help to his men. He will try to involve the officer in conversation, create a friendly atmosphere, perhaps stack up in front of him a few of his favorite magazines. Sometimes he may shrewdly introduce a cigarette or a piece of cake— but always in such a manner that the officer will not get the impression that he is being bribed.

In addition to the formal inspection by the barrack leader in charge of a particular barrack, there are numerous informal ones by other officers. These informal visits are even more dangerous, because there is not that familiarity which arises between the senior and the officer in charge. A barrack may have satisfied one inspector and be reported by the next for "outrageous disorder."

In Dachau at eleven o'clock the prisoners march home for lunch. Again they sing on the way. Before entering the barracks, they have to remove their shoes (the floor is waxed). There is only a small hallway, and in bad weather, when the men cannot take their shoes off outside, there is fighting and growling. They also fight for a place in toilet and washrooms. There is not enough room, and everyone wants to get through as soon as possible, so that he can have a few minutes rest.

A few men from each room are dispatched to the kitchen. They march in military order, pick up the vessels with the food, and march back in military order. This is not easy. There are about 320 food carriers, with every three men carrying two vessels of about eleven gallons each between them. The hot soup slops over the edges and burns their hands. But they are not allowed to put the vessels down. An SS officer on a bicycle drives them on, and if there is too much disorder, he makes them drill. Once we had to march around the big square with the full vessels. Another time we underwent ten minutes of heavy drill—"Up, down, run, fall on your face ..."—while the camp waited for its food.

The senior distributes the food. According to my observations, he usually tries very hard to be fair. To the best of his ability, he divides the fishable objects equally.

Going for the food and returning the empty vessels takes up much of the precious noon rest and is, in addition, heavy work. Some barracks have revolving shifts. Others put the job on a voluntary basis, with a slight reward for the men—they are the first to get what may be left after everyone has had his share.

The men eat hurriedly. As soon as they have gulped down their food, they run to the washroom to clean their dishes. There are twelve faucets with cold water for a hundred men, whose aluminium dishes must shine like mirrors.

Those unfortunates whose beds the inspecting officer has torn apart spend most of their noon rest remaking them. Often whole barracks must do this and lose their rest period.

As soon as the dishes are cleaned, the men are chased out of the barracks. They spend the rest of the noon period in the open, even though it may rain or hail. The barrack detail immediately begins to clean the room for afternoon inspection.

A number of errands have to be done during the noon rest—at the infirmary, the barbershop, the clothing department, the canteen, and so forth. There is not much time for real rest.

At 12:30 the whistle blows and roll call is repeated, but much more informally this time. Then the prisoners march off to work again.

In Buchenwald the noon rest lasts for only half an hour and is spent on the working grounds. Brown water is distributed (half a mug per man), and the men eat what they have left of their "rations" of sausages, cheese or fish, and some bread. These "rations" are distributed with dinner the night before. Only a few working groups are fortunate enough to spend their noon rest under cover. Most of the men have to eat where they happen to be standing, even though it may rain throughout the whole period.

The afternoon drags on again, but anticipation of evening makes it seem to pass a little faster. The prisoners are not supposed to know the time, but the day passes faster when you are able to keep track of it. They contrive all sorts of methods to do so. They count the number of trips made by tipcarts, wagons, even wheelbarrows. They watch the length of the shadows and the position of the sun. When there is an opportunity, they build real sundials. They send men to camp with trumped-up excuses for tools or something else, to "bring the time." It is a common saying among the prisoners that "these are the two wishes in concentration camp: throughout the morning, that it may become noon, and throughout the afternoon, that it may become night."

In Dachau at 6:00, in Buchenwald at 4:30, the official working day is over. The men march back to camp, again singing on their way. This eternal singing is as much a part of their life as it is of the military life of their guards who impose it upon them.

In Buchenwald every man who returns at night from a place outside the fence has to carry along a heavy stone, nicknamed the "good night stone." The stones are needed inside for building roads. About five thousand stones are thus brought into the camp every day. Carrying the stones on their shoulders, they must sing as they march, and are greeted at the gate by the blare of a brass band playing military marches and the Buchenwald song.

The band originated when prisoners were brought from penitentiaries, where they had been allowed to keep musical instruments. Commander Rödl, who was an enthusiastic lover of music and songs, organized them into the band. Later, he even occasionally permitted the purchase of new instruments. However once, when he collected contributions from the whole camp to buy new instruments and took in many thousands of marks, no new instruments were bought, and we never knew what happened to the money.

Immediately after return from work, there is roll call again. It lasts considerably longer than morning roll call. Announcements are made. The commander arrives late. In Dachau, men who have been sentenced to an hour on the "tree" are hung up during roll call. Fifty-five hundred men listen to their screams. In Buchenwald, the "twenty-five" is executed during roll call. Ten thousand men stand at rigid attention while a few scream in pain—or endure in silence. Often the 10,000 have to sing lusty songs while the sentence takes its course.

After roll call the food carriers go to the kitchen. The punitive workers, who must work overtime, and the "door duty," who must stand at the gate all evening for punishment, report to their tormentors, and then the official day is over. However, in Buchenwald during the summer there are two more hours of work after dinner, so-called "night work" inside the fence. This work is less strenuous than that during the day. On many working grounds the men do not work at all, but just stand around. The reason for this is that the officers don't like to go down into the camp and watch men after dinner. They want to have their time off, and even driving men becomes tiresome and a nuisance when you have to do it in your leisure time.

When roll call and work are over, the prisoners spend the rest of the evening either inside their barracks or on the streets talking to their friends. As at noon, there are a number of things that have to be attended to, such as going to the infirmary, the clothing department, and so on. But in the evening the queues are much longer, and the major part or all of an evening's spare time may be spent waiting in line.

Shortly before nine o'clock punitive workers and the "door duty" are sent home. The whistle blows and everyone hurries toward his barrack. Shortly thereafter, a second whistle blows. It is "lights out." Anyone who leaves the barrack after lights out is shot without warning "on attempt to escape." This is a method of suicide, as good as any other.

And now the camp sleeps.

However, there is no such thing as undisturbed quietness at night in a concentration camp. Again and again there are interruptions. In earlier times it frequently happened that, with or without apparent reason, the guards in the machine gun towers fired into the camp. During my time it happened only once. One night Commander Schneider, extremely drunk, made the rounds through the barracks in Dachau and had men whose feet were dirty reported for punishment. Another night Commander Rödl appeared and threatened to shoot anyone who made a move. He was trying to catch homosexuals.

One night the sirens began to wail in Buchenwald. Over the loud-speaker came Commander Johnny's voice. "Within five minutes I want to see the whole gang up here." It was about two o'clock in the morning. We formed in marching order, ten men abreast, took each other's hands so as not to slip in the mud, and stumbled up the roll-call square. In the shine of the huge searchlights, a bloody corpse was lifted up. Johnny announced over the loudspeaker, "And that will be the fate of every bird who tries to fly to freedom. Get off with you!" And we marched back to bed, not the least concerned about the dead man—we did not even know whether it was a genuine attempt at escape or a suicide—only grumbling because our sleep had been disturbed. For all we cared, he could just as well have chosen the morning to die.

Chapter 5

The Daily Routine

The Work

The bulk of work in a concentration camp consists of digging and carting away gravel, clay, sand, humus, and stones, and the transport of other building material such as cement, bricks, lime, rubbish, and so forth. Digging is done with shovel and pickaxe; carrying by wheelbarrow, handbarrow, man-drawn wagon, and human shoulders.

Since no skill is required, no care is taken in the selection of men to do this work. Everyone who, by his presence on the roll-call square, has demonstrated his ability to get there, is automatically considered able to do a laborer's heavy work. Only those few who, after a rigorous process of selection, have finally been certified by the infirmary as incapable of work, are permitted to stay away. Old and weak men and invalids who are certified as such are, at best, attached to easier jobs, apparently in order that able-bodied men will not have to be used for the easier jobs. This is corroborated by the fact that old men and invalids who don't happen to get the easier jobs are driven at their digging jobs just as hard as the strong and young.

Some kinds of work require a certain amount of skill: concrete mixing, helping the masons, transporting breakable material such as slate, and so forth. Here there is a certain amount of selection, since the administration is interested in having the job done well. Then, too, the capos, as far as they are able to influence selection, try to get capable men, because the capo is held responsible if a structure breaks down.

There are a certain number of skilled workers used in the construction of barracks and buildings and in the repair shops—masons, carpenters, cabinetmakers, tilers, furniture builders (in Dachau there is a factory with modern machinery), shoemakers and tailors (doing repair work for the whole camp), and so forth. In addition there are, of course, a number of specialists at work on all the odd jobs that accompany construction work—electricians, pipefitters, stokers, and so forth. But there are so few of them, among the thousands of men, that they are hardly worth mentioning, except to make the point that the whole camp is actually built by prisoners.

Among the jobs that do not require any special skill and yet are special jobs are those in the camp kitchen and as house personnel for SS officers.

There are also jobs which are given preferably only to invalids and old or injured men. An example is the "nail bench," where men straighten out old nails with a hammer or an odd bit of iron. They work on an iron table, and the resulting din is unbelievable. There are not too many nails, and the workers try to husband their small stock. When not watched, they hammer away at one and the same nail for hours or even days. The noise prevents them from speaking to one another and from thinking or daydreaming. Their minds become blank and dull. But life, dear life, is prolonged a little. There are always about ten to fifteen people at this job in Dachau.

"Brick cleaners" remove the concrete from old bricks so they can be used again. This work is done with a crowbar. The noise is less intolerable, the men can speak to each other, and the job is more sought after. They, too, have to husband their supply. They carefully avoid knocking off too much of the concrete at one time. I remember a man who cleaned a single brick for three days, hiding it every night so nobody could steal it. When the sad moment arrived when the last speck of concrete was gone, he took a last farewell of his friend of three days and, with a solemn little speech, smashed the brick to pieces.

Nail bench and brick cleaning are more characteristic of Dachau. In Buchenwald one of the most typical invalid jobs is stone cutting. The stonecutters sit in huts or in the open and use bigger stones to knock smaller stones to little pieces, to furnish material for decorating flowerbeds. Other invalids carry the product away in tin cans (old jam containers holding about two gallons). If there is not enough to carry, they carry regular stones from the quarry, but only take small ones and are not harried much by SS officers, as long as they are on the move at all.

This enumeration of various activities should not lead the reader to believe that prisoners in concentration camps do all sorts of things, such as mending, building, digging, etc. The only generalization that may be permitted is this: For the most part the prisoners dig, dig, dig, and dig again. If they are not digging, they push wheelbarrows, and push, and push, and push. If not pushing the wheelbarrow, then they carry hand-barrows, and carry, and carry. Only a few of them do work which is a little better. The rare exception, when someone works at skilled labor or in a sheltered room, might as well pass unmentioned, especially in respect to the Jews.

Because there is one supreme law: No Jew in a skilled job; no Jew under a roof. The only exceptions are a small number of invalids and those Jews who, for a time, can smuggle themselves into a better job without being noticed. As soon as an officer discovers them, they are out digging again.

In addition, there are a few very general rules concerning some of the special jobs. Kitchen workers in both camps are taken almost exclusively from the "asocials." Practically all the skilled work in Dachau is done by political prisoners, especially the work in the furniture shops. In Buchenwald, all skilled and special work is divided between the professional criminals and the political prisoners. In Dachau, the personnel in the officers' mess and houses are taken from the politicals, and in Buchenwald, from the politicals and the Jehovah's Witnesses.

Clothing and Personal Belongings

The administration issues to each prisoner one set of clothes, which consists of trousers, jacket, shirt, underwear, stockings, shoes, and a cap without visor. It also issues one set of dishes, which, in Dachau, includes an aluminium pot, aluminium plate, fork, knife, spoon, and drinking glass. In Buchenwald it includes only an aluminium bowl, aluminium mug, and spoon, with no fork or knife. One towel is furnished in each camp. The prisoners have to buy their own toothbrushes, tooth powder or paste, and soap. Occasionally toothbrushes are distributed to men who have no money, and occasionally soap is distributed. The assumption seems to be that men without money can get theirs from those with money. The same applies to shoe polish and shoe oil, which is also usually bought in the canteen, but occasionally distributed by the barrack. In Dachau each man is given one or two shoe brushes. In Buchenwald there are only a few brushes for each room.

In Dachau each prisoner has a change of shirt, underwear, and socks in his locker. However, he is not allowed to use it under any circumstances until the regular two-weeks period is up, no matter how dirty or wet he may be. If, in the meantime, his shirt gets too dirty, he must wash it or he will be punished. In Buchenwald, where there are no lockers, the change of clothing is given on changing day, and the men undress and re-dress right at the table.

The same shirt is worn day and night. When clothing is torn, it may be exchanged for mended articles in the clothing department.

During the winter in Buchenwald, after many men had died from the cold and others had lost hands and feet because of frostbite, sweaters, gloves, and scarves were brought to the camp. The Jews had to buy them at their own expense; the non-Jews got them free. Among the Jews, those with more money bought the garments for those who had none. Never, not even during the coldest winter and snowstorms, did we receive overcoats.

To protect ourselves from the cold, we used to put newspaper in our shoes, and we "tailored" cement bags, which were made of rough paper, and wore them under our jackets. This was forbidden and severe punishment was in store for those who were caught. Even so, the practice was widespread—a cement bag could often save a life.

In addition to his official belongings, there are several other items that the prisoner may buy in the canteen or acquire otherwise. In Dachau these most commonly include a pair of wooden clogs, in Buchenwald a bread bag; also a few handkerchiefs, which, however, are only old rags in many cases; cleaning material, such as polishing rags, steel wool, and sandpaper; perhaps needle and thread, only occasionally a pair of scissors; occasionally a machine for rolling cigarettes; in Buchenwald perhaps a knife, made from a tin can; a few odds and ends such as strings or cord, a little piece of wood especially carved for the purpose of scraping dirt off the trousers, some odd piece of wire, perhaps, or the rubber stopper of a glass bottle. The prisoners acquire a surprising instinct for picking up any sort of material that might be of further use. But only a very small amount of it can be kept, or a man may be hanged by his wrists for "making a junkyard out of his closet."

In the closets at Dachau and in the breadbags at Buchenwald, the prisoners keep whatever food and tobacco they buy from the camp canteen and whatever "durable" food the camp issues, such as the bread ration for three days or, in Buchenwald, the cheese ration for next day's lunch.

Beyond that, there is a minimum of more personal belongings, primarily the last few letters from home (officially only one letter is allowed, but the men usually manage to save three or four of them), pencil and paper, and stamps. Then there are exceptional belongings, such as the horseshoe a man found and carried home, hoping it might bring him luck. I myself carried with me as one of my most precious possessions two passages from Joseph Conrad's *Youth,* which I had asked Lucie to write me in a letter, but that was an unusual case of individual property.

Money is usually carried in a little purse, either in a pocket or on a string around the neck. The purse can be bought in the canteen.

Mail

The prisoner is permitted to write and receive two four-page letters a month. Those which he writes, on camp stationary, have eleven four-inch lines to the page. But this is only a theoretical maximum. In Buchenwald, for example, where outgoing mail is censored by the barrack leader, experience taught us to write only two pages–otherwise the mail did not go out for weeks. Very often only a postcard (eight lines) is permitted, and occasionally a mail day is omitted completely.

Every letter carries an imprint with detailed regulations about mail, including the following statements:

Parcels are not permitted as the prisoners can buy everything at the camp.

Applications to the camp administration concerning release from protective custody (*Schutzhaft)* are useless.

Permission to converse with or to visit prisoners in concentration camp is absolutely never granted.

The Buchenwald letterhead also carries the following statement:

The day of release cannot yet be told. Visits to the camp are forbidden. Inquiries are useless.

The prisoner has to give the name of one person with whom he wishes to correspond, and if he desires to get in touch with anyone else, it must be through this person. It is practically impossible to correspond directly with people in foreign countries. Prisoners who want to do so usually address their letters to someone inside Germany, who then sends a copy abroad.

Prisoners are not allowed to request or receive information about steps their relatives may take to secure their release. During our whole stay in Dachau, we were not allowed to correspond on the subject of emigration. In Buchenwald, we were told to do so. Censorship applied to these two topics and, of course, to any sort of report about treatment or living conditions. Prisoners were not allowed to report about their own health. When my hand was seriously injured and I had to have my letters written by a friend, I could not even say as little as, "Don't worry, the hand is still there." For weeks my relatives thought that it had been amputated, until I was able to hint in a roundabout way at the real state of affairs.

The number of ruses employed by prisoners to get information through in either direction is legion. But so is the number of letters which are confiscated, cut in half, or of which nothing more is delivered than a line with "Dear Heini," and perhaps another line with "your mother."

Censorship is also applied to the emotional content of outgoing mail. Sentimentality, "gushiness," and also signs of moral strength and resistance are frequently censored. The ideal letter contains nothing but "thanks for the money, thanks for the mail, I am well, everything is all right, your Hans." Contact with the outside world is thus limited to the minimum both in frequency and intensity, and whatever the prisoner wants to tell or find out, he has to interpret shrewdly using every single word. The picture he gets of his own people thus becomes completely distorted. Every mother or girlfriend turns into a clever lawyer whose every word is ambiguous, equivocal. No word is taken at its face value; hidden meanings are sought in every little line. The most fantastic rumors about impending mass release or changes in the political situation or anything else can often be traced to nothing but a friendly greeting from a relative that has been misinterpreted.

Bath and Barber

The prisoners get a shower once a week in a big bathhouse with showers for several hundred people. Usually two or three barracks take showers simultaneously. The water runs for about three minutes. In Dachau the commander himself turned the water on and off because he enjoyed working the mechanism. But his presence meant that perhaps three hundred and fifty men had to bathe and change their clothes in icy silence. If a word was spoken, the whole barrack to which it was traced had to do punitive exercise right after the bath—"Up-down-up-down-jump, roll in the dirt-up-down"—and the effect of the bath disappeared.

In both camps, the bathhouse was installed long after our arrival. In Buchenwald, with its lack of water in the barracks, many men were unable to wash for the first few weeks. Because of the universal dirt in Buchenwald, lice flourished. A machine for delousing was set up in the bath. Men from barracks where lice had been found were marched to the bath and took a shower. Meanwhile their clothes were sterilized in the machine. But since nothing was done to clean the barracks themselves, the nuisance kept recurring.

In Dachau one barrack is set aside for the barber's salon. About fifteen prisoners work as barbers. The equipment is adequate. Every prisoner goes to the barber at least once a week, for if he lets his beard grow too long, he is punished. Although it is against regulations, it is customary to leave a small tip for the barber. Because the men must go during their free time, and because they have to wait so long in line, they consider it a great nuisance.

Illegal barbershops are therefore installed in the barracks. For a few pfennigs, the prisoner can get his shave in the barrack and save a precious half-hour in line. The equipment, however, does not come from the barbershop, for razor knives are used there, while in the barracks they use safety razors. Most of these are smuggled in through the SS.

In Buchenwald each barrack has its own barber, who is a member of the barrack detail.

The barber also clips the prisoners' hair. Anyone who lets his hair grow longer than two millimetres (about one-tenth of an inch) is threatened with punishment for attempt to escape. This was not taken very seriously in Dachau, but was very much so at Buchenwald.

There seem to be three reasons for requiring that the hair be cut off. It is hygienic; it prevents escape (one ill-fated attempt was foiled because of the man's clipped head); and it is intended to add to the deep humiliation of the prisoner. It is a traditional concept that the slave's hair is cut, while only the free man wears his long.

Food

The food situation was very different in the two camps. Dachau was located in an agrarian section with a rich food supply. Buchenwald was in an industrial region. The period that I spent in each camp also made a difference. I was in Dachau during the spring and summer of 1938, in Buchenwald from the fall of 1938 through the spring of 1939. We arrived at Buchenwald during the days of Munich, which foreshadowed the outbreak of the war.[1] The German economy was geared almost completely for war production, and food, particularly meat and fat, was scarce.

In Dachau in the period around 1938, the food was about the same as in an ordinary prison. Usually it was sufficient, both in quantity and quality, to keep the prisoner alive under the strain of hard labor. In the morning, there is "coffee" and bread; at noon, about a quart of some *Eintopfgericht,* that is, a thick stew of potatoes, peas, or beans, with another vegetable and meat or fish, all cooked together. In the evening there is "tea" (a sweet brew, the ingredients of which we were never able to identify) with bread and one of the following: herring, cheese, sausages, prunes with rice, porridge, etc.

In Buchenwald the food is basically the same, but the quality is much worse. The "stew" is actually nothing but a heavy soup, with only a few solid items to the quart. A recognizable piece of meat is considered a sensation.

The difference in the food supply is reflected in the canteen. Prisoners are permitted to receive some money from their relatives and to use it to buy additional food and various necessities such as toothbrushes, shoelaces, soap, etc. from the canteen. The canteen in Dachau is well supplied with butter, sugar, cookies, chocolate, canned fish, jams, and artificial honey (molasses). In Buchenwald the canteen is poorly stocked. Its chief articles are canned fish and stale bread, left over from a bakery in Weimar.

To sum up, Dachau has about enough food, if one takes into account the fact that canteen food is redistributed to a certain degree; that is, those who can buy more canteen food often give away part of their regu-

---

1. Editor's note: In September 1938, British Prime Minister Neville Chamberlain, French Prime Minister Edouard Daladier, Italy's dictator Benito Mussolini, and the German Führer Adolf Hitler met in Munich and came to an agreement. The British and French governments agreed to accept the seizure of the Sudetenland in Czechoslovakia by Nazi Germany, and Hitler promised not to make any further territorial demands in the future. The policy which led to the Munich Agreement became known as "appeasement."

lar camp food. But "enough" means, of course, only that it is sufficient to keep men alive. The individual man is very often hungry.

In Buchenwald there is far too little food, and the canteen offers only negligible supplements. The men are continually hungry. Hunger and food are the chief subjects of conversation among the majority of the prisoners. When they paint a picture of their release, it goes like this: "First, when I get to Weimar, I'll buy myself a loaf of bread, and eat it right away. That gives a good foundation. Then comes a square meal with two servings of meat, and lots of potatoes, and then ..." Wife or girlfriend enter the scene embarrassingly late—the hunger is too great.

The food is insufficient not only in quantity, but also in quality. It does *not* keep men alive. Hunger is not usually the direct cause of death, but physical resistance is lowered by bad food, and the men fall victim to the first illness or infection, diseases that under ordinary circumstances would hardly keep them in bed a day or two.

Money

Prisoners do not, of course, receive any payment for work done in a concentration camp. Any money they have comes from relatives, who send it by money order. It is either paid out to the prisoner immediately, in which case a close check is kept so that no one receives more than the amount permitted per week, or it is entered on a personal account, from which the prisoner may make withdrawals at stated intervals. The former method is used in Dachau, the latter in Buchenwald. In Dachau the prisoners are permitted to receive up to fifteen marks per week (sixty-five per month), in Buchenwald ten marks every ten days (thirty per month). Actually, only a small proportion of the men receive the full amount permitted. Ten or fifteen marks is a considerable amount, since a skilled worker or office worker makes about thirty-give to forty marks a week. Those who receive ten or fifteen marks are considered the "rich."

In Dachau the men buy directly from the canteen, which is located in a barrack on the roll-call square. In Buchenwald, where the canteen is outside the fence, each barrack has its "canteener," a man who takes orders and money and buys supplies for the whole barrack. He is a member of the barrack detail. At a certain hour of the day, all barrack canteeners gather and, led by the "camp-canteener," march to the canteen and do their shopping. Since they obtain only a small fraction of what has been ordered, the meagre supply must be distributed arbitrarily, and conflicts often arise. Rackets develop, and goods are sold and re-sold, until the ultimate consumer often pays several times the original price.

Here are some of the prices of the most common canteen goods, as an indication of what a few marks may mean to a man. (One mark is a hundred pfennigs.) The prices in Dachau are fairly constant; in Buchenwald they vary considerably with the supply. The canteen itself asks different prices at different times, and the number of resellings before the goods reach the ultimate consumer varies with the extent of the shortages.

Lump sugar: ten lumps, ten pfennigs.

Cookies: one-half pound, thirty pfennigs. (These are cheap, ordinary cookies and are sold in large amounts in Dachau, where the canteen sells no bread.)

Cookies in boxes: about one mark per box (one-half to one-quarter pound). These are fine cookies, which are sold in Buchenwald.

Fish in tin cans: sizes as in the American market, usually kippered herring, herring in tomato sauce, or sardines, forty pfennigs to one mark. The latter is for the usual large oval can, which is a staple in Buchenwald. In times of scarcity such a can can cost up to two marks.

Jam in glass: sizes as in the American market, about one-and-a-half marks, sold only in Dachau.

Two white rolls: five or ten pfennigs, sold only in Buchenwald.

Butter: one-quarter pound, fifty pfennigs, sold only in Dachau.

Artificial honey (molasses): seventy pfennigs.

Cigarettes: packages of twenty-five, or the equivalent in tobacco, seventy pfennigs to one mark, the prices being higher in Buchenwald where, in times of scarcity or when smoking is forbidden, the black market prices go as high as thirty or fifty pfennigs per cigarette.

Cigars: small and cheap sort, five pfennigs each, also running up to fantastic prices on the black market in case of scarcity.

Thus, in Dachau a man who receives five marks a week (or seventy pfennigs per day) might perhaps buy the following things:

Sunday: a package of cigarettes .70
Monday: one-quarter pound butter, one-half pound cookies .80
Tuesday: a can of fish .50
Wednesday: molasses .70

Thursday: some personal article, such as soap, shoe laces, or toothpaste	.30
cigarettes	.70
Friday: cookies	.30
Saturday: fish	.50
	4.50

This leaves about forty-five pfennigs, of which he pays five or ten as tip for his weekly shave. (He may even pay twenty pfennigs and be shaved by a room barber.)

The rest may go for some extraordinary expense, such as any of the things that have to be bought illegally—wooden clogs, belts, "tools" for making beds, steel wool, sandpaper, etc. Extraordinary expenses may also include bribes, although they were not so much in evidence in Dachau as in Buchenwald.

Actually, instead of buying an item each day, the man would do his shopping on two evenings and on Sunday morning, in order not to have to line up so often.

The man who receives ten marks regularly does not simply buy twice as much food. He spends part of his additional money for a newspaper subscription or other "extraordinary" expenses, and buys things that the man with five marks can practically never buy, such as a glass of jam. And of course he can smoke a great deal more.

When a man gets eight to ten marks a week, he may buy additional food from the canteen to replace regular food. Men who have enough money give away their salt herring, tripe, or other unpopular food. Also, beginning at eight to ten marks, bribery plays a more serious role. So does payment for regular services. A man who receives fifteen marks weekly can afford to pay another man two marks for making his bed or shining his shoes, or taking over some of his regular cleaning chores. In a political barrack, some of his money may be paid into a fund to help those who don't receive any money.

In Buchenwald, where seven marks per week is the maximum amount a man may receive, the difference between "rich" and "poor" is much less, especially in view of the serious shortage of canteen goods. The shortage results in one of two conditions: Either there are no goods, and the money is almost useless, or the goods are very expensive, sold in the black market, and the money is therefore worth even less.

The average amount of money received per week differs greatly among the various categories of prisoners. So does the regularity with which the remittances come. Gypsies receive almost no money. Of the asocials, only a small number receive any, and those few at irregular intervals. Many of the political men do not receive any money at all, but those whose relatives can afford to send any money get it at very regular intervals, no matter how little it may be. Those from the higher economic levels, particularly the professionals, receive from ten to fifteen marks a week regularly. The great bulk of the professional criminals receive little or nothing, but a few of them receive quite high remittances regularly. On the average, Jews receive more money than non-Jews, since among the Jewish prisoners there are more middle- and upper-class people. This fact, added to the popular belief that Jews are rich and corrupt, leads to serious consequences in the relations between groups, particularly in Buchenwald, where there is more corruption to begin with.

The total amount of money in the hands of the Dachau prisoners on any given day around the fall of 1938 may be estimated to have been approximately 3,500 marks.[2]

In Buchenwald the amount of money varies considerably, because money is not distributed in a regular flow of money orders, but rather on particular "paydays." These occur at irregular intervals, about once every four to six days. As soon as the news spreads that the cashier is giving out money, prisoners who have accounts gather in front of his barrack after evening roll call. Sometimes money is given out on a "first come, first served" basis, and on some days only those whose initials are in a certain part of the alphabet are served. Since it is never announced in advance which system will be used, thousands of men gather in vain and, in the ensuing confusion, are driven away with threats and blows. Hundreds of men who are actually entitled to money on a particular night may not get it, because they are driven away with the rest. And as soon as the cashier runs out of change (only coins are permitted

---

2. This estimate was arrived at as follows. There were 5,500 prisoners at the time. Of these, the 500 in the punitive company received almost no money; they were permitted only ten marks every third month. Perhaps half of the rest never received money, or so seldom that they were almost always without any. Those 2,500 who actually got regular remittances seldom received less than ten marks a month; most of them got at least fifteen, while quite a number got twenty and more, up to the full limit of sixty-five a month. It seems safe to assume that five marks a week may have been the average for these 2,500 men. That leaves them with 70 pfennigs per day. Assuming that each man had on the average two days´ spending money left (that is, about 1.40 marks), including those who were just out of money and those who had just received fifteen marks, there were about 3,500 marks in the camp.

in the camp, no bills), payday is ended, and those still waiting are chased away.

Thus there is a great deal of money circulating on payday, and the amount decreases considerably before the next payday. The total may be estimated at about 14,000 marks on payday, dwindling to about 2,000 marks just before the next payday.[3] If the interval between paydays is longer than about five days (at times it is as much as two or three weeks), and then there are three paydays within one week, it may well happen that there are 30,000 marks or more circulating at one time–and the word *circulating* should be stressed. The canteen does not double its volume of goods on these days, nor does it double its prices. Thus the extra money begins to circulate among the prisoners. The goods that come in are resold more frequently, prices go up, bribes are more frequent and larger, and a regular inflation takes place inside the barbed wire.

Sickness and Death

The death rate in a concentration camp is extremely high, but the number of men who die from direct mistreatment or who are shot is considerably smaller than people outside seem to assume. The camp usually

---

3. This estimate was arrived at as follows: There were 9,800 prisoners. Of these, 400 second-termers, 400 Jehovah's Witnesses, and 400 men in the punitive company received almost no money; they were permitted only ten marks every third month. Of the remaining 8,600, only about 4,000 received money regularly. In contrast to Dachau, this was less than half, because in Buchenwald about a fourth of the prisoners were non-Jewish asocials and gypsies, who received very little money, while the same groups comprised only about one-fifth of the Dachau prisoners.

Those who received money regularly seldom got less than ten marks per month. No one received more than thirty (in contrast to sixty-five in Dachau). Thus the average was probably seventeen or eighteen marks per month (in Dachau, about twenty-two), or a total of 70,000 marks for the whole camp. If this amount was distributed on six paydays, then approximately 12,000 marks poured into the camp on one such day. Thus, each of the 4,000 money-receivers had, on the average, about 50 to 60 pfennigs per day. Assuming that on payday each had about one day´s spending money left, there were about 2,000 marks left, which, together with the new money, would add up to 14,000 marks.

These estimates have been checked with others made by former prisoners. From them it appears that the actual amounts might have been from one-third less to one half more than my estimates.

kills its victims in less spectacular ways. It is comparable not so much to a ferocious murderer who runs amok, as to a dreadful machine that slowly, but without mercy, grinds its victims to bits.

The greatest number of deaths are due to the general conditions; usually, it is difficult to define exactly what killed a person. When one hears of a man's death and asks, "Anything special the matter with him?" the answer, more often than not, is, "No, nothing special. Buchenwald has swallowed him."

People are overworked, underclothed, and underfed. They work in every kind of weather, in rain and snow and burning sunshine. Wounds and illnesses are not treated until they have reached a stage where they are immediately apparent, and treatment is discontinued before the patient is actually cured. Almost no treatment is given for internal diseases, because those who complain of illnesses that cannot be seen are considered fakers. No special diet is available for those with intestinal diseases, except for the few cases that are taken into the infirmary. There is no insulin or other treatment for diabetics, no treatment ordinarily for cardiac cases or for illnesses of the respiratory tract. Only fully developed pneumonia is acknowledged, and the death rate from that is about sixty to seventy percent. Arthritis is an unknown sickness, because you can't see it. So are practically all nervous diseases. Only actual insanity is given some recognition—and then, not in the form of treatment, but in the form of segregation. Those who are undeniably insane are put into special groups and work together.

Because of weakened body resistance, injuries and small infections immediately develop into large festering sores. Men must continue to work in the dirt, until finally the affected limb will no longer function. Blood poisoning sets in, and the infected cellular tissue begins to rot away. This is one of the most typical concentration camp diseases— "cellulites," or a "phlegmon." Then the infirmary intervenes and cuts. Sometimes that stops the rotting process. If not, they amputate fingers, hands, arms, or feet.

When the men have colds, which ordinarily would keep them in bed for a few days or perhaps only make them uncomfortable for a while, they have to work on until the fever has gone up to at least 103 degrees. Then, if they are lucky, they are taken to the infirmary. But frequently it is then too late, and pneumonia has already set in. During the winter, frostbite reaches the proportions of a catastrophe. Men come in by the hundreds with frostbite, and there are too many for the infirmary to treat. Most of them are sent away. Some receive the only treatment available—bathing their hands in lukewarm water for an hour a day. Then back to work. In exceptional cases, they are granted a few days off from work.

During the summer the prisoners are not allowed to drink water. Instead, they are driven to speed up the work. Many die of sunstroke or general exhaustion.

It is amazing that under these conditions there were not more epidemics than was the case. In Dachau there were none while I was there. In Buchenwald a typhoid epidemic developed during the spring of 1939. For two months it ravaged the camp. The prisoners in charge of the infirmary fought a terrific battle to hide from the administration the fact that there was an epidemic. They knew that releases would be stopped immediately if it became known. But at length it could no longer be hidden. All releases were stopped for six weeks.

The administration, fearful that the disease might spread to the SS camp and the surrounding country, had all the men in the camp vaccinated three times. A few infirmary attendants stood on the roll-call square and vaccinated the men, who lined up by the thousand. No hypodermic needles were exchanged or sterilized between the individual vaccinations. The administration was afraid that this might cause the spread of veneral diseases, and they were also afraid that men who feared vaccination might be able to escape getting vaccinated. The only measure they took was to threaten, "Anyone who has syphilis and is vaccinated, gets 'twenty-five.' Anyone who does not get vaccinated, gets 'twenty-five.'" Actually, no one was given "twenty-five" for either of these two reasons, but many, including syphilitics, were whipped for disorderly conduct while lining up. Others, especially gypsies, who were afraid of the hypodermic and therefore hid in the forest, were punished for loafing.

It was a relatively light attack of typhoid. There were only about 350 cases (that is, about four percent of the total number of prisoners), of which about 180 died. The germs did not stop at the fence, and the SS men and some of the neighboring villages got their share of typhoid.

In December 1938, an epidemic of an intestinal disease developed. It was not lethal and ended when the heavy frost set in, which apparently killed the germs. An epidemic of meningitis was stopped in January 1939, after it had cost fifteen lives. This time the administration took effective action and provided first-class serum. The danger was too great.

At the beginning of the typhoid epidemic, and on other occasions as well, the SS doctor's first tactic to halt the disease was always to kill the

49

germ carriers by injecting an overdose of morphine. This policy of individual murder was continued until either the disease had disappeared or the epidemic had taken over the camp. This fact, unknown to many prisoners, was told to me by a man who worked in the infirmary. He repeatedly witnessed scenes when the SS doctor ordered the prisoner-attendants to kill a particular germ carrier, and when, on the next inspection, he found the sick man still alive, the doctor himself performed the final injection.

The infirmary at Dachau consists of two barracks with about eighty beds, that at Buchenwald of three barracks with about 170 beds. In Buchenwald it is divided into two completely separate units, one for the non-Jews (120 beds) and one for the Jews (fifty beds). The non-Jewish infirmary is inside the barbed wire in the forest below the camp; the Jewish infirmary is in one of the regular camp barracks.

In both camps the infirmaries are under the supervision of the SS doctor, who is also in charge of the SS infirmaries. But he either does not have much time or does not worry much about the prison infirmary. Most of the time the infirmary in Dachau is run by two SS attendants and a few prisoners, and in Buchenwald almost exclusively by prisoners. These prisoners are ordinarily not former doctors, of whom many would be available, but men of other occupations—a printer, a carpenter, and so forth. These men train each other in the treatment of wounds and sickness and, after years of training, they achieve a surprising ability. They perform major operations, such as the amputation of arms and legs. How the first of them ever learned it, I do not know.

During my time the head attendant of the Buchenwald infirmary was an ex-printer, and the man who performed the most complicated operations was a former cabinetmaker. It is not quite clear why former physicians are practically never selected as infirmary attendants. The reason frequently advanced, namely, that the administration wants to keep them from thinking that they are better than the rest of the prisoners, does not seem very convincing.

At any rate, the men in the infirmary develop a great professional pride and a guild spirit that makes it rather difficult for them to consult with former doctors among the prisoners. Such consultation takes place only infrequently and through personal channels.

The infirmary gives clinical treatment in addition to taking care of men who are hospitalized. There is a minimum of medical supplies and instruments and medicines. The number of injured men seeking help is usually greater than can be treated during the rest period at noon, at night, or on Sunday, and those for whom there is no treatment are simply sent away. If they come back, they are beaten, perhaps with sticks and clubs—and if then they are afraid to come back until the wound has become too bad, they are blamed for not having come earlier, when the treatment would not have taken so long.

The infirmary issues passes which certify that the bearer need not work. The free time thus gained must usually be spent sitting in a clearing in the forest, rain or shine. However, during the winter a barrack was given over to the sick men. Of course only the worst cases receive such passes. Frequent checkups by SS officers weed out those who get into this crew by pretence or bribery. Other passes entitle men to do special work, such as mending socks, repairing shoes, etc.—work that has to be done, but which is easier than the regular work and is therefore available only to invalids.

The atmosphere in the infirmary is rough and harsh. The men are "hard-boiled." They have seen the utmost in human suffering. No man can observe what they must without either breaking down or becoming callous. They are callous and ruthless with most of their patients. But when special action is required, they rise splendidly to the occasion. When it is a question of saving a life that they want badly to save, they will take every risk. Their attitude will be no less rough, but they will smuggle and steal whatever supplies are needed, risking their own good places in an effort to save the man. Ordinarily this is done with the greatest discrimination, primarily in favor of political prisoners. But when the worst catastrophe of all befell the camp—when the Jews were forbidden treatment for weeks during the November pogroms in 1938—these men offered all their help indiscriminately for the thousands of Jews.

The total number of deaths is unknown, but a few figures obtained from men who worked in the infirmary may indicate the extent of fatalities. Between November 12, 1938, and February 22, 1939, about 900 men died in Buchenwald. At the beginning of this period, the camp contained about 20,000 prisoners, and at the end about 10,000. The difference is accounted for by the Jews who were brought in during the pogroms, most of whom were released within a month or two. During the second half of November, when the Jews were brought in and treatment in the infirmary was forbidden to them, there were about fifteen deaths a day. About the same number died per day during the first half of December, when there was a bitter cold wave. The maximum was thirty-two during a single day, when the prisoners stood for half a night on the roll-call square while a search was made for two fugitives. Seven dropped dead from the cold while we were still on the square. During the summer of 1938, about 1,600 Jews from Berlin were brought to Buchenwald, 130 of whom died during the month of July.

When a man dies, a case history is written by one of the men in the infirmary. This case history is written in medical terms, reporting that he died of heart disease, or arteriosclerosis, or tuberculosis, or any other sort of internal disease. It contains a detailed description of how he was delivered to the infirmary with such and such symptoms, how on such and such a day his condition became worse, a crisis arrived, and then he passed away. This case history is written no matter what the man actually died of. He may have been killed in an accident, shot, beaten to death, or forced to commit suicide; he may have died of blood poisoning due to a wound, or of the after-effects of a leg amputation, or anything else. The only connection between the deceased and the alleged disease is that for the most part, diseases are attributed which seem fairly plausible in view of the patient's age, such as arteriosclerosis for an old man and tuberculosis for a young one.

This case history is then added to the man's personal dossier, and from then on for all future reference, he has died of cardiac disease, or arteriosclerosis, or whatever the SS doctor happened to dream up for him. The men in the infirmary, of course, have to write these reports as ordered.

This information about forged case histories of casualties, unknown even to most former prisoners, was given to me by one of the men who wrote the reports. He quoted to me both actual case histories of dead men, and the faked reports he wrote about them, which were kept on file in Buchenwald.

The same queer bent toward formal legality runs through all Nazi terror. Everything has to have its place in a file box where it can be looked up, so that anyone can convince himself that all the due legalities were observed and that no illegal means were used to bring a man from life to death. If he happened to be a cardiac case, too bad for him—don't blame it on the concentration camp!

Chapter 6

The Prisoners

The prisoners were divided into categories according to the type of "crime" they had committed—for instance, political prisoners, professional criminals, the work-shy. These categories were identified by triangular colored badges, which were worn on jacket and trousers, along with the prison number. Jewish prisoners wore in addition a yellow badge, which, together with the other badge, formed a six-pointed "Star of David." Later on, the meaning of the categories seems to have changed from the type of crime committed to an indication of the authority under whose jurisdiction a man had been sent to camp, such as the Gestapo, criminal police, criminal courts, or public welfare oranizations.[1]

Prisoners within each category were more homogeneous than the camp as a whole. This homogeneity was due not so much to the type of crime committed as to the common social and political background of the men

---

1. This change was never officially announced, but could be inferred from many observations. When the Gestapo rounded up 2,000 Jews in the streets of Vienna in May 1938 solely because they were Jews, they were given the red or "political" badge. The "work-shy" were referred to by the administration also as "welfare prisoners," indicating that they were held by request of a welfare authority. Jews who were rounded up in Berlin in June 1938 by the criminal police on the basis of previous minor convictions, received a brown or black badge and were referred to as "cri-po prisoners" (criminal police prisoners).

in each category. It was made more evident by the fact that men in the same categories were usually housed in the same barracks.

As the meaning of the categories changed, prisoners falling into the same category showed less and less homogeneity of background and behavior. But the administration to a large degree continued to use the old concepts, which created a great deal of confusion among the prisoners. Men with black badges were still referred to as "work-shy," although many of them were skilled workers, who had been arrested for absenteeism, for instance, or because of nonpayment of alimony. Men who came from a penitentiary were given a green badge and treated as "professional criminals," although many of them were political cases. From time to time, the Jews had to fill out cards recording their previous convictions. Those who had any convictions at all received the green badge of the "professional criminal," even though the conviction may only have been the result of a traffic accident or of insolvency.

There was still worse confusion regarding the red or "political" badge. Originally it was given to political prisoners, but later to everybody who was arrested by the Gestapo. That included not only serious political opponents of the Nazis, but also any nonpolitical small businessman who had expressed his dissatisfaction with any of the numerous local trade authorities, and workers who had come into conflict with the *Arbeitsfront*. The red badge was also given to Nazis who were arrested in the course of internal conflicts within the party, or to SS men who were sent to the camp for violation of disciplinary rules. The real political men found it more and more difficult to keep their distance from those they considered "trash," and to keep their own dominating position.

The worst confusion was caused when the 2,000 Viennese Jews were given the red badge. In this flood of red badges, the older political prisoners almost completely disappeared. The camp began to identify the red badge with nonpolitical Jews. Only the political prisoners themselves made a sharp distinction between a "Jew," meaning a nonpolitical Jew with a red badge, and a "comrade," meaning a socialist or communist.

Political Prisoners: Red Badge, Arrested by the Gestapo

Social Democrats and Communists

In the beginning (1933), most of the prisoners were members of the workers' parties, the trade unions, or one of the numerous organizations connected with them. In Central Europe the workers' parties fulfilled, besides their immediate political pursuits, a number of social and cultural functions that served their political goals only indirectly. The individual party member found himself in a vast realm of suborganizations; he was usually a member of two or three of them at the same time, and he spent the greater part of his social life in them. There were all sorts of organizations—children's homes; boy and girl scouts; women's clubs; travel clubs; trade clubs; dancing and theatre groups; philosophic circles; study groups in economics and history, mineralogy and medicine; and clubs for any sort of education, hobby, or pastime, from fishing to breeding canaries.

Both the political and the nonpolitical organizations were run by the members themselves, with a great deal of local autonomy. They elected their own officers and respected them, because those who were not in office had been so before, or might be in the future, or at least had the power to unseat the incumbent if they didn't like him. And if a member so pleased he could always leave the organization.

The whole setup trained the members in a high degree of cooperation. Voluntary subordination under self-elected leaders and frequent sacrifices for the organization or for a common political goal were basic requirements. When members of these parties were brought to the first concentration camps to live under crowded and disorganized conditions, they acted in accordance with their previous cooperative training. They elected, in a very informal way, seniors or chairmen, and under their leadership began to organize the daily routine in cell and room and barrack.

The first leaders were perhaps chosen because they were known to the men from their previous political life. If it was discovered that an able political leader was not necessarily an able senior in the camp, new men were chosen. The men not only organized the daily routine such as cleaning the room, getting the food from the kitchen, etc., but they soon developed a sort of authority in other matters. They were called upon to settle controversies and to interpret the latest orders from the administration. They were also asked for their opinion about developments in the outside world. They took it upon themselves to give courage to those who needed it and to keep alive the spirits of all their fellow prisoners.

Around the senior who thus developed into a leader (or the leader who was chosen senior), there usually grew up a clique which formed the dominant elite of the little community. When this clique became exclusive, the rest formed groups and subgroups.

Thus, in the first stages of the concentration camp, a social life developed which had its roots primarily in the previous organizational life of the prisoners and their training in cooperative behavior. They were held together by a common ideology and by the fact that they were being persecuted together for this ideology.

Later, when other sorts of prisoners were brought in—nonpolitical opponents of the Nazis, professional criminals, and so forth—the political prisoners were the ones who were best organized as a group. When the administration set up its system of barracks seniors and work capos, they first took political prisoners, because they already knew their way around. All the power connected with these positions thus came into the hands of political prisoners. They also developed quickly into the moral elite of the camp. They dominated the rest of the prisoners both by their numbers and by their better organization. Usually, this domination was not contested by the other groups.

The majority of Social Democrats and Communists were skilled industrial workers, white-collar men, and officials of party and trade-union organizations. The Communists had a larger proportion of unskilled labor among them and the Social Democrats a larger proportion of white-collar workers. Both income and educational levels were somewhat higher among the Social Democrats, who had a larger following among the middle classes.

The industrial workers usually brought with them from their jobs a good deal of training and teamwork. White-collar and middle-class people had less of this training at their place of work, but had usually been quite active in organizations. Professionals among them showed more individualistic features at times, but ideologically they were well prepared for voluntary subordination, once they had made up their minds to join the workers' parties. The intellectual and educational level of the political prisoners, including the conservatives and liberals, was superior to that of any other group in the camp. Only some of the nonpolitical Jews were on the same level.

Conservatives and Fascists

Conservative parties in Central Europe were much less strongly organized than their socialist counterparts. Their members did not go through as much cooperative training in daily organizational life. When brought to the concentration camp, they found themselves a small minority among the well-organized mass of leftists. The Socialists treated their former enemies with great distrust in the beginning. The individual men were not accepted at face value, as political comrades were, but had first to prove that they were reliable. Many were never accepted and lived a lonely life.

Most of the conservative prisoners had been high-ranking party officials, by profession lawyers, teachers, physicians, business executives, journalists. They were more accustomed to rule than to subordinate themselves in daily cooperation. This made adjustment to camp conditions more difficult for them. Most of the Socialist prisoners were rank–and-file members, used to voluntary subordination. The reason for this difference was that the Nazis arrested those whom they knew, or who were pointed out to them, as members of certain parties. Socialists and Communists frequently appeared in public meetings, in street demonstrations; often they appeared in uniforms. Thus they were easily recognizable, and one did not have to be known as a leader to be betrayed to the Gestapo as a "red." Conservatives appeared considerably less in public, seldom marched in the streets, hardly ever wore uniforms. Thus one really had to be a leader in order to be known at all to people outside one's own party. Consequently, the Nazis arrested more of these leaders and fewer rank-and-file members.

The situation was different for the members of the Austrian fascist organizations, who had ruled the country before the Nazis took over. They had frequently marched around in uniforms and were easily recognizable. Thus a greater proportion of rank-and-file members were arrested. They had not gone through the cooperative training of the democratic organizations, but had at least the military training of subordination in organizations of which they themselves had chosen to be members. This rendered adjustment somewhat easier for them.

One important difference between the leftists and the conservatives was that the former still could hope for a share in the coming revolution, while the latter were a completely defeated group. The Socialists, considering themselves the representatives of the working classes, put their hopes in the fact that although the fascists could suppress the workers as a political group, they could not annihilate them—they needed them in their factories. There the workers could reorganize themselves for a future fight. Most of the conservatives in the camp had lost their political goals. They could not, as the conservatives in other occupied countries could, consider themselves the imprisoned representatives of a class that still fought the national enemy outside the barbed wire. They represented only one wing of a class, ousted by the rest who had joined up with the Nazis. They were truly defeated.

The Liberals

The liberals usually had had some party contacts in their previous life, very often with the cultural and educational workers' organizations. Thus many of them were known to their more outstanding political fellow prisoners. They had lived more individualistic lives than the ordinary socialist party members, but they had approved of and often aided the workers' organizations. They did not find it too difficult to find their place in cooperative groups, which were dominated by men whose general political leanings they approved. The political prisoners generally accepted the liberals who were thrown in with them in the camp, as they had many ideas and ideals in common. They helped the liberals along as well as they could. The liberals represented the highest educational and intellectual level in the camp. Most of them had advanced academic training and belonged to highly specialized professions.

Others

This classification included the many nonpolitical people who had been arrested for complaining about rising prices and falling wages or about restrictions upon the general freedom to move and act. These were the so-called "Miesmacher und Kritikaster" (spreaders of discontent and carping critics).

The Gestapo also arrested people against whom there was no concrete charge, but who were under general suspicion for approving of anti-Nazi activities. Others were sent to a concentration camp when a regular court trial might have revealed military or political secrets. Often participants in minor labor quarrels, which usually consisted only of mild grumbling, were sent to a camp—it seemed the safest way to nip any further developments in the bud. In times of political crisis, the Gestapo rounded up thousands of people who were known to have participated in political movements years before, even if they had given up all activity since.

More and more SS men were brought in for graft, violation of disciplinary rules, and sometimes for political unreliability. Other Nazis were brought to camps as the result of factional fights within the party—Röhm men, Strasser men, and other true Nazis who had believed their leader's pseudosocialist phraseology and had expressed too freely their disappointment at the outcome.

The red badge was given to all 300 men in the first two transports of prisoners from Austria, although many were nonpolitical people. Finally, it was given to the 2,000 Viennese Jews.

These various groups cannot be described as having some common characteristics in their social, economic, and cultural backgrounds. They had almost nothing in common except the fact that they had been arrested by the Gestapo. They came from all walks of life. But the political prisoners among them, by means of all sorts of connivance and trickery, managed to keep the majority of their own people together in a few "political" barracks. Thus they retained their organization as the leading group in the camp.

Professional Criminals: Green Badge, Sent by the Criminal Courts

The designation "professional criminal" was originally given to men who had served one or more sentences for serious crimes—murderers, habitual thieves, pimps, forgers, counterfeiters, rapists, killers, robbers, and others. Most of them were held in the camps for the purpose of segregating them from the population after they had served their terms. The great majority of them came from the lower educational and income levels; many of them had never held any regular jobs. But many were mentally alert and had strongly developed personalities. In spite of the fact that they were recruited mainly from urban areas, the number of skilled workers among them was surprisingly low.

In spite of what the phrase "professional criminal" may convey, most of them were not habitual criminals, nor had they belonged to organized gangs. They had committed one or several crimes, with or without accomplices. However, there were a few members of famous Berlin gangs.

Usually, they had not previously belonged to any large political or social organization. Many had been members of small clubs for boxing, wrestling, etc. They had a fair number of social contacts, but not the sort that would train them in cooperative behavior. Neither did their jobs, if they'd had any.

Later on, the green badge was given to most prisoners who were brought in from a penitentiary, although this often included political men who had been involved in street fights and convicted of murder when the fight resulted in casualties. When the Gestapo decided from time to time to "cleanse" the German nation of its criminal elements, they rounded up anyone who had a major conviction on his record, regardless of the type of crime or whether the criminal had in the meantime become re-established as a member of his community. In still later roundups, they went after the "criminal Jews," and previous conviction was no longer a reason, but merely a pretext for arrest. Any conviction, no matter for how slight a crime, was enough. A growing number of SS men were brought in whose graft was interpreted as a "professional crime."

Thus the professional criminals became a less homogeneous and perhaps less vicious group than they had been originally. But the camp, both the administration and the prisoners, treated them as a group on the basis of the original meaning of the phrase, and on the basis of behavior that was observed in those who were justifiably given the name.

As a group they were largely rejected by the camp. This rejection was not based on their crimes—nobody cared about things like that—but upon a widespread and often well-founded assumption that it was difficult to cooperate with them because they had no cooperative training. Even if it worked for a while, it was always dangerous. When faced with a crisis, they were not willing to make personal sacrifices to save the group, but instead sacrificed the group to save their own skins.

When a big scandal was uncovered—for instance, corruption or an organized slowdown or smuggling—the same thing could always be observed. If political prisoners primarily were involved, the investigation would soon peter out. No torture, no blackmailing, would yield more than five, six, or seven of the men involved. When professional criminals were the main participants, they betrayed each other by the dozen. While the political prisoners were deeply imbued with the principle, "Never betray the group," the professional criminals were restrained only by the fear that the group might avenge itself.

Common treatment by the administration and common rejection by the prisoners helped to transform the professional criminals from an atomized agglomeration of men, who had nothing in common but the green badge, into a group with a well-developed "we"-feeling. This was strengthened by the fact that the "greens" as a group did not fill the lowest position on the social ladder. By feeling himself a member of his own group, the individual criminal had an opportunity to look down at the great mass of the work-shy. He could hardly have enjoyed this privilege if both categories had been treated merely as collections of individuals. If that had been case, he might very often have proved inferior to one of the work-shy.

Cri-Po Prisoners: Brown Badge, Arrested by the Criminal Police

The meaning of this category was never quite clear to us, but neither was it to the administration. The "browns" took an intermediate position between the professional criminals and the work-shy. Most of them were rounded up as undesirables by the police, apparently on the basis of minor convictions. This was particularly true of a group of 1,600 Jews from Berlin. But others received the brown badge without any previous conviction. The administration usually mixed them up with the work-shy, and when the clothing department did not have enough uniforms with brown badges, they gave them black ones, but occasionally also green ones.

Work-shy and Asocial: Black Badge, Sent by the Welfare Authorities or the Gestapo

Originally this category designated vagabonds, loafers, vagrants, habitual beggars, and so forth. This original concept gave the group its name and its social position in the camp. These men represented the very lowest level of income, education, and intelligence, although a number of fairly shrewd individuals were among them.

Later on, when the meaning of the categories changed, more and more men fell into this group who would otherwise have been sent to public workhouses for failure to support their families, divorced wives, or illegitimate children. It also included drunkards and quarrellers. This group consisted primarily of unskilled laborers, with a small proportion of skilled workers.

Men were also sent to camp as work-shy who had come into conflict with the *Deutsche Arbeitsfront* because they had changed jobs without permission, or had been out of a job for some time, or had quarrelled at their place of work. More and more, semipolitical motives played a part in the arrest of people for minor labor disputes.

When the Nazis began to force people into the growing armament industry, they suddenly and without any warning banned certain occupations and put several hundred people who worked in these occupations into concentration camps in order to terrorize the rest. These included dancers, waiters, proprietors of nightclubs, small shop-owners and craftsmen who had clung too long to what was left of their independence, and others. Along with them they sent others who had never done anything but live on their fathers' money.

When all these new groups were brought to the camp, the intellectual and economic level of the "asocials" rose somewhat. But the overwhelming majority still belonged to the lowest level, and the proportion of feeble-minded persons among them remained large.

Of all the prisoners described so far, these had lived the least cooperative life. Still, it would be incorrect to call them the most individualistic category. As a group, they were the most apathetic among the prisoners, with the most poorly developed sense both for cooperative behavior and for individual action. In the camp, they more or less ceased to be human beings; they lived a sort of animal existence, trying to keep physically alive without any thought of the why and wherefore. Their fellow prisoners thought of them as the most unreliable and the most stupid group in the camp. This was not always justified, for among them were hundreds of ordinary citizens who had simply happened to stand in the way of some authority; however, it was justified for the vast majority. It was usually considered dangerous to have "blacks" in any forbidden activity, such as organized shirking or smuggling. They were less alert than others and therefore frequently caught. And when put on the spot, they were apt to give away their accomplices, not only to save their own skins, but also because of sheer stupidity and helplessness.

The lack of individuality in most of the "asocials" prevented the development of any "we"-feeling among them, even though they were housed together and rejected as a group, as were the professional criminals. They were absolutely unable to organize any group life among themselves, beyond the minimum routine prescribed by camp discipline. Those who resented their social position in the camp tried to improve it by making friends with other prisoners, preferably political ones, and by dissociating themselves from the "trash" in their own category.

The black badge was also given to gypsies. Living on the borderline of law and society, they constituted an element of disorder that the Gestapo would not tolerate. The gypsies were put into concentration camps to make them "settle down." Most of them came from neighborhoods of Berlin, but a whole tribe numbering 300 came from Burgenland, the formerly Hungarian part of Austria. The chieftain was an old man of more than ninety years, almost blind, who used to be led around by two sons, both well over seventy.

The gypsies fitted even less than the other "blacks" into any sort of cooperative situation. They hardly understood why they were in a concentration camp, and they did not care about anyone else. When they saw an advantage for themselves, they denounced others without compunction. Therefore, the others rejected the gypsies and were wary of them.

Practically all of the "asocials" mentioned so far were non-Jews. Jews were arrested more indiscriminately by Gestapo action and were given the red badge. But hundreds of the Jewish cri-po prisoners from Berlin who had originally received a brown badge ended up with a black one. They were not treated as regular "blacks" by the camp, but rather in the same way as other nonpolitical Jews.

Jehovah's Witnesses: Violet Badge, Arrested by the Gestapo

Jehovah's Witnesses were incarcerated primarily as conscientious objectors to military service. In addition, their resistance to totalitarian demands on men's souls, when organized in religious communities, was always a latent political threat.

Most Jehovah's Witnesses were tradesmen and little shopkeepers from small towns. They belonged to a social milieu that bred individualism, but this individualism was outweighed by their membership in a religious community which had cooperation and willingness to sacrifice as one of its basic principles. Their educational level was not high. They were of average intelligence, but often underestimated because of the peculiar notions they had about the world and its political course. In the camp, they were one of the groups that had the highest morale, as helpfulness to their fellow men was part of their religious creed. They organized themselves into a smoothly cooperating community.

The concentration camp authorities led them to believe that if they resigned from their organization, they would be released. Actually, only a few cases are known in which men were released after renouncing their religious principles. Others, who also resigned, were not released. However, the fiction was believed for a long time, yet practically nobody signed the paper of renunciation. We were told that the few who did were not members of the organization, but people whom the Nazis had confused with Jehovah's Witnesses because they were against the war.

I repeatedly asked Jehovah's Witnesses why they refused to sign the paper. They gave various explanations: "It is a sin to betray the Lord. You can't change your convictions like your shirt. What good is it, they won't release you anyway. Soon the Lord will establish his Kingdom on Earth, we want to be part of it. The neighbors would point with their fingers at me and say, 'He used to witness for Jehovah, but now he has failed Him.'"

The last two reasons were most frequently given. The latter indicates the terrific social pressure upon a man who has been known as a fighter for a certain ideal. When he gives in under pressure, his community will treat him like a traitor, even though the community did not share his conviction. The other reason indicates the source from which the Jehovah's Witnesses drew their strength—their absolute certainty that Jehovah's Millenium was near. The Witnesses quoted long passages from the Bible, they interpreted prophecies, they divided the number of the prophets by the number of letters in their names, and they calculated the exact year when the Lord would come. There were many, many ways to arrive at the true year. Since it was always close at hand, corrections were sometimes necessary. These were made by reinterpreting the Holy Writ.

These men were not as pacifistic as they seem at first sight. They were waiting for the Day of Judgment, when God will descend on those scoundrels "up there" and annihilate them with fire and sword in a frightful Armageddon. But their knowledge of the approaching Day of Judgment and their firm belief in their role as executors of His will gave the Witnesses a moral power of resistance that was far superior to that of any other political or religious group. Every hardship, every torture they underwent, was only a test by Jehovah to discover the really faithful. And they proved faithful, one by one.

Jehovah's Witnesses were the only ideological group in the camp that was treated more or less as such by the administration. They were referred to as "Bible students" (*Bibelforscher*), as they call themselves, or by one of their slang nicknames, such as "Bible stallions" (*Bibelhengste*) or "comedians of heaven" (*Himmelskomiker*).

They were housed together and, to a certain degree, subjected to special treatment. They were permitted only one letter and ten marks every third month, and they were not allowed to smoke. In Dachau they were in the "punitive company," and aside from these restrictions, they sometimes received better treatment than the rest of the camp. In Buchenwald many of them were assigned to special skilled jobs or kitchen duty, or as officers' servants. In the punitive company at Dachau they were not hounded as much as others who were there for disciplinary reasons.

Sometimes they fared worse. One morning, for example, Commander Rödl in Buchenwald had the potato peelers line up. With a threatening undertone in his voice, he asked, "Do you still believe in your Jehovah? Step forward every man who does not!" Not a single man stepped forward. "Now I will teach you to believe in your ... Jehovah. All of you to the quarry, on the double!"

Another commander used to chide them, "Where is your Jehovah now? Why doesn't he get you out of here? Is he perhaps afraid of us? Or of the barbed wire?"

Incidents like that achieved the opposite of what was intended. They helped strengthen the feeling of these men that they were the outpost of His kingdom—and for the commander they had only silent contempt.

Social Democrats and Communists might also, technically, have been treated as separate groups, but they were not. They were referred to only by the word "politicals," which for the administration included everybody who wore a red badge. Words like "Socialist" or "Communist" were, in our time, practically taboo for the administration. The difference in treatment had its political reasons. The Nazis considered Social Democrats and Communists a powerful threat to their government. Treating them in the camp as a special group (as was done during the first year) would have implied recognition of them as an organized enemy. But that was just what the Nazis wanted to avoid. They wanted to destroy in these men the feeling that they were the representatives of a group, a force that was still fighting. Therefore they tried to depersonalize them.

Jehovah's Witnesses were a considerably weaker threat. There were not too many of them. Before their persecution began, there were never more than a few thousand in each of the larger regions of Germany. The average citizen and the authorities looked on them merely as slightly peculiar and off the right track. If it had not been for their refusal of military service and for the latent danger posed by the existence of independent organizations, nobody would ever have thought of persecuting them.

Homosexuals: Pink Badge, Sent by the Criminal Courts

Prisoners in this category had served a sentence for homosexuality and then been transferred to a concentration camp. Practically all of them were non-Jews. In Dachau they lived together in one barrack. The few who were Jews lived among the other Jews. In Buchenwald they were part of the punitive company. Homosexuals were treated by their fellow prisoners in about the same way as they were treated outside—accepted individually but regarded in general with a certain degree of prejudice.

Aside from those with a pink badge, there were, of course, prisoners who fell into other classifications and happened to be homosexual in addition. And there were others who turned homosexual under the abnormal conditions of a purely male society. The administration knew this was going on, but avoided interference. Apparently it did not quite know how to handle the problem. In flagrant cases, a thrashing of "twenty-five" was considered an appropriate solution.

In December 1937, the Jews in Dachau were locked up in their barracks for many weeks with the windows blackened. They were forced to write letters home announcing that they were now subject to harsher treatment, which would become much worse if their relatives did not stop spreading "atrocity stories" in foreign countries.

The barracks were terribly overcrowded and not ventilated; not enough food was distributed, and many died of disease. The political men among the prisoners began to organize courses in languages, history, and politics. Some of the men began to practice homosexuality, which, under the circumstances, could not be concealed from other men in the barrack.

When the so-called "isolation" was lifted in January 1938, the story came out. The administration, instead of admitting directly the existence of political activity in the camp, clamped down on the homosexual affair and tried to involve the political leaders in it. Two of the leaders committed suicide. Six other alleged homosexuals received "twenty-five," and later in the spring were handed over to the Criminal Court in Munich. The Court, considering the peculiar circumstances under which this "homosexuality" had occurred, did not apply the full severity of the law. The men were sentenced to a few months in prison each, which they welcomed gladly as a change from the much harder life in the concentration camp. However, after the trial, they were brought back to Dachau and kept there in the dungeon for months. Along with the other prisoners, they were sent to Buchenwald in the fall, and in spring of 1939 they were handed over to a prison to serve their few months.

Emigrants: Blue Badge, Arrested by the Gestapo

Most of these men were Jews who had come back from foreign countries, either after failure to establish themselves or simply in the ordinary course of business travel. Their actions naturally seemed less stupid at the time it happened (1934 and1935) than it does today. Some were extradited from neighboring countries because they happened to escape the Nazis without first obtaining a passport from the Gestapo. During my time, the Netherlands in particular provided inmates for Buchenwald in this way. Others were expelled from their guest countries because citizens of the guest country had been expelled from Germany. If they were Jews, they ended up in a concentration camp. Unfortunately, here too, the Netherlands provided new inmates. Others of the emigrants were regular political cases, men who had worked as propagandists against the Nazis and were caught by the Gestapo. Non-Jews in this group were primarily former members of the French Foreign Legion. In Buchenwald these legionnaires wore the red (political) badges.

Race Polluters: Black Outline, Sent by the Criminal Court or the Gestapo

Men in this category were held under the Nuremberg race laws, which forbade sexual intercourse between Jews and "Aryans." Evidently, only Jews who violated these laws were prosecuted. "Race pollution" seemed to be considered immoral only when Jews practiced it. The only "Aryan" in this category was a former SS man, and he was given a special classification—*Artvergessen* (forgetful of one's own kind).

Many of the "race polluters" were old men of 60 or 70 who, for one reason or another, had not married the women with whom they had lived for decades. Others were youths who, for romantic or other reasons had ignored the law. One of the most touching cases was a bricklayer, a particularly ugly man, good-natured but very stupid. For years, he had lived without any sexual intercourse. One night he had visited a prostitute. The next morning she denounced him to the Gestapo. He was sent to a concentration camp because he, a Jew, had violated the honor of a German woman.

Most of these men came to the camp after having served terms in a penitentiary. Practically all of them were nonpolitical middle-class people. When many of them lived together in one room, they had the organizational difficulties that corresponded to their individualistic backgrounds. When only a few of them lived in a room with others, they did not attract attention as being different.

As far as their "crime" was concerned, nobody gave it a second thought. After all, they had done what everybody else does; it was made a "crime" only by a peculiar twist in the German concept of justice.

In Dachau they lived together with the other prisoners. For a long time, that was also the case in Buchenwald. In the spring of 1939, both they and the homosexuals were put in the punitive company.

Second-Termers: Colored Bar, Arrested by the Gestapo

A bar the same color as the badge indicated that a man was in the camp for the second time. Practically all the second-termers were Social Democrats or Communists. In the beginning, there were some Jews among them, but later on, no Jews were added, as Jews were released from the camps only on the condition that they would leave the country.

The second-termers—150 in Dachau, 400 in Buchenwald, and hundreds and hundreds in other camps—were proof, more than words can be, of man's undying fighting spirit. They were men who had gone through the hell of Dachau and still continued to fight for their ideals. Too little seems to be known about them in countries where the existence of an anti-Nazi movement in Germany is often doubted.

In the camps they represented the very elite of the prisoners; their colored bar was referred to as the "badge of honor." In Dachau they were kept in the punitive company; in Buchenwald they had a barrack among the others, but were subject to the same restrictions as Jehovah's Witnesses (one letter and ten marks every three months, smoking forbidden).

Idiots: White Armband with the Imprint "Blöd" (idiot)

Most of the "idiots" were non-Jewish, work-shy imbeciles and halfwits whom the welfare authorities wanted to get rid of. The few Jews among them had lost their minds under mistreatment on their way to the camp or inside it. There were about twenty-five men in this category in Buchenwald. The category did not exist in Dachau.

They lived together in one room and were assigned to easy jobs. No one paid much attention to them. With empty eyes they trotted along behind their capo, the only man who could really talk to them. Most of them had not the faintest idea where they were and what was happening to them. Still, they were regular prisoners in a concentration camp.

Jews: Yellow Badge, Combined with Another Color

The definition of a Jew was not very clear. When prisoners were brought in who had been arrested on charges other than that of being Jews, the order was given, "Jews, half-Jews, quarter-Jews, and so forth, segregate." And the men segregated themselves according to their previous knowledge of what the Nazis considered to be a Jew.

The Nazi concept followed not religious but racial lines. A half-Jew was a person with two Jewish grandparents. A quarter-Jew had one Jewish grandparent, and the mechanically spoken "and so forth" included combinations such as three Jewish great-grandparents. Occasionally, one Jewish great-grandparent was enough.

The men evidently segregated themselves under the impression that the Gestapo knew everything. People who had been Catholics or Protestants for generations, whose closest friends did not know about their Jewish grandmothers, would obediently step out of the ranks and become Jews. There were only a very few cases known in which men who fell under the classification did not comply with the order.

The camp made its own rules about races, following the strict standards of the SA.[2] In ordinary Nazi courts, a "quarter-Jew," was treated as a non-Jew, provided that he did not adhere to the Jewish religion and was not married to a Jew. In the concentration camp, he was a Jew.

Thus from a racial point of view, the "Jews" were a very mixed group. They were still more mixed as far as their religious and cultural backgrounds were concerned. There were hundreds of baptized Christians among them, and other hundreds who did not adhere to any religion. Others, by the hundreds and thousands, belonged legally to the Jewish faith because their parents happened to be Jews, but had had practically no contact with Jewish religion or culture. Only a small minority were orthodox Jews.

In some parts of Germany, the process of assimilation between Jews and non-Jews had proceeded so far that even the Nazis had difficulty separating them. This was particularly true of Vienna. Hundreds of these men, singled out as Jews, were married to non-Jewish women, or were the sons of mixed marriages, and their children were treated as non-Jews outside. So far had the mixture of races gone that some of the men

---

2. Editor's note: The SA (Sturm-Abteilung, also known as stormtroopers or brownshirts) was one of the private armies of the Nazi movement. The SA played a crucial role in the street flights in Weimar Germany, but lost influence after 1933 due to factional rivalries between several branches of the Nazi movement.

who were forced to wear the Star of David in the camp had been fervent anti-Semites outside; some of them had even been members of the Nazi underground movement during the Dollfuss period in Austria. I still remember the grotesque sight of a man with the star of the Jewish professional criminal on his trousers—which were held together by the belt of the SA unit of which he had been a member before he wound up in Dachau.

Since the Jews were such a mixed agglomeration of people, the fact that they were Jews was not an incentive to self-organization. They established their group relations on the basis of other common interests. Political men stuck together; so did liberals who had known each other personally or by name. So too did orthodox Jews, who shared a religious creed and resented the fact that the others did not revert to the faith of their fathers, while they were made to suffer for it. So did the few anti-Semites among them.

Relations between Jews and non-Jews in the camp hardly followed the racial concept at all. Most relations were based on membership in other groups such as the Socialists and Communists, or simply on personal acquaintance between individuals made on the working grounds. In Dachau, where the political prisoners dominated, anti-Semitism played only a very small role. It was more important in Buchenwald. Problems involved here will be treated in a later chapter. We may anticipate by saying that the administration did not succeed in creating more anti-Semitism than some groups had brought with them from the outside.

Chapter 7

The Guards

The Common Guards

There were about 6,000 men of the *SS Verfügungstruppe* in Dachau and three thousand in Buchenwald. The daily guards and sentinels were taken from this reservoir, but not the permanent staff of the prison camps, who were especially appointed to their jobs.

Outsiders often ask, "How could they ever get 6,000 sadists together in one spot?" They didn't get them. They made them. The conditions under which these SS men were trained made the system independent of the available supply of psychopaths. However, there was a certain amount of self-selection of sadists involved; not everybody applied for service in the SS.

The SS was established in 1925 as a bodyguard for leading party members, a gang of hooligans who were used in street fights and to break up political meetings. In the late twenties, it developed into a strong military and political body, used for battles inside and outside the party. After 1933, when the power apparatuses of Reich and party were amalgamated, the SS took over more and more of the political tasks of the police.

Originally, the SS was made up chiefly of people for whom service in the SS was a pastime. When it became necessary to have reliable troops always at hand in case of civilian outbreaks, a military body of SS men was established, the *SS Verfügungstruppe.*

By 1938, admission to the SS was no longer a process of selecting tough individual hooligans; it had become a routinized procedure, subject to certain qualifying conditions, as is common for elite military units everywhere.

The prospective SS recruit was about 18 or 19 years old. He often preferred service in the SS to the army because it offered certain privileges and a respected position in the Nazi state. He had to prove physical fitness, his "Aryan" ancestry back to 1800, and four years of membership in the Hitler Youth and other party organizations. His application had to be accompanied by letters of recommendation from his superiors, describing him as a good Nazi.

Here we see an element of selection. A "good" Nazi was supposed to be an especially tough fighter, an aggressive and devil-may-care fellow. He was supposedly obsessed by an "idealistic spirit" that made him willing to fire upon father and mother and to sell out brother and sister, when it served the glory of party and Reich.

Applicants for service in the SS usually did not know whether they would serve in a concentration camp. Some of them may have known from their friends in great detail what was going on inside the camps, while others may not have known anything about it, or if they had been told, dismissed it as a pack of lies. But all of them knew one thing beyond doubt—they were going to belong to the toughest body in the German Reich, the one that dealt most harshly with Jews and Reds and all other opponents of the Nazi system. Men who, knowing this, voluntarily applied for admission, may safely be assumed to have represented the toughest part of German youth. It also seems reasonable to assume that the expectation of cruelty and mistreatment attracted a larger proportion of real pathological cases and sadists than were attracted by any other organization.

The social background of the SS men varied in different sections of Germany. In Dachau most of them (perhaps 80 or 90 percent) were sons of Bavarian peasants or farmhands. They constituted one of the most uneducated groups one can imagine in a modern state, with a deeply ingrained hatred of all that smelled of "city" and "intelligentsia." This added greatly to their hatred for the prisoners, the vast majority of whom were *Stadtfrack* (city slickers).

In Buchenwald, too, a large proportion of the SS men came from the countryside, but there were also a certain number of lower-middle-class people and workers. Thuringia, where they came from, was more highly industrialized than Bavaria.

The young recruits in the SS camp underwent regular military training, perhaps with more stress laid upon Nazi indoctrination than was the case in ordinary army camps. When the camp happened to be combined with a concentration camp, duty as guards for the prisoners at work was part of their daily routine.

The life of the SS man was poverty-stricken. Their salary enabled them to spend only an occasional weekend in Munich or Weimar; the rest of their leisure time was spent in the camp. Actually their lives were almost as closely tied up with the camp as were the prisoners', and it did not help them very much that they were sitting outside the fence and the prisoners inside. They were still close to the fence most of the time.

They were on good terms with the youth of the neighborhood; the boys tried to prevent the SS men from stealing their girls. That restricted their sex life to a minimum; sometimes they could resort to a prostitute in the nearest city, but usually not, for the salary was too low. In the meantime, they waited months for a furlough and dreamed about the girls back home.

The common guards came in contact with the prisoners on the working grounds. There they formed chains of sentinels, surrounding a large or small area, primarily in order to prevent riot or escape. Where they were close enough to the prisoners, they also drove them on to work, mistreated them, yelled at them, made them carry out all sorts of exercises, threw stones at them, or did whatever they thought fitting. Sometimes they left the prisoners alone. A sentinel was not supposed to leave his place. If he wanted to mistreat a man, he either waited until the man, in the course of his work, came close enough, or he called the man to him.

Particularly in Dachau, the sentinels were close to the men all the time. Each working group outside the barbed wire had its own chain of sentinels, very often placed at a distance of not more than two yards from the prisoners, seldom farther away than ten or fifteen yards. And usually all the guards could simultaneously observe each other and all the prisoners. That gave a great deal of publicity to each act, and this publicity seemed to play a large role in the amount of mistreatment or teasing the sentinels accorded the prisoners. Apparently, the individual guards wanted to show off to their friends and comrades, sometimes to their superiors, and prove what tough guys they were.

Some of the guards obviously mistreated the prisoners from sadistic and pathological motives. One could see how their eyes grew gloomy while they were beating or kicking a man. Some of them invented the subtlest finesses to the game. Still others looked upon what they did to a prisoner less as an act of fiendish cruelty than as a boyish joke: You yelled at a man and the man began to run. You yelled some more, and he got frightened and ran some more. You could feel like a young puppy, barking with joy at an object that moves.

Most of the guards mistreated and teased the prisoners because they were bored. For four hours at a stretch they stood in the glowing sun or in the rain, rifle in hand, watching wretched prisoners digging gravel or pushing wheelbarrows. They may have even envied the prisoner his free- dom to move a few steps back and forth. And they began to give orders to the prisoners, just to make the time pass. Some made their victims work faster, faster, and faster. Others had them carry out tricky exer- cises—fifty kneebends, somersaults, and so forth. In earlier times it was a popular game to have a prisoner somersault back and forth until he lost his sense of direction, then have him somersault through the chain of sentinels, and then shoot him "on attempt to escape." In our time this seldom happened; murder had become better regulated.

Most of the games had little connection with the outsider's idea of torture. If, for example, a prisoner wanted to "step out," he approached the nearest guard, stood at rigid attention at the prescribed distance of six yards, took off his cap, and said, "Protective-custody prisoner so- and-so begs Herr Wachtmeister most obediently to be permitted to step out." Ordinarily, the guard would nod his permission, but sometimes he would pretend not to have understood. The prisoner would repeat his request; the guard still would not hear. The prisoner would yell at the top of his lunge—to no avail. He could not simply turn away and give up, because he might be called back and fare worse. So he would keep yelling until finally Herr Wachtmeister graciously granted his request.

This game could be refined. The prisoner had to stand exactly oppo- site the guard. When the guard turned to the left, the prisoner had to run around an arc of six yards radius, to face the guard again. If the guard then turned to his right, the prisoner would again run around a semi- circle. This running game, combined with the yelling game, provided "amusement" for as long as ten minutes.

The language of the SS men was on similar level. It consisted of the most unprintable obscenities, but lacked the spark of originality that is characteristic of the slang in big cities. The same few curses and obscenities were yelled in endless repetition; not even the order varied much. It began with "dirty hog of a Jew, dirty," ran through a few more unprintable profanities, and wound up with one of a few standard remarks, such as, "Why don't you go hang yourself? Want me to get you a rope?" or "Want me to send a bullet through your head?" Once a 72–year-old man answered with, "Yes, Herr Wachtmeister, I most obediently beg you to do that." But Herr Wachtmeister changed his mind—"Costs about a nickel. You aren't worth that much."

When the guards faced the prisoners individually, rather than as part of a large chain of sentinels—that is, when two guards followed a small detail of prisoners about the camp on some special work assignment—contact between the guards and prisoners often took on a completely different complexion. In this situation the guards seldom mistreated or harassed the prisoners; most of the time they left them alone. Often, lengthy conversations developed, usually with the capo of the group, sometimes with individual members. Lack of publicity for acts of abuse seemed to decrease considerably a man's desire to mistreat his charges.

The attitude of the SS men toward the prisoners was greatly influenced by the way they themselves were treated. They lived under the harshest military discipline, their officers treated them roughly, and the punitive drill they had to undergo for the ordinary misdemeanors that occur in any military camp was not much easier than that of the prisoners. Fully armed, with rifle and heavy bag, they were chased around, undergoing the same "up-down-up-down" that was so frequently inflicted on the prisoners. Their drill was all the harder because they could not be subjected to corporal punishment, and all the coercion that could be applied had to be put into this drill. When the drill was over, the SS men were as exhausted as the prisoners after their drill, and crept away in the most pitiful manner.

But the next day, when they were rested again, they took it out on the prisoners. A company that had undergone punitive drill in the afternoon was a very dangerous body the next morning. Naive souls sometimes wonder why, after the men were mistreated in this way, they didn't sympathize more with the prisoners. They didn't. Mistreating the prisoners seemed to relieve their own tension after the humiliation they had undergone.

In Buchenwald, for a short time, we had two companies of Austrian SS men, most of them from Vienna. They showed a certain tendency to fraternize with the Austrian prisoners. Not that they were not good Nazis, but they did not like the German regime and despised their fellow

SS men as "damned Prussians." Much discontent could be observed, from quarrels about the lousy food to behavior bordering on mutiny. Their sentimentality was touched when prisoners spoke the familiar Viennese dialect, and Viennese prisoners had a somewhat easier time.

Events in the outside world influenced the behavior of the guards to a certain degree. When the political situation became critical, the guards got jittery, and mistreatment became more frequent and more violent.

Among the thousands of guards there were all shades of personalities, from exquisite sadists to relatively good-natured fellows, with sadists and brutes being in the majority. Some of the guards didn't beat prisoners unless they knew they were being watched by their comrades; some beat only occasionally; most of them beat and chased the prisoners frequently. Some of them were pathological cases, who apparently found deep satisfaction in mistreating a man.

To the prisoners, the guards were a great herd of animals without any individuality. Usually weeks would pass before one would see the same guard a second time. And usually prisoners did not recognize the guards unless one had been mistreated by a guard in a rather spectacular way. After all, you don't remember every dog that barks at you in the streets, but you will certainly remember the one that bites you.

The Staff

The staff consisted of thirty to forty noncommissioned and a few commissioned officers, including the technical staff, such as the chiefs of the kitchen, post office, bureau of construction, etc. Most of the noncommissioned officers were in charge of several barracks each and were called "barrack leader" (*Blockführer*).[1]

Most of the barrack leaders were "old fighters" (*alte Kämpfer*) who had proven themselves valuable gang leaders during the political twilight between dying democracy and rising fascism. By 1938 they were in their late twenties or early thirties, with a few older men among them. Others had come up from the ranks of the common guards after 1933 and were in their early twenties in 1938.

In the beginning (1938), the staff members were taken from the local SS and SA units who had made the first arrests. Later, however, the

---

1. This should not be confused with "barrack senior," which designated the prisoner in charge of discipline.

central authorities of the SS took over the appointments. We do not know the principles according to which these men were selected. Judging from the examples we were faced with in Dachau and Buchenwald, one is led to believe that they were selected most carefully for toughness, brutality, and sadism, and that it was only an accident when occasionally a lesser devil slipped through. This belief is supported by the terrible zeal exhibited by new barrack leaders, especially those who did not yet have their final appointment. Great diligence in mistreating the prisoners seemed to increase their chances for promotion.

The main activity of the officers was supervising the work. In Dachau each working group had one or two officers, who usually were in charge until the particular job was finished. Their job, apparently, was to drive and hurry, beat and yell, throw stones, file reports, and incite the capo to urge his people on; in addition they also supervised the technical part of the work, at least insofar as it could be supervised without technical training. The more involved technical work was under the supervision of special officers. When a particular job lasted for weeks, a relationship would develop between officer and capo, similar to that between officer and senior in the barracks. But the contact was not so close, because the chain of sentinels, the higher officers who happened to be passing by, and, what is more important, all the prisoners, could see what was going on.

In Buchenwald the whole working area was surrounded by one large chain of sentinels. The prisoners were under no supervision by the sentinels, unless they happened to work close to them. Supervision was in the hands of the capos and a dozen officers, who ran all day long in the huge area, going from place to place, and of course getting tired in the process. They occasionally felt that they had had enough and would retire into one of the numerous toolsheds; one of the more powerful capos might join them for a little chat and a cigarette. For some time the work would go on relatively quietly. Then both officer and capo would decide that it was about time to give the prisoners hell; they would emerge from their shed, raise havoc among the men, and perhaps retire again.

Since the individual officer in Buchenwald was under much less observation than in Dachau (the chain of sentinels was far away in the forest), a great deal more depended on his personal mood. If he was ambitious, he would expend much energy trying to keep things moving forward, particularly if he knew that the capos were doing the beating and yelling, so that there was no danger of the commander's finding anything wrong on his occasional tours of inspection.

When the commander made his rounds, all officers and capos in the neighborhood turned wildly upon their prisoners, for they themselves were under observation. If the officer and capo were "good," the prisoners would warn them when the commander was approaching.

Officers in charge of special work, such as the kitchen, carpenter shops, and sawmill, were usually on relatively good terms with their prisoners and particularly with their capos. After all, they worked together for months, sometimes years, and they did skilled work which cannot be sped up if it is to be done properly.

The officers, who served on the staff of the camp for many years, were very distinct personalities to the prisoners, although many of them, particularly those who had come up from the ranks in recent years, were little more than brute animals who would hardly be considered worthy of attention in the outside world. But there were some officers, particularly among the "old fighters," who were most distinct personalities even when measured by the standards of civilian life. Some were dangerous killers, some cruel sadists, others were simply nervous and jittery, easily irritated. Occasionally, there was one or another who was relatively good-natured, which meant that he did not beat more than he considered necessary to maintain his own position. And there were the "white ravens"—one in Dachau and one in Buchenwald—who never beat a man. This was so extraordinary that every time one of these rare specimens was found, a whole mythology was immediately built around him. The one in Buchenwald, for example, was believed to be a sort of hostage, who had joined the SS in order to free his aristocratic family from the suspicion of being anti-Nazi.

Some of the more famous and outstanding of the officers, like Lutgemeier, Zeuss, Hoppe, and Sommer, have been carefully described in all their exquisite devilishness by other authors.[2] Below I shall just sketch some of their features.

There was the man who could not pass a working group without having them do some exercise, such as making them "frog" through a gravel pit, the most exhausting exercise ever invented. Another could not count the prisoners at roll call without kicking or boxing every fifth prisoner as he passed along the rows. Another had a juristic turn of mind; whenever he wrote a report for punishment, he had the man he was reporting countersign it. Another officer, who was very short, particularly enjoyed hitting in the face men who were a head taller than he. Another used to

---

2. Bruno Heilig, *Men Crucified* (London, 1941); Peter Wallner, *By Order of the Gestapo* (London, 1941).

sneak around the forest in Buchenwald, observe prisoners from behind a tree, and when he caught one at a misdeed, he became pedagogic. He would ask the man whether he had done something forbidden. If the man confessed, say, to having eaten, or having spoken, or having been lazy, he let him go. If he did not confess, he reported the prisoner for being a liar. Another was a lyrical soul, who made well-known composers or authors sing or recite. The author of the popular song, "I Lost My Heart in Heidelberg," often had to give a performance on the spot.

One officer in Dachau was relatively quiet, occasionally even helpful when prisoners were injured in accidents. I was astonished and asked old-timers how it happened to be so. "Oh, he killed so many of us in the past—he used to be one of the worst. Perhaps he got tired of beating and killing." Political prisoners who had some contact with him thought that he might have become tired of Nazism too, but that was only a guess.

Those who had their peculiarities were well aware of them and preserved them carefully as part of their personalities. They were very proud that an idiosyncrasy distinguished them from the common run-of-the-mill man. Even their language showed some originality at times. Lutgemeier used to enrich the German language every now and then by a coinage of his own. Jews, for example, were "Jordan splashers" (*Jordan planscher*).

One of the worst killers in Dachau during my time was a man whom we had known in the spring as a guard and who had become a temporary barrack leader. He killed several men at the very beginning of his career. One of his killings I observed myself. It was during the days when the Viennese Jews were brought in. One of these men was hurrying past him with a fully loaded wheelbarrow. Just in front of the killer, he broke down. A kick with a boot brought him to his feet again. He staggered forward a few steps, broke down again. He was kicked again. Broke down again. This was repeated three times. The whole scene happened close to the "neutral zone." Finally the killer shouted, "Why don't you jump into the canal and have it over with." I do not know whether the newcomer knew what the "neutral zone" meant. My impression was that he was simply frightened and went where his tormentor's hand pointed. He took two steps in the grass toward the ditch, whereupon the killer drew his revolver and fired three shots, killing the man instantly "on attempt to escape."

On the whole the conclusion seems justified that the staff members were a group of evil demons, in spite of the fact that one or another may perhaps not have done more evil than was his proper share.

The Commanders

The SS camp was under the command of an officer whose rank corresponded to the number of his troops. The 6,000 men in Dachau were commanded by a major general, the 3,000 men in Buchenwald by a colonel.[3]

The prison camp had its own commander and deputy commander, whose military ranks apparently had nothing to do with the commissions they were holding. In Dachau at one time, the commander was a captain, and his deputy a major. In Buchenwald the commander was a lieutenant colonel, and his deputy a second lieutenant.

The commander of the SS camp was also the supreme commander of the prison camp. He was concerned less with the prisoners' daily lives and more with the general policy of the camp. Colonel Loritz in Dachau interfered relatively little, since Commander Koegel was extremely capable of organizing the prisoners for death. In Buchenwald, where Commander Rödl with his primitive brutality was not quite up to the standards of organized mass murder, Colonel Koch was a frequent guest at roll call.

The commanders were carefully selected specimens, experienced bloodhounds and killers. They certainly did not have to be mistreated and indoctrinated before they turned against human beings. The crime of National Socialism in these cases consisted not in creating the men, but in having them as leaders. Gangsters like these were the creators.

Colonel Loritz at Dachau was the son of a former high state official in Munich. To us prisoners he appeared as a brutal and uneducated man, who raced through the camp on his motorcycle like a whirlwind, raising hell here and there, and then disappearing again. He loved his dog and his swan. Once we watched him trample a prisoner half to death, and, while still wiping the blood from his boot, whistle for his beloved dog and pet him.

Captain Koegel, commander of the Dachau prison camp, was believed to have been formerly a petty employee of the city of Augsburg. He was a very capable organizer, who routinized the hell of Dachau into a well-rehearsed play. He frequently inspected the barracks himself, and when he could not find a speck of dust, he took a nail file and scratched dust from between the planks. Then he made the men do punitive drill because their barrack was a pigsty. When one of our friends committed

---

3. All ranks are given in approximation to United States Army ranks.

suicide by hanging himself on a window beam, Koegel came to inspect the situation. The floor was soiled under the corpse and, the first thing we knew, he was threatening us with all the punishment of hell if such a thing happened again. During the Röhm affair in 1934,[4] Koegel commanded the corresponding butchery in Dachau. He was probably the most cold-blooded mass murderer we met during our time there.

Koegel's deputy, Major Schneider, was a silent man who did not interfere much. Occasionally, a prisoner had a chance to get away from him without punishment. This made him seem almost human, and a legend was spun around him—that he had been sent to Dachau to check Koegel's reign of blood to a certain extent, because at that time the Nazis did not want to provoke too much scandal in Paris and London. This legend did not seem very convincing to me.

The man who replaced Koegel was a Prussian, formerly commander of concentration camp Sachsenhausen, whose name I do not remember. We did not have a chance to get to know him well because we were sent to Buchenwald soon after his arrival. But the few days with him made us fear that, in spite of everything we had been through, there was a possibility that Koegel could be surpassed.

Major Schneider was replaced by Captain Grünewald. In comparison to Koegel, he seemed almost human, and therefore a legend also grew about him—that he was a former Reichswehr officer, who detested his fellow commanders. At any rate, his sleeve mark identified him as an "old fighter." The first thing he did was to go around the camp for days without saying anything, getting well-acquainted with the situation. Not until some weeks had passed did he begin to interfere in our life. He was a capable organizer. In the days when the 2,000 Jews were brought from Vienna and there were not enough tools to keep them busy, he arranged relays of wheelbarrow pushers, thus keeping thousands of men busy with a few hundred wheelbarrows.

By and large, he did only things that conformed to his own code of honor. To organize people to death, to make them do work that killed them, to let a man hang on the "tree" for two-and-a-half hours because he refused to betray a friend, to spill the water a prisoner was trying to

---

4. Editor's note: The *Night of the Long Knives* (a phrase from a popular Nazi song) on June 29, 1934, diminished the influence of the SA. During this purge, dozens of SA leaders were murdered by SS troops, including the leader of the SA Ernst Röhm. The SA was accused of planning a conspiracy against Hitler. The official rhetoric that legitimized the purge made use of the phrase "honorless people," with a subtext referring to the homosexuality of leading SA men.

give to a few Jews who were dying in the sun—all that fit into his code, and he did it. But to formally sentence and punish a man for something that he clearly had not done—that did not fit into his code, and therefore he did not do it. I experienced this myself once when I was charged with sabotage, mutiny, and impudence to the capo and guard. When I denied the charge, the commander yelled at me that I was a liar, but when I firmly denied it again (which was extraordinary in itself and could never have happened with Koegel), he let me go. My calm admission that I had torn a bag of plaster with my heel while being thrown off a car by an angry capo, apparently convinced him that the whole story about sabotage and mutiny had been invented out of whole cloth.

Colonel Koch, supreme commander in Buchenwald, was a very refined sort of killer. He was from Berlin, and the language he spoke led us to suppose that he must have had some higher education. He seemed to be a pathological sadist, with a queer saluting obsession, on account of which numerous prisoners got their "twenty-five" for not having saluted him fast enough. He interfered frequently with the daily routine; days without meals, punishment of hostages, and other disruptions were often due to his interest in our lives.

Lieutenant Colonel Rödl, commander of the prison camp, was Koch's exact opposite in appearance—an uneducated brute who couldn't speak a single word of literary German. On account of his unintelligible dialect, we dubbed him, in allusion to a certain type of language book, "One Thousand Words of Bavarian." By profession he was a concrete mixer, and was probably quite good at that job. He seemed perhaps the kind of man who could be quite good-natured during the week, and then on Saturday get drunk and beat his wife. His frequent drunkenness was the source of the most unpredictable happenings. In that state, for instance, he might go through the forest and search for shirkers. Two men had to walk behind him carrying a stand, and when he found a shirker, he laid him personally over the stand and gave him "twenty-five" with his riding whip. If he did not find any shirkers, he took anybody he met. Captain Koegel in Dachau did a similar thing, but he did it as a well-planned campaign of terror and he took care not to soil his dirty hands. He had barrack leader Wagner do the whipping. But out of Rödl's drunkenness, we once gained a double ration of sausages and at Christmas a pair of frankfurters for every prisoner. He was a lover of songs and had the whole camp practice new ones. He liked the band, and on Sundays occasionally had the conductor sing sentimental popular tunes over the camp loudspeaker.

As an organizer he was completely incompetent. He apparently did not even comprehend the size of the city in which he was lord over life and death. He once gave a most amazing demonstration to the camp, when he wanted a pile of about 2 million bricks removed from the roll-call square. On a Sunday morning he ordered two Jewish barracks (600 men) to the job, and promised them that they could go to their rooms when they were through. Actually it took the whole camp six weeks to remove the pile.

Rödl's deputy Johnny Hackmann was certainly the most refined product of this hell, a devil deluxe, so to speak. He proudly spoke the most precise German in the world, Hannover German, and he produced the most finely turned phrases while hitting prisoners in the face. He took great care never to get soiled in any of his actions and always looked as if he had just come from the tailor.

Johnny was in 1939 a young man of about 25. Some old-timers had known him years before as a common guard in the peat-bog camp Esterwegen. It was not quite clear how he achieved his spectacular career. One rumor had it that he was a relative of a Nazi Gauleiter[5]; another made him the homosexual partner of a high Nazi official.

I once saw Johnny playing the following game. In a forest clearing, about twenty-five prisoners were hanging from trees by their wrists, some of them screaming for father and mother, others beseeching Johnny to take them down, promising they would behave well in the future. Johnny, arms crossed and his face a stony mask, watched them carefully and did not move. Particularly he watched one man whose feet were fairly close to the ground. With a tremendous effort the man managed to get a little pebble under his feet, which took some of the weight off his wrists. As soon as the man had the pebble under his toe, Johnny gave him a terrific slap in the face. The man dangled in the air and did not utter a sound. As soon as he came to rest and thought that Johnny was not watching him, he again worked the pebble under his toe. But Johnny had been waiting for just that moment. As soon as the pebble was in the right position, he again gave the man a frightful slap. I saw the scene repeated once more.

On another occasion Johnny appeared in the Jewish infirmary during the time when the death rate was at its highest. Several dead Jews were

---

5. Editor's note: A Gauleiter was the highest ranking Nazi official at the regional level of a Gau, a German province similar to a state in the United States. The official would be similar to a U. S. governor.

lying in the lavatory, two were still in their beds, one was just being carried away. Said Johnny, "It is a true pleasure to observe how these sons of Abraham perish."

Altogether, there can be no doubt that these commanders, whether they had intellectual and organizational ability or not, were highly specialized, pitiless murderers, who were fully conscious of what they themselves were doing and what was being done under their orders.

Chapter 8

Crime and Punishment

No institution in which men are held together by force can be understood without a knowledge of the type of regulations an inmate may violate and the type of punishment that may be the consequence of such violation.

In ordinary prisons and penitentiaries, the prisoner receives a set of rules which tell him what is allowed and what is forbidden, and what punishments will follow if he misbehaves. It outlines the procedure leading up to a sentence and punishment, and mentions the few rights which are left to the inmate to protect him from complete arbitrariness. "Dos and don'ts" are established primarily to keep order and discipline, and the man who obeys the rules is for the most part left alone. Seldom do the regulations contain rules which the prisoner necessarily must break if he wants to survive as a human being. He usually has a fair choice between following or breaking the regulations, and a fair idea of what the consequences will be. The most common violations of rules, such as smoking at work, taking food to the cells, smuggling articles from cell to cell, are usually punished by temporary withdrawal of certain privileges, such as smoking, correspondence, or time in the open air. Imprisonment in the dark cell and corporal punishment are usually reserved for more serious violations or constant repetition. There is, within the restrictions of the institution, a certain balance between deed and consequence.

Rules and punishment in a concentration camp are established not only in order to keep discipline but also for the purpose of terrorizing the inmates and the people outside. Since one of the main tasks of a concentration camp is to break the prisoner as a human being, two of the first prerogatives of a human being are withdrawn from him: the right to expect that there shall be some reason in the way he is treated, and the right to influence his own fate by reasonable behavior. Instead he is subject to completely arbitrary treatment. When he behaves well, he is not entitled to be let alone, and when he behaves badly he is not entitled to a fair trial. He is entitled to nothing. Not to food or clothing, shelter, life, or death. All of these are given to him for expediency's sake, and withdrawn when expediency happens to suggest otherwise, or simply on the spur of the moment. When the commander's whim dictates a day without food, there is no food. When an officer wants to hang you from a tree by the wrists for an hour because he happens not to like your nose—you hang from a tree. When a guard wants to drive you to suicide, he mistreats you until you cannot stand it any longer; when he wants to kill you immediately, he does it; but when he wants to prevent your suicide, you will get a thrashing of "twenty-five" if you were not successful.

Whatever influence the prisoner has upon his own fate is not due to abiding by the rules, but to his cunning and luck, and to certain technical restrictions of the situation. There are only a few dozen officers attached to a camp of many thousands of prisoners, and these officers have a vast supervising job, which does not allow them to stay too long at any one spot and mistreat individual men. Hence all the administration can do is make the general living conditions very hard, and pick for individual mistreatment as many as it is technically possible to abuse. And for this purpose they prefer to pick people against whom there is some sort of claim. This preserves the fiction of justice, which seems to suit their taste better. (That it is only a matter of taste, not of principle, is clear when one remembers the previously mentioned inscription on the gate: "My country right or wrong.")

Considering the ridiculous rules and the horrible punishments that follow any infractions, the conclusion is obvious that the rules are made in order to be broken, and thus provide this machinery of fake-justice with a never-ending supply of men against whom there is a claim.

Under these circumstances, rules and punishment are no longer what the words may suggest to the civilian mind: regulations which you may follow or break after due consideration, and pre-announced punishment if you decide to break them. In a concentration camp most rules mean nothing except vaguely channelized arbitrariness, and punishment means nothing but organized mistreatment. This becomes especially evident at times when the capos and seniors are slow in reporting prisoners for punishment. At such times they are called before the commander and told, in front of the whole camp, "I want to see reports!" (*"Ich will Meldungen sehen!"*), and they are threatened with punishment should they not comply with this order.

Where arbitrariness is a goal in itself, regulations concerning the procedure that leads to punishment are superfluous. As far as any order in the procedure can be observed, it is a ritual developed for purposes of expediency or out of mere habit. And of course any provisions for complaints about arbitrary mistreatment would be completely meaningless.

The civilian mind seems to be unable to grasp a state of perfect arbitrariness. The citizen of a free country is bound to ask "why," and he expects a reasonable answer. "If a man is punished, he must have committed a crime. If he can't adjust himself to rules and regulations, that is his own fault. After all, he knows what sort of a place he is in." This is about as logical as the saying you hear inside the camp dozens and dozens of times from officers and guards: "You are not in a sanatorium here"—which covers everything from hard labor to lack of food to being slowly beaten to death. And eagerly this civilian mind grasps the few cases where there has actually been a serious violation of a reasonable rule. When three men dug themselves into a heat shaft every morning and stayed there until roll call at night, their action would have been punished in any institution. But the civilian mind, in its search for rhyme and reason, immediately generalizes from these few cases—which usually are romantic exceptions—and says, "See, I knew they would not punish them for nothing." But they do punish people for nothing.

Punishment

The following description of the reasons for which men are punished should not mislead the reader into believing that even these insignificant reasons are always given. To pick them out and put them into words is a concession to the outsider who cannot possibly accept a description of the dreariness of meaningless yelling and beating and mistreatment that goes on all day long. The SS guard or officer does not need a reason for beating you. The fact that you are here is reason enough. If he beats you, and not your neighbor at the same time, it is because he has only two hands and because he mistreats those who attract his attention. To work more slowly than the next man is just one incidental way of attracting attention. Other ways are having a big stomach or being very tall, and so forth. Working hard and fast but fussily attracts more attention than working slowly but regularly, and consequently attracts more beating. To this extent prisoners are right with their overused generalization: "If you are afraid, then you get beaten." The sentence should read: "If you are afraid, you get nervous. If you are nervous you get fussy. If you are fussy, you attract attention. If you attract attention, you get beaten. Or 'reported for punishment.'"

The reader should, however, be reminded of one thing. The countless beatings and mistreatment on the spot—when men are trampled half dead, when their limbs and skulls are injured or broken by heavy blows from sticks and stones and rifles—have no name. They are all considered more or less as "accidents"; the prisoner concerned is more often than not glad that at least he was not "reported for punishment." "Punishment" is the name of mistreatment only when it is administered in one of the standardized forms, such as "one hour on the tree" or "twenty-five," after a thirty- to sixty-second "hearing" before the commander.

The more common punishments:

Overtime: punitive work during spare time.
Door duty: standing at the "door" during spare time.
The tree: hanging on a pole or tree by the wrists.
Twenty-five: twenty-five heavy blows with a stick.

Special and irregular punishments:

Punitive working group: a group that works under particularly hard conditions.
Punitive drill.
Punitive company: a segregated part of the camp, or special barracks, whose inmates are subjected to harder living conditions.
Sunday without meals.
The dungeon: darkened cell.
The outlaws.
The black dungeon: darkened barrack with especially hard living conditions.

Overtime: Two additional hours of work at night and work on Sunday, when the rest of the camp has time off. In Buchenwald this punishment is hardly ever used. On weekdays the whole camp works until dusk, and also on Sunday part of the time. Also it would be difficult to guard this special work. In Dachau in the summer of 1938, overtime was replaced by punitive drill, due to the lack of work.

Overtime is usually given for a period of six to ten weeks, or frequently "until further notice," which means months, often years.

Door duty: After roll call at night until "lights out" and the greater part of Sunday, the men who are sentenced to this punishment stand bareheaded at rigid attention in front of the "door." They receive no evening meal. In the glowing sun on summer Sundays, they faint and suffer sunstroke. During the winter, they suffer frostbite. In Buchenwald men who are caught in some misdemeanor during the day are brought to the "door" and stand there until evening roll call, when they receive "twenty-five." After that, they are to stand there until lights out, often with their hands clasped behind their heads, sometimes with their knees bent at the same time.[1]

Door duty is a regular punishment used more frequently in Dachau than in Buchenwald. It is usually given for several weeks at a time. Sometimes larger groups, especially whole barracks, get door duty combined with extra drill.

The tree: The victim's hands are tied behind his back, and he is then hung by his wrists with his feet off the ground. In Dachau men are hung on special poles in the dungeon yard; in Buchenwald they are hung on trees in a clearing in the forest. The main strain is felt in the wrists and the shoulder joints. Tendons and nerves in the hands are often damaged for weeks and months, sometimes for years.

In my time the "tree" was a regular punishment, usually given for one hour at a time. In addition, it was used as the most common means of extorting confessions whenever an investigation was underway. In earlier times, the "tree" was used more irregularly; men were hung on the nearest tree whenever an officer deemed it advisable. They were often left hanging for hours, sometimes until they died.

---

1. This is called the *Sachsengruss* (Saxon salute). The general belief seems to be that Charlemagne demanded this humiliating posture of the conquered Saxons. However, I am not certain that this explanation is correct.

Twenty-five: The victim is strapped to a stand and given twenty-five heavy blows with sticks. The blows are given by barrack leaders (officers); sometimes one man beats the victim, sometimes two do it alternately. Sometimes a blanket is put over the victim's head so that his screams cannot be heard.

In Dachau the "twenty-five" is given with heavier instruments, and usually combined with four days in the dungeon with one meal per day. It is considered the heaviest of ordinary punishments. The administration provides a great deal of pomp for this occasion. Ordinarily it takes place in the dungeon, in the presence of a platoon of eight SS men in full war paint, with steel helmet and rifle. Sometimes it is administered on the roll-call square or in the main street. The whole camp or some selected barracks have to line up on three sides of a quadrangle; the fourth side consists of a company of SS men. They beat the drum and a formal verdict is read that so-and-so has been sentenced to "twenty-five blows on the back and buttocks" for "outrageous laziness at work." If the victim screams, he is given more. We once counted thirty-three blows. During the beating everyone has to look at the stand. He who fails to do so receives the same punishment immediately.

In Buchenwald the "twenty-five" is an unceremonious, everyday affair. No guards, no drums, no verdict. Men who are caught in some misdemeanor during the day are brought to the "door," and in the evening, when Rödl is informed at roll call of their offenses, he says, "Just give 'em twenty-five." They are beaten at once, while the others are still singing the "Little Village." Thus no time is wasted.

In Buchenwald the "twenty-five" is the most common of all punishments. Every evening about half a dozen people receive it, sometimes as many as twenty. On extraordinary occasions considerably more victims go "over the stand."

As the blows are given "on the back and buttocks," it frequently happens that the men's kidneys are damaged. The results of this punishment are sometimes apparent for many years.

Punitive working group: Each camp has one working ground where the conditions are particularly hard and which is under the supervision of some special Satan of a capo. In Buchenwald it is the quarry, in Dachau one of the gravel pits under Capo Sterzer, one of the most famous killers we ever had.

Sentences to this type of punishment do not follow any regular scheme. A commander may be enraged by a man's "laziness" and send him to the gravel pit immediately. A capo may send a man there, thus exercising a kind of justice of his own. Frequently newcomers are sent there during their first days or weeks in camp in order to teach them how to be prisoners.

The capo for this place is selected only for his brutality and sadism. His function is not to keep the work going, not even to keep the men on the run. His function is to break their spirits.

In other parts of the camp, the fiction that he who works hard can escape mistreatment is upheld. It is not always true, but it works to some degree. Not so under Sterzer in the gravel pit. Other capos, by and large, avoid killing or breaking men's limbs advisedly (although it happens often enough). Sterzer does not mind. All day long he is on the run, beating his victims, yelling, swearing, beating again—with a whip, with a rod, with an iron chain. No hard work can placate this devil. The victim is to be taught that he is nobody and nothing, that he cannot influence his fate, neither by doing well nor by doing evil. He simply is beaten.

Here is a typical case. One man from our first group of Austrians fell sick after a few days in camp. Even the infirmary recognized his illness. He was excused from work, his hands wrapped in heavy bandages and splints. The very first day he returned to work, his arms not yet healed, he was sent to Sterzer. He was beaten all morning. During lunch he complained a little, but did not say much. He was in utter despair and did not see how he could possibly live through the afternoon. After the noon rest he was missing at roll call. He had hanged himself from a window bar in the dormitory.

Punitive drill: This type of heavy drill is a veritable hell. It is usually given to large groups, such as a whole barrack. One officer, sometimes with the assistance of others, commands it. When Rödl commands drill for the whole camp, he is assisted by his whole gang of underlings.

The officers shout the orders and the crowd executes them: Lie down! Stand up! Forward run! Down on your face! Maggot! (This means creeping forward on elbows and belly.) Roll left! Roll right! Stand up! Bend knees! Frog! (This means hopping forward with bended knees.) Hop forward! Right turn! Left turn! About face! Frog! Up! Down! Up! Down! Assemble in the right corner! Line up in the door! Disperse! Lie down! Up! Down! Up! Down! Do this! Do that! Do this! Do that!

It is difficult to describe just why this is so hellish and why it differs a great deal from an ordinary military drill. Sometimes it is the cruelty of the exercises, like frogging, rolling, maggotting. Sometimes it is the ground—deep mud, pools of water, sand, pebbles, or snow. The worst thing about it is the terrific speed. Up-down-up-down-up-down. Sometimes merely running at this speed is enough to kill the spark of life in men. And to all this is added the perfect arbitrariness and meaninglessness of the procedure.

The drill is still worse when old and invalid men are not allowed to leave. They are a hindrance to the rest. They drop and faint and thus disrupt the running crowd. Sometimes they die.

Punitive company: This is a group of prisoners who, for disciplinary or other reasons, are forced to live under harder conditions than the rest of the camp. In Dachau their barracks and working grounds are separated from the others by barbed wire; anyone who speaks to them is himself sent to the punitive company. In Buchenwald their barracks are not separated, and during leisure time they are free to mix with others.

Prisoners in the punitive company are permitted to write and receive one letter and to get ten marks every third month (compared to the two letters and thirty marks per month in Buchenwald and twice as much money in Dachau, for the rest of the camp). They are not allowed to smoke. They receive less food. In Buchenwald on Sunday they get no dinner and stand "door duty" when the others happen to have the afternoon off. In Dachau they are forbidden to speak to each other during working hours. (Theoretically this holds true for the whole camp, but only in the punitive company is it actually enforced.) In Buchenwald, due to the working conditions, such enforcement is technically impractical. There, the punishments for misdemeanors are more severe. "Twenty-five" and the "tree" are practically their only punishments, and they are given more frequently.

Prisoners in the punitive company are there for one of three reasons:

1) Disciplinary reasons inside the camp. This classification principally includes men who have committed serious misdemeanors or who have previously undergone several ordinary punishments. Occasionally men are put there for a slight first offence.

2) In Dachau, Jehovah's Witnesses and second-termers, and in Buchenwald homosexuals and "race polluters" are in the punitive company. (As mentioned earlier, Jehovah's Witnesses and second-termers in Buchenwald were subject to the restrictions concerning money, mail, and smoking, but otherwise lived like the rest of the camp.)

3) Newcomers who are sent to the punitive company without ever entering the ordinary camp. Presumably the "crime" which brought them

to camp, was particularly serious. However, in Buchenwald I met a great many men who had been in the punitive company in Dachau from their arrival in camp, and there seemed to be nothing peculiar about their "crime." They were Austrian opponents of the Nazis, just like the rest of us who were picked up at the beginning.

In Dachau, being sent to the punitive company means a complete change of one's life. All relations, sometimes ones which have lasted for years, are broken. It means a sort of social death, because even the experienced prisoner has difficulty imagining how life can begin again behind that barbed wire. Of course it does. There is a social life there which absorbs him exactly as did that in the general camp. The stay in the punitive company is for an unknown period of time, usually years.

In Buchenwald the change is not so radical. Men who are sent there for disciplinary reasons are in many cases sent back after a few months. During their free time they can meet their former friends, who sometimes provide them with extra food and other necessities. In Buchenwald, barrack and room seniors and the whole barrack detail are not themselves members of the punitive company. Through them the social forces of the camp influence to some degree life in the punitive company. This is hardly the case in Dachau. (However, being based on the same kind of background as the society in the general camp, the society in the punitive company develops in a similar way.)

Sunday without meals: This was a regular event in Buchenwald but did not occur in Dachau during my time. On such days no food whatsoever was served for twenty-four hours except for a little brown coffee-water.

In the beginning these fast days were preceded by some threat, such as, "The work of the camp (or, the work of the Jews) has been lousy this week. If it does not improve a hundred percent, there'll be no grub next Sunday." The capos at first took the statement quite seriously and drove their men to greater speed. But after a few times it became quite clear that no effort could avert these fast days. Hence the capos made common cause with their men, and the threat of a fast day was considered merely an announcement and an invitation to a general slowdown. The administration then realized what was happening and no longer announced these days in advance. It simply happened that on Saturday night the food carriers would be driven away from the kitchen and told not to show up again until Sunday night.

Whereupon the camp took it for granted, after some experience, that approximately the third Sunday of each month would be a fast day, rain

93

or shine. We tried to keep on hand a can of fish and a piece of bread for such days and, for the rest, stopped worrying. You can't worry about such regular occurrences. We assumed that the fast days were due to some irregularities "up there," since one day's food for ten thousand prisoners, however little they are fed, amounts to quite a bit of money. Days without food were explained by the camp with "Koch's white horse needs some oats."

The dungeon: Called the "bunker" in camp slang, this structure consists of dark cells for solitary confinement. In Dachau a special building is reserved for the dungeon; in Buchenwald it makes up one wing of the "door." Confinement there is usually not employed as a regular punishment in Buchenwald; rather, men are held there to extort confessions about affairs under investigation inside the camp. In Dachau, as already mentioned, four days in the dungeon usually accompany the "twenty-five."

When men are brought there for confessions, the most cruel tortures are applied. This is the place where things happen in the "third degree" manner which outsiders usually have in mind when they think of concentration camps. Men who have gone through it speak of it to their fellow prisoners with the same hesitation as the prisoner speaks to the outsider in Germany about his stay in camp.

Many people die in the dungeon. The exact figures are not known, since men who are placed there, are removed from their barrack rolls. Rumor probably exaggerates the figures, but it is this very uncertainty that makes the dungeon a strong weapon in the hands of the administration. The prisoners think of it with the same horror and fear as the whole German nation thinks of the concentration camp—as a place where you are tortured beyond the limits of imagination, where human beings do not exist, and where your innermost secrets will be wrung out of you.

A friend of mine was put into the dungeon in the course of a letter-smuggling affair. On his return, after four days, he was a pitiful sight. He avoided talking about the treatment he had undergone, but described his cell to me in the following words: "There are four walls and the floor and the ceiling. The window is blacked out by a board from the outside. There is a rope hanging from the window bar, and there is the prisoner—and he is nude. He and the rope are all the furniture." He told me that he could hardly have resisted for a fifth day the temptation to make the proper use of the rope.

Sometimes newcomers disappear immediately into the dungeon, only to leave it as corpses. One of these was the executioner from Vienna who had hanged the Nazis that killed Dollfuss.[2]

The Outlaws: In early 1939 in Buchenwald, discipline was at a low. The battle against the professional criminals was in full swing, corruption was at its peak The prisoners had grown too familiar with the "twenty-five." New punishments were invented, two of them by the camp senior Hubert Richter, a professional criminal.

One was to outlaw prisoners for certain violations. The barrack senior was to announce the punishment, and from then on no prisoner would be allowed to speak to the man. Smoking and canteen privileges were withdrawn.

The first attempts were made with prisoners whom everybody disliked. But to no avail. The men understood too well what was happening. They realized that this was a threat against the society as a whole. Everybody talked to the "outlaws" in order to demonstrate that it was impossible to isolate any man within this society against the will of the others, no matter how much he was disliked.

The new punishment was quickly abandoned and forgotten. Still it deserves to be remembered. The man who invented it, had found the point where his fellow prisoners were vulnerable: Break a man off from his social relations, isolate him within his society, and you will be able to break his power of resistance, his will for life.

The black dungeon: The other of Hubert Richter's inventions was carried out more successfully. An entire barrack was emptied of furniture and the windows blackened. The victims were given light summer uniforms (it was a grim winter with deep subzero temperatures during the night), no underwear, no beds, no blankets, nothing but the walls. They were given one meal a day, consisting of half of the ordinary dinner ration. Nothing to drink. Nothing to smoke. No mail. Once a week they were let into the open, taken up to the "door," given "twenty-five," then returned to darkness. Cut off from light and life. Buried alive.

They could not sleep in the cold. To warm up a little, they kept running around in circles in the darkness. We don't know how they managed not to sleep. We heard them running day and night. Those who

2. Editors note: On July 25, 1934, Austrian Nazis started a coup d'état to overcome the authoritarian government under Engelbert Dollfuss. During the failed putsch, Dollfuss was murdered by the Nazi insurgents, and thirteen of the assassins were afterwards sentenced to death. Two of them were hanged on July 31, 1934.

tired, dropped in a corner, but were soon trampled upon by someone else in the darkness. They ran for weeks. They fell sick. They got avitaminous furunculosis. Covered with terrible sores, they were led to the infirmary to get their wounds dressed—then returned to darkness.

One day one of these luckless fellows was to be released from the camp. He was dressed in his civilian clothes, together with others to be released that day. But this was the very day when the camp was put under quarantine because of typhoid. The released men were put into prison clothes again and sent back to work. And this man was sent back to darkness.

We were used to many cruelties—but this incident shocked us. This man had actually been freed by the Gestapo. It was the mere coincidence that his fellow prisoners happened to be dying of typhoid which prevented him from gaining his freedom. Still he was sent back to the worst punishment, for some crime he had committed against the disciplinary rules of a camp from which de jure he was released.

This martyrdom lasted for weeks and weeks. One day it was over. The dungeon prisoners were sent back to their barracks, the windows were opened, the room cleaned and refurnished. The whole thing belonged to the past. We don't know why.

Crime

There are very few things expressly forbidden in a concentration camp, and few things expressly ordered. There seems to be a general assumption that a prisoner naturally knows how he ought to behave, and if he does anything an SS man happens not to like at the moment, then it turns out to be forbidden. And for the rest, if there is any question about it, everything is forbidden in concentration camp.

The following enumeration of misdemeanors, vaguely divided into a few major groups, is not a sort of penal code, but simply a general description to indicate what actually happens.

Misdemeanors against general discipline in the camp and barracks: A man does not march smartly enough. He does not salute quickly enough. He does not press his fingers straight enough against his thighs at roll call. His shoes are dirty. His shirt is dirty. His clothes are torn. His hair is too long. He is unshaven. He talks to his neighbor during roll call (everybody does, or tries to). He does not sing loudly enough. His bed is badly made. His eating dish is "dirty" (it does not reflect the officer's face). His toothbrush is dirty (it shows a speck of dust). His shirt is folded the wrong way, or his underwear. His water glass stands where his plate should be. His socks lie at the right side of the shirt instead of at the left.

He has smoked in the barrack. He has laughed while an officer passed by. He has claimed to be sick and is thought to be malingering. He has … He has … He has … He has always done something.

Misdemeanors against discipline at work: A man is lazy. Between two shovels of gravel, he tries to take a breath. He sets down a fully loaded wheelbarrow for a moment. He does not toss up enough gravel. He takes four bricks when he is supposed to take five. He takes five when he is supposed to take six. He does not run fast enough with an empty wheelbarrow or with an empty water jar. He gets kicked, falls over his wheelbarrow, can't pick himself up in a hurry. He is lazy.

You are always lazy, when the question comes up. No man can accelerate his tempo all morning. After a few minutes of acceleration, you are at your top speed. But any boy of eighteen can yell at you for hours: "Faster, faster!" if only he has a rifle in his hands and is ordered to stay beside you.

A 63–year-old man told us a curious experience one evening. He had taken a breathing spell. All of a sudden an officer was beside him: "Are you crazy! I have been watching you for a whole minute! For a whole minute you haven't done a thing!" The prisoner, whose hair was completely white, answered, "I am an old man." The officer let it go at that. But his amazement was characteristic. A white-haired old man had dared to stop for a minute!

There are more definite crimes, such as smoking and eating during work time. (Breakfast is at four in the morning, and noon rest at twelve!)

And there are an unlimited number of people who are really lazy and shirk whenever they have a chance. Why shouldn't they? The job isn't theirs, they get no wages, they can't even make sure that they won't get beaten. People used to say, "In concentration camp, you have to work with your eyes and ears." I am sorry to add that the newcomer who takes this neat proverb too literally will soon find out that hands and feet and shoulders and back and the whole body are involved. But of course the general tendency to shirk makes it easier for any officer always to find men who actually are shirking.

Forgotten rules: In all of the cases recorded so far, the overt appearance of "justice" is preserved; a man has really broken some rule, when he had at least some chance of not doing so. But there are numerous rules which he simply must transgress because of the sheer necessities of life. And there are others which he violates because everyone does, quite openly, in front of the officers and guards, until suddenly one of them on a mere whim reports a man for violating the forgotten rule.

Practically everyone speaks to fellow prisoners at work. Usually nobody pays any attention. Then one day a man is reported for having "engaged in conversation." A man walks instead of running, when he is not carrying anything. Nobody can run all the time. Ordinarily this is settled by a curse, perhaps by a stone thrown at the culprit, or a blow. But occasionally it turns up as a report for "strolling around with the most outrageous slowness."

In this classification belong rules forbidding the production and trading of a great number of articles such as wooden clogs, "flatirons" for making beds, sandpaper for cleaning the closet, steel wool for polishing dishes, breadbags, and so forth. Production is illegal, as it is done at work, from stolen material. Trade is illegal, as all trade is forbidden. Usually transporting the articles from the place of production to the camp is also illegal, but possession is usually considered legal. Nobody can do without these articles. The officers see them thousands of times. But occasionally a corruption scandal involving one of these articles is brought to light, and without warning, men are punished for having produced, smuggled, sold, or bought it.

Then there are some completely forgotten rules. No one is allowed to keep more than one letter from his relatives, but who throws away the dearest possession he has. For months no attention is paid to the matter. Then one day there is a general inspection, and men are punished. In Buchenwald nobody is allowed to carry more than ten marks with him. But if you happen to possess more, you have no place to keep it. Usually nobody cares. But someday you may be punished. In Dachau the carrying of any tobacco or food in one's pockets during work time is prohibited. Nobody cares. Then one day an officer may stroll along and have the splendid idea of searching pockets. In Buchenwald the men produce slings with which to carry the handbarrows. They make them of wire, cord, potato bags. Sometimes their use is allowed. Then again, it is forbidden, but nobody knows it except those who are punished for having them. Nobody cares much either.

It is theoretically forbidden to enter any barrack other than your own. Everybody does, nobody cares. But one day you may be punished for it.

Special crimes: There are always a number of real violations of definite rules—deliberately planned offenses, committed in a shrewd way. In the course of time, because of the great number of prisoners, all these peculiar crimes are repeated and become part of a pattern. But the individual case always falls outside the norm. The most famous stories about the camps belong here.

In Dachau for a short time, milk could be bought. A barrack senior made some money out of it, with the help of high prices and much water. Result: punitive company and suicide.

In Buchenwald twenty men formed a fake working group. They wandered through the forest with empty boxes. Result: "twenty-five."

A man broke a gold tooth out of the mouth of a dead fellow prisoner. It was valuable currency. Result: "twenty-five" and punitive company.

A non-Jew was discovered among the Jews. For two years he had pretended to be a Jew. Someone had told him that this way he had a better chance of release. Result: punitive company.

A man with heavy bandages was unmasked as a malingerer. Result: punitive company.

Here belong all the famous corruption and smuggling scandals.

During the winter in Buchenwald, the administration made a tremendous profit by selling us pullovers, gloves, shawls, and ear-muffs. Many seniors grew rich by raising the prices still more.

The smuggling of articles from the infirmary is endless. We could continue for a long time with this enumeration of special crimes. Still it should always be kept in mind that these more interesting cases are only a small proportion of the crimes for which punishment is given. The bulk of the prisoners have committed nothing more than one of the standard "crimes," such as making their beds badly or having a speck of dust on their toothbrush, or being lazy.

Chapter 9

Differences

After having spent half a year in Dachau, where everything ran smoothly and cleanly and the administration had such a firm grip on discipline that hardly a breath went unnoticed, it was greatly surprising to find conditions which were exactly the opposite prevailing in Buchenwald. Everything there was dirty and disorganized, the administration hardly knew what was happening, and discipline was lacking. This did not mean that the terror in Buchenwald was weaker than in Dachau. It was only less smoothly organized.

Among the specific differences we noticed immediately after our arrival in Buchenwald was the role of the political prisoners. In Dachau the political prisoners exercised a well-established domination over the rest of the camp, while in Buchenwald, in the fall of 1939, most of the important administrative positions were in the hands of the professional criminals. We were surprised at the great amount of autonomy the prisoners in Buchenwald exercised in the administration of certain services, such as the infirmary, the special workshops, the clothing and other supply departments—and the tremendous amount of bribery and racketeering that went with it. In Dachau everything was under close supervision, and racketeering among the prisoners was kept within relatively narrow limits.

After some time we found that the social organization, too, was much more complicated in Buchenwald. The various categories of prisoners were often divided between those who aligned themselves with the politicals and those who were more inclined toward the professional criminals, while in Dachau we had seen a fairly rigid hierarchy of the various categories.

Differences in the natural conditions, the backgrounds of the prisoners, and the state of construction in the camp led to differences in the whole administrative organization—that is, in the time schedule, the working conditions, and the guard system. The combination of these factors largely accounts for the difference in the social structure of the two camps. Some minor factors, such as the ability of the camp commander, the size of the camp, and the geographic location of the camp modified or emphasized the differences.

Guard System and Organization of Work

In Dachau every working group outside the barbed wire had its own guards, who formed a circle around the working ground. On the level, meadowy land, all of the guards could usually watch all of the prisoners at the same time, standing close to them all day long. The guards could harass, abuse, torture, and drive the men as much as they pleased. The supervision of the work and the technical direction were usually carried out by an officer. The capo was there primarily to keep things going by yelling, cursing, and beating. Only in the case of specialized and skilled jobs was he concerned with the direction of the work.

This guard system, with the guards close to the men all day long, led to the famous "Dachauer tempo," which forced the prisoners to be on the move without interruption, always double quick, never pausing for a moment's breath.

In Buchenwald, with its forest, this system would have required a tremendous force of guards in order to surround and effectively watch every individual working ground. Instead, the whole area on the top of the mountain, containing the main working grounds, was surrounded by one large chain of about 600 sentinels, who stood at their posts, ten to fifteen yards apart. Inside the chain there were only a few officers who were on the run all day to keep the prisoners at work. Thus only those groups who happened to work close to the chain came in contact with the guards; the majority of the prisoners hardly saw them all day long. The guards themselves seemed to be more rigidly bound to their places than had been the case in Dachau. Their chief source of amusement was to throw stones at the prisoners or to order them from a distance to do gymnastic exercises (such as fifty kneebends, etc.)

Since the officers could not be everywhere at the same time, the supervision of the prisoners at work was actually in the hands of the capos and an elaborate system of sub-capos and capo's aides. Most of the technical direction of the work was also handled by the capos, with one officer from the bureau of construction as head supervisor.

Under these circumstances, shirking, particularly organized shirking by a whole group, was much more frequent than in Dachau. So was racketeering, because of the tremendous amount of personal power in the hands of the capos and their underlings.

The administration and the officers knew of course that all of this was going on and that the work tempo was slow in most places—that is, slow for a concentration camp! As a countermeasure they prolonged the working hours (thirteen hours during the summer, compared with ten hours in Dachau), and they exerted their terror more indiscriminately against whole working groups, since it was more difficult to discover and punish individual culprits.

When we came from Dachau and saw the slower working tempo, we thought we had made a good bargain. But we soon learned that the long working hours (with only half-an-hour's noon rest, compared with two hours in Dachau) could exhaust a man as thoroughly as the terrific speed in Dachau, especially since the food in Buchenwald was so much worse and there was practically no drinking water. We never knew which to prefer; perhaps the death rate from simple exhaustion was somewhat greater in Buchenwald, and that from actual mistreatment somewhat greater in Dachau.

An important difference in the working conditions arose from the fact that Dachau was situated on level ground and Buchenwald on a steep mountain. In Dachau the transportation of great masses of material, such as gravel, sand, and stones, was accomplished by using wheelbarrows over short distances and men-drawn wagons over long distances. In Buchenwald, neither of the two was used to any great extent because of the steepness of the mountain. Instead, most of the material was carried in handbarrows—wooden boxes on two long poles carried by two men like a sedan-chair. Sometimes four men carried one on their shoulders.

This led to a difference in organization and treatment. The men who carried gravel in wheelbarrows over short distances could be abused individually without holding up the rest of the camp. An officer or capo could jump on a man, kick him, or beat him so that he fell over his wheelbarrow. It seldom happened that the material was spilled this way. A man with an empty wheelbarrow could be made to run on the double, and if he did not speed up, he could be made to run with a full load.

Two men with a handbarrow could not be forced to speed up to any great extent, because they would then spill the material in the box. Hence they looked less inviting to an individual officer than did men with wheelbarrows. In addition, the material in Buchenwald was usually transported over long distances, through the forest and between the many side streets of the camp. If the prisoners were to run these distances individually, almost no supervision would be possible, unless literally companies of guards were employed. Hence, large columns of fifty to a hundred or more carriers were formed, with a capo and one or two sub-capos in charge. The columns marched in single file. Officers seldom attacked individual men in a column, because that would have brought disorder into the ranks. For this reason, service in a carrier column was usually considered not too bad a job.

Since the columns often moved over distances of half a mile and more, rest periods had to be given at the discretion of the capo, lest the men drop the boxes and spill the contents. These periods ordinarily didn't last long—when an officer was around usually a minute or so—but they are worthy of notice because they provided a basis for shirking in groups. A column could prolong its rests considerably if it kept on the lookout and was ready to start up again soon after an officer appeared. When a column met a commander or passed the gate, or was asked by any officer, the capo had to report the destination and purpose of their trip. A capo with presence of mind and a fairly well-organized column could lead it almost anywhere with empty boxes. This did not mean that life in a carrier column consisted of nothing but idle strolling in the sunshine (or in a snowstorm, for that matter). But it did mean that there was a possibility for occasional excursions and evasions, and the combination of these possibilities in various working groups was the basis of the administration's inability to control the situation. For example, a fake column of twenty men, with ten boxes and a fake capo, was once found strolling around in the forest. They had been strolling for about three work days, until an officer grew suspicious, because he never saw them with anything in their boxes, no matter from what direction they came. They got their "twenty-five" each immediately. This case was an exceptional one, but it is significant because it indicates the lack of contact. Almost any column, even one without boxes, could have been "on its way to the lumber yard for boards to be used in building 'troop-garages.'"

This advantage was offset by steady attempts of the officers to trip columns on fake missions. Columns without handbarrows were especially subject to suspicion and often to mistreatment. They were often given extra exercise when they encountered an officer, even if they were on perfectly legal business.

In Dachau, material was usually transported under the eyes of the guards who surrounded a working ground, and the slightest attempt to fake business with an empty wheelbarrow was impossible. When material was carried over great distances, each man-drawn wagon was accompanied by two guards. Any ruse the crew employed to ease its lot had to be carried out either in silent agreement with the two guards, or by deceiving them while they were present and looking on, which was difficult and seldom successful.

Working groups in Buchenwald outside the chain of sentinels had their guards with them and therefore worked under the same close supervision as in Dachau, while also enduring the long working hours of Buchenwald.

An indirect consequence of the guarding system was the arrangement of the lunch hour. In Dachau the guards stayed with the prisoners for a period of five hours, then marched them back to camp for lunch, while other guards took the watch for the afternoon. In Buchenwald the chain of sentinels could not leave their posts until the prisoners were inside the fence and roll call had been taken to make sure that nobody had escaped. This took up too much time at noon, and therefore the lunch hour was spent on the working grounds.

This led to another conspicuous difference. In Dachau all food and tobacco found in a prisoner's possession during working hours was contraband. This was a frequent source of punishment. In Buchenwald every prisoner had a breadbag in which he carried his noon rations. Only a large quantity of food and tobacco aroused suspicion. With the help of the breadbag, a tremendous amount of smuggling and trading went on all over the area, and the administration was practically powerless to stop it. It was simply impossible to search ten thousand breadbags a day.

Two major differences between the two camps had to do with the fact that in the summer of 1938, Dachau was practically a finished camp, while Buchenwald was still under construction. In Dachau almost no work was left to be done inside the fence. If the administration did not want to call out the guards to escort the men to the outside working grounds, the men had to be let alone. Actually, no Sunday work had been done since Easter 1938. (Before that time there had not been a single free day for years.) Hence on Sundays and every evening after roll call during the summer, the prisoners were sent to work inside the fence, which kept them busy and yet required only a dozen officers to supervise the work.

The other important differences lay in the type of work. In Dachau, approximately 3,500 of the 5,000 men did nothing but digging, pushing wheelbarrows, and the crudest sort of road-building work. About 500 men were employed in the furniture factory, and about a 1,000 worked at house construction, that is, as masons and their helpers, carpenters, tillers, plumbers, hodcarriers, and all other kinds of semi-skilled and skilled labor. All of these latter jobs were reserved for non-Jews, and all of the more desirable ones were in the hands of political prisoners. The mere fact that there was only a small number of "better jobs," made their holders an elite group, in a position superior to that of the rest of the camp. Belonging to certain groups (especially to the politicals) was almost identical to having a good job. For example, the furniture factory was manned almost exclusively by politicals—and almost every non-Jewish political who did not hold a special job or position somewhere else found a place in the furniture shops.

In Buchenwald the main work was not road-building but the construction of houses and garages. That, of course, required a tremendous force of workers who did nothing but dig—dig foundations, dig shafts, dig in order to level sites for building purposes. But it also required an enormous number of workers for the actual construction of the houses. There was so large a need for builders that the preferences, both of the administration and of the prisoners, were less rigidly observed. The administration wanted to keep the Jews out of every job that was not digging. But there were fewer digging jobs than there were Jews. And there were more semi-skilled jobs to be filled than there are non-Jews. This meant not only that a certain number of Jews got semi-skilled and occasionally skilled jobs, but also that there was no control over the distribution of jobs. Again the administration was helpless and could only try to keep the Jews out of the best jobs and see that the worst jobs were always held by Jews. There was a great deal of mobility—in part growing out of individual action, in part caused by the organized action of certain groups of prisoners.

Perhaps 6,000 of the 10,000 prisoners in Buchenwald were connected in one way or another with building work, and, in contrast to the situation at Dachau, there were considerably fewer men who, by their status as Jews or members of other groups, were excluded from it. Thus there was not such an apparent elite of semi-skilled workers, and it was only the skilled ones who formed a fairly exclusive elite. The political prisoners and the professional criminals, whose organization gave them influence over the distribution of jobs, could not take care of all the thousands of semi-skilled jobs and other jobs which were preferred for various reasons. Hence there were thousands of jobs that were more or less on the market—that is, which were filled without organized influence from the administration or the prisoners. It was primarily in this sphere of semi-skilled jobs that most of the racketeering on the working grounds took place. Capos and sub-capos were bribed or imposed tributes; men used all sorts of private connections and ruses to shift from one working place or working group to another. Change of working place without permission of the officer in charge of construction, or at least of one of the leading capos, was forbidden in both camps. In Dachau this law for the most part could be enforced, and it was an exception when it was broken. In Buchenwald it was practically impossible to enforce it, no matter how terribly individual violators were occasionally punished. Every day hundreds of men changed their working places. That did not mean, of course, that there was a consistent movement toward better jobs. If a capo with 150 bad jobs on his hands found himself short, say, thirty men some morning, he went to the officer, asked for thirty men, and was told to take them "from carrier column number 2" or some other designated group. Off he went, told the capo there (or maybe did not even bother to tell him), and took thirty men, without listening to their protests. This happened every day in almost every working group except for the very worst ones and the specialists. This extreme insecurity in respect to working place was, more than anything else, indicative of the general insecurity in Buchenwald. Once you wangled a good job for yourself, you didn't know whether you would keep it tomorrow or not, and you seldom stayed longer than a few weeks at any one job. But of course, once you were in a bad spot, there was always hope of getting out of it again. In Dachau these things were considerably more permanent. Good jobs were more difficult to get, but easier to hold. And the man who ran into a bad job, was more permanently stuck.

Order and Hygiene

In Dachau the prisoners were tortured with overregulation and supercleanliness, in Buchenwald with disorganization and mud. It was this difference that made it so difficult for the prisoner to answer the question, which of the two camps was worse? They were too different in many respects. They both were "worse."

The cleanliness/mud difference was primarily due to the fact that Dachau stood on gravel, a relatively clean material with which to work and with plenty of good water for keeping things clean, while Buchenwald stood on clay, which smears and sticks and penetrates everything. And there was an accompanying shortage of water, so that the prisoners couldn't even wash their hands every day, to say nothing of keeping their clothes clean. In Dachau after a rainfall, the streets were dry in a few hours; in Buchenwald the clay turned into a quagmire and stayed that way for days, ankle deep. Throughout the whole winter the mud never dried up, except on days when it was frozen.

For these reasons, it was possible in Dachau to enforce a great number of rules of cleanliness which simply were not applicable in Buchenwald. In Dachau shoes had to be taken off before entering a room, and washed under the faucet before being put away. It was strictly forbidden to come to roll call with dirty clothes or shoes. An enormous part of the prisoners' spare time was wasted on keeping clean, scrubbing, washing his shirt, washing or scrubbing his locker, his dishes, and so forth. And since it was possible to keep the barracks clean, this was turned into a torture too. The men of every barrack spent most of their spare time on Saturday afternoon and Sunday morning polishing the hardwood floor, polishing the freshly laquered beds, and so forth.

In Buchenwald there was not enough water nor enough room to do all this cleaning. The mud could not be cleaned from clothes until they were dry—but when were they ever dry? It was impossible to keep shoes clean. All one could do on inspection days was to put a heavy layer of shoe cream on top of the clay, so that it lasted for the two hours of inspection.

This eternal mud, that stuck to shoes and clothes, that crept in between stocking and foot and between shirt and body, finally penetrated men's minds. If one cannot sit down on a bench, nor touch another man's arm, nor go to the washroom or any other place without getting muddy, then eventually the mud permeates conversations, thoughts, habits, everything. A great majority of the prisoners gave way intellectually and physically to the mud. Only a minority made a moral issue of keeping clean.

Lack of water affected health and hygiene, not only because the prisoners could not keep clean, but also because they could not take care of little wounds. Many a small wound, and often larger ones, could be taken care of in Dachau with the help of water and a few pieces of clean linen. In Buchenwald a wound much more often resulted in blood poisoning. Dachau was free of any kind of vermin, while in Buchenwald occasionally a barrack was infected with lice.

The water shortage also helped to slow down the tempo. Men simply cannot be accelerated without limit if they cannot get any water. In the glowing sun they will break down and die like flies, and the work will not be done. This was amply demonstrated in July 1938, when 1,600 Jews were brought from Berlin to Buchenwald. This time the administration was less interested in the work than in torturing the men. One hundred and thirty of them died within the first months, most from mere exhaustion.

Size of the Camp

Both in number of prisoners and in the size of the project under construction, Buchenwald was vastly larger than Dachau. In the fall of 1938, Buchenwald had 10,000 regular prisoners, to which were added (in a special fenced-off area) 10,000 Jews after the pogroms around November 10, 1938. Dachau had 2,400 prisoners during the spring of 1938 and about 5,500 by fall. This sudden increase of 3,000 men caused the administration almost to lose its grip on discipline and created, to a certain degree, conditions which were similar to what we found later in Buchenwald.

The prisoners' camp in Dachau consisted of thirty low barracks. The fence ran close around them, and included only the barracks, the roll-call square, one big building in front of the square, and the greenhouse in the back. The barracks stood in two rows, and from the machine gun towers, every side street could be watched. One officer strolling down the main street could inspect the whole camp in ten minutes.

In Buchenwald the forty-eight barracks stood in eight rows, the fence encircled a large area, and the guards on the machine gun towers could not look into the camp. In the criss-cross of side streets, it was possible for whole working groups or, during spare time, for individuals to avoid encounters with officers simply by turning around a corner. During free time the prisoners were practically alone, for no officer liked to go down to the camp, where he got his uniform and polished boots muddy. This added greatly to the freer development of a social life among the prisoners.

The main projects in Dachau at the end of summer 1938, were road-building around the camp, finishing some housing projects for SS officers, and levelling the grounds, especially drill places. All these projects were easy to watch, usually they were separated from each other, and the working groups were ordinarily not larger than 50 to 150. Only one or two of them had as many as 300 or 400 men. Even an inexperienced observer could readily understand what was going on in most of the jobs, and whether the men were doing what they were supposed to do.

The main projects in Buchenwald were the construction of large stone barracks for the prisoners inside the fence, and outside the fence, the building of thirty-six big garages and a big repair hall for the trucks of a motorized regiment; sixteen two-story houses for one company each; a few big barracks to house several hundred SS men each; the necessary storehouses, dining room, kitchen, hospital, and so on for all these SS men; villas for the SS officers; and in addition, all the streets, sewers, etc., for both prison and SS camp. All of these projects were on the mountain, inside the chain of sentinels. Working groups were seldom less than 100 men; many of them had as many as 300 and several up to 500 or 600 men. Their working areas overlapped, and the work comprised so many different activities and projects in themselves so complicated that in all but the digging jobs, only the experienced officer in charge of construction could tell whether the men were doing their prescribed work.

As a result, in Buchenwald considerably more of the work was entrusted to the capos and to organized sub-groups. For this reason groups that had influence inside the fence could exert this influence directly on the working grounds to a much larger degree than in Dachau. And the shrewdness and boldness of individual men had much greater scope—which made possible so many of the incredible happenings that are crystallized in the saying, "Everything is possible in Buchenwald."

Prisoners

The chief source of the difference in the social structure between the two camps was the difference in the categories of crime according to which the prisoners were distributed.

Concentration camp Dachau was established in 1933 as a camp for political prisoners. Even after the influx of all sorts of other prisoners, the politicals remained for many years the largest group. This changed considerably during the summer of 1938, when 3,300 Austrians were added to the 2,200 Germans.

Table 9.1 gives the distribution in March 1938, before the first Austrians arrived, and in September 1938, after the Austrians had arrived and before the Jews were sent to Buchenwald.

The two major divisions, Jews vs. non-Jews and politicals vs. nonpoliticals, changed, so that the Jews, who in March had been only a small group, became by September almost half of the camp, and the politicals (Jews or non-Jews), who had made up more than a third of the total, made now only a little more than one-fifth (as shown in Table 9.2).

These major divisions overlapped considerably; for example, there were 1,250 nonpolitical Austrian Jews with a red (political) badge.

Concentration camp Buchenwald was established in 1937, with 1,000 non-Jewish professional criminals as the first inmates. During 1937 and 1938 several hundred of them were sent away to other camps, while political prisoners, large numbers of non-Jewish "asocials," and several thousand Jews were brought to Buchenwald. In the fall of 1938 the distribution was as follows:

1,450	politicals
2,650	nonpoliticals with the red badge
900	professional criminals
3,900	"asocials" with the black or brown badge
100	emigrants
400	Jehovah's Witnesses
150	Foreign Legionnaires
100	race polluters
9,650	

Table 9.1

March 1938		September 1938
900	Political prisoners	1,250
300	Nonpoliticals with red badge	2,100
200	Professional criminals	850
400	Asocials (black or brown badge)	900
50	Emigrants	50
150	Homosexuals	150
150	Jehovah's Witnesses	150
50	Race polluters	50
2,200		5,500

Table 9.2

March 1938		September 1938
300–2,200	Jews vs. non-Jews	2,300–3,200
900–1,600	Politicals vs. nonpoliticals	1,250–4,250
0–2,200	Austrians vs. Germans	3,300–2,200

The three major divisions, which had developed in Dachau during the summer, had a different weight in Buchenwald:

Jews vs. non-Jews: 3,800–6,000
Politicals vs. nonpoliticals: 1,450–8,350
Austrians vs. Germans: 2,300–7,500

To these was added one more division that played no particular role in Dachau: professional criminals vs. politicals. The total numbers (900–1,450) do not accurately represent the situation, because they included Austrians and Jews, both of whom were involved in the conflict only to a minor degree—the Austrians because they arrived at a time when the struggle between professional criminals and political prisoners was already nearing its climax, and the Jews because they did not have power enough to enter the struggle. Thus the conflict was primarily fought out between about 400 professional criminals and 1,000 political prisoners, both groups consisting of German non-Jews.

Chapter 10

Kaleidoscope

When they are released, most prisoners are completely unable to verbalize the monotony of everyday life in camp. How could one relate the eternal sameness of fifteen-hour days that in the main consisted of nothing but carrying 120 loads of gravel over a distance of 100 yards, or throwing up 1,500 shovels of clay from a shaft? How could one describe the yelling that went on, when it varied no more than a switch from "Lazy bag, lazy" to "Lazy swine, lazy" to perhaps "Dirty Jewish swine, dirty," and each of these variations was repeated about 300 times a day? What should one say about the beating, when on an average day it consisted of nothing but a few kicks, or perhaps on a lucky day a man was not beaten at all, and his neighbor got only one slap in the face and a stone thrown at his head, but the stone was not very big, so he did not even bleed?

The pressure of the situation consists not so much of the actual mistreatment one has to endure (which after all is over in a few minutes or a few hours), but of the everlasting presence of mistreatment. If you are not beaten yourself, then you see somebody else being beaten, and you know it is only your good luck if the officer does not pick on you. Your eyes and ears and every thought and every nerve are strained and watchful; every fiber in your body is put to serve one single goal—to work ahead as calmly and inconspicuously as possible, so that you don't attract the attention of one of the many devils around you. You know there are more devils than you can watch at the same time, and one of them may crash down on you—and there is nothing you can do about it. If it hits you, it is not like a relieving explosion, after which you know that there is now security for some time; it is much more an invitation to redoubled watchfulness, for the man who has beaten you now has his eyes on you, as long as he is there. To be beaten is in itself a reason for being beaten more. And if he goes away, others may have watched him beating you, and now they pick on you. If you are lucky and the first man goes away, and nobody has watched him, then you are in the same position as before. You see other people being mistreated and are watchful so that it won't be you. And you know you can't prevent it anyway.

This situation is difficult to describe to outsiders who want to hear a story. It is made more difficult by the fact that the former prisoner and the outsider speak different languages. When the outsider asks, "Did they beat you very much?" he perhaps has in mind a milder form of beating than does the man who has actually experienced it. But the former prisoner, who still has the distorted logic and standards of the camp in his head, will say, "No, I got away very cheaply." He will not elaborate on this statement. It may actually mean that during several months in the camp he went through about thirty personal attacks from officers and guards and capos, during each of which he was pushed around, hit with a stick, kicked in the sides, or slapped in the face; every one of these attacks may have lasted anywhere from one to ten minutes, but none of them left visible traces. Only the standardized "twenty-five" or the "tree" or the "dungeon" or some extraordinary mistreatment counts in the camp. The former prisoner would be ashamed to face his fellow prisoners, if he went around bragging about a little blood he lost under an officer's boot.

So he searches his memory for stories that have a beginning and an end, and a point to them. And certainly there are enough. He tells about the "big things"—when Peter Forster was hanged on the gallows, and when the wolf was killed by snowballs, and when they would not release us without selling us a pair of suspenders because they made one mark apiece, when the Jews were brought during the pogroms and they dashed the brains out of about sixty of them who had gone insane under the mistreatment. He tells about the little ruses he used to secure himself a soft spot for a week or two—"Yes, and then I found one sub-capo, who was quite a nice chap, he did not notice me at first, but then I met a friend of his and through him we got acquainted, and I gave him a few cigarettes and he put me on a fake job—oh boy! What a time we had! For a whole week we did nothing but roam about the forest with a half-filled bag of sawdust. And when somebody asked us where we were going, we would report very seriously, 'We are transporting sawdust from the lumberyard to the infirmary for a repair job.'

"And one day there was a man who gave the warning 'eighteen, eighteen,' but suddenly an officer appeared behind him and added, 'and seven makes twenty-five,' and reported him. And when they whipped him in public, they made him yell 'eighteen, eighteen' every time the whip went into the air. And when it crashed down, he would moan, but they made him yell again 'eighteen, eighteen.'

"And one day they whipped a man who had stolen some duck eggs from the commander's garden. And the commander chuckled at every stroke, 'Quack, quack, quack' and 'Did you like those eggs?' and 'What a taste for luxury our little fellow has.'

"And there was a man who used to beg and scream that they should not beat him. The officers knew him and when they came across him they threatened him. And he would break out in tears, fall on his knees, throw up his arms, and beseech, 'Dear good little Herr barrack leader, have mercy on me, don't beat me, please, I beg you.' And he would slide around on his knees and try to embrace the officer's boots. And after having had some 'fun,' the officer would graciously release him with no more than one kick or perhaps none at all. And the man would come back, grinning from ear to ear and boast, 'See, I escaped again.'"

People who listen to these stories get a completely distorted picture of life in a concentration camp. It is not these stories, but the 120 loads of gravel and the roll call and the construction of the bed and other routine jobs, which dominate the prisoner's life. In order not to let the stories outweigh the routine, I have carefully avoided reporting them in the context of this book. But they must by no means be left out. They are just as much part of the situation as is the routine.

Every once in a while the drab monotony of primitive labor and mistreatment is interrupted by some extraordinary event. There are highlights in the prisoner's life, where all the cruelty of hell, or all the madness of a lunatic asylum are condensed into a single hour of horror or craziness. Sometimes hell and asylum form a mixture of such utter grotesqueness that, were it not for the suffering and the death of human beings, one could not help laughing. And the prisoners, used to mistreatment and death, expecting it for themselves every hour and every minute, seize their opportunity and laugh. They are glad to have something extraordinary to talk about, and to spice a little the poor gossip of the camp.

What are highlights to the prisoner who has spent weeks or months in a concentration camp become typical events to the man who has been there for years. Since I spent fourteen months there, certain things had already become typical to me that were exciting exceptions for one who had been in camp for only three months. A public whipping in Dachau, with all its pomp, is, to a man who has seen it but once, something unforgettable, surpassing by far the ordinary cruelty of the camp. I have seen several of them and when speaking of the scene use the nickname which it has among the old-timers.[1] But I have seen only one man hanged on the gallows, while people who had been in camp for almost six years at that time gritted their teeth and swore revenge, because "Now they have done it once more."

After about a year in camp one begins to understand that the extraordinary is in itself part of the routine. The individual events may be exciting, but taken as a whole they represent in condensed form the most characteristic element of the situation—insecurity and complete unpredictability. The fact that the extraordinary can be expected at any minute, and that it always comes, makes it so much a part of the prisoner's routine life that the old-timer shakes it off with a shrug of his shoulders: "Something is always bound to happen." And if it may look a little out of the way even to him, he may add, "Everything is possible in Buchenwald."

To him it seems a waste of energy to try to distinguish between the various events or to get excited about new ones. To him nothing is new under the sun. He has seen some executions, some escapes; he has watched several people trampled to death in public; he has stood a few winter nights on the roll-call square; suicides of prisoners are an old tale to him; men digging themselves into a heat shaft, thus producing the most complicated shirking story of the year, draw only a smile from him—he knows that this is bound to happen every time a new heat shaft is dug. He has seen commanders come and go, and for every new superbeast he remembers one that was worse. He has seen the greatest smuggling scandals uncovered, and he knows about things which never came

---

1. The nickname is *Öffentlicher Schlageter*, which is a pun against the Nazis that cannot be translated. *Schlagen* is the German verb meaning "to beat"; Schlageter was a man who was shot by the French for sabotage in 1923 during the Ruhr occupation. The Nazis subsequently made him a hero.

to light and for which, if they had, people would have been shot by the dozen. Sometimes the lore of the camp includes sagas from the old past, that is, two or three or more years before the narrator's time, which are so horrible and so grotesque that I do not dare to mention them in this book because I would not know how to verify them. But I have asked old-timers in the camp, and every one of them says, "Sure, those things happened," and immediately tells similar stories from his own experience.

In the following I will relate a few of these more extraordinary events. Each of them happened during my time, and I was a personal witness of every one.

Buchenwald, Winter 1938

During roll call Rödl made us sing the "Little Village." The second-termers apparently were not singing loudly enough. Lately they had become a little too powerful, and Rödl decided to teach them a lesson.

After roll call he had them remain on the square. For a full hour he commanded personally one of the most frightful punitive drills I had ever heard of. For a full hour we heard his orders over the microphone: "Up-down-up-down-roll-jump-up-down . . . "

When he thought that they had had enough and had learned their lesson, he sent them off. They gathered in formation, all 450 of them, and marched through the camp. Their barrack was way down in the last row. On the march they began to sing the "Song of the Pirates." It is one of the romantic songs that German youth used to sing, with an inspiring rhythm that can enliven the most depressed crowd. The text is nonpolitical, and the song is occasionally ordered in camp.

But the second-termers made a political demonstration of it. They began with the last instead of the first verse, which thus immediately became symbolic:

And when the last shot is fired
And all our fighting done.
Then we shall steer our rotten boat
With cheers to hell straight on!
And if Satan himself won't like us there
Then the fire we'll light ourselves,
For we were the lords of the world,
And want to be lords down in hell!

It rang through the camp like a tocsin.

Rödl became infuriated. He ordered them back and for ten minutes continued to drill in the most terrific way. But when he sent them off again, they marched again in full battle order through the camp and with mighty voices repeated the third verse:

Wir waren die Herren der Welt,
Und wollen's beim Satan noch sein!

It was the most inspiring experience I had during my stay in camp. Even the old-timers were impressed. After they had finished their song, they spread out over the whole camp, shouting jovial greetings and jokes in the barracks. The voice of one of them still rings in my cars. A giant of a man with a voice like a waterfall, he put his hand into our window and, laughing with his whole being, said: *"Uns kann det allens nich erschüttern!"* ("All this can't shake us!")

Buchenwald, January 4, 1939

The week between Christmas and New Year's had been a crazy time. At Christmas we had had two days off—the first time in years. We were allowed to draw some extra money from our accounts and order extra food from the canteen. On Christmas day we were given a pair of frankfurters each and even something similar to cocoa. During the next few workdays, the general atmosphere was lighter than usual, after all, there was one more holiday to come. On New Year's Eve a few of Austria's foremost cabaret artists, who were among the prisoners, gave a show, which aroused the interest of the SS. The camp was quite exhilarated. I remember how on that evening an Austrian SS man staggered through the camp, extremely drunk. He yelled something unintelligible at a prisoner. The man snapped to attention: "Yes, Herr barrack leader." "Where are you from?" "From Austria, Herr barrack leader!" "Where from?" "From Vienna, Herr barrack leader." Whereupon the drunken officer slapped the man on the back: "Cut out that damned 'Herr barrack leader.' Just call me Joe. But don't tell them goddam Prussians about it!"

Liquor was smuggled in, and the Herren Capos enjoyed a drink. The camp was full of rumors about it, but it might never have come out had it not been for Commander Koch's greeting obsession. He ran into two professional criminals who did not salute him. He became infuriated and had them receive "twenty-five" each, immediately. It turned out that they did not understand in the least what it was all about. They were dead drunk.

Koch first had them whipped into soberness, then threw them into the dungeon and there had confessions whipped out of them.

On January 4, after evening roll call, he announced over the microphone: "There are some among you who thought that they needed a little New Year's celebration. They even thought that they needed liquor on that occasion. All right, you had your share. Now I want to have a little celebration of my own."

He ordered several working groups to the "door"—potato peelers, plumbers, dishwashers, electricians, and so forth—about 250 men. Because of their close contact with the SS, they were apparently the ones he suspected of having smuggled in the liquor. He had them count off by fives. And every fifth "went over the stand."

And since he happened to have an old grudge against a few other groups such as the shoemakers and carpenters, among whom there was some corruption that had not yet been completely uncovered, he decided to clear that up too, and had them count off by fives.

And some men had their "twenty-five" coming that day in the ordinary course of events, so that all told he had about eighty men whipped that evening, while ten thousand men stood by at rigid attention for two hours.

Dachau, Summer 1938

Four hundred SA functionaries had come sightseeing. One troop was led by Koegel, one by Grünewald. Beaming with pride they demonstrated how clean *their* prisoners kept their barracks, how mirror-like were the dishes and the floor, how spick and span the closets. The demonstration was somewhat disturbed when Grünewald displayed a particularly well-made bed: "And there is no other means used, but the straw in the bag, as you readily see." With his fist he hit the edge of the bed—and a curse slipped from his mouth. He had hurt himself on a wooden edge which the prisoner had placed in the straw bag to keep it straight.

But otherwise everything was wonderful. The visitors were in the world of their dreams: everything was alike, everything was in its place, and people did only what they were told.

Somehow they avoided the eyes of the prisoners. They were not as well-trained in facing their victims as our guards were. They approved of what they saw, but they didn't want to get their fingers dirty. "Strong hearts, but weak nerves."

We prisoners stood at attention and were inspected. But among us circulated an old story in amiable Viennese dialect: "Poppa, why do these monkeys keep jumping around in their cages all the time?" "Well, you know, boy, they see the bars, and that makes them think that we are imprisoned. And that makes them happy."

Buchenwald, Spring 1939

Morning roll call. "Caps off!" For two minutes the camp was silent, while the count was reported to the commander. From the dungeon came some noise. The board which darkened the window was thrown off from one cell. A mighty voice shouted over the square: "I am Pastor Schneider, and Commander Rödl has kept me here in darkness, because I preached the Gospel of the Light of God. I am going ..."

There are noises, yells, screams, we hear a man being beaten and Rödl shouting, "That old idiot again! Shut up!"

Buchenwald

All beeches and oaks inside the camp were being felled. Only one mighty oak in front of the kitchen was carefully preserved. Anyone who did any harm to this oak got "twenty-five" immediately, because under this oak Goethe was said to have composed his poem, *"Ueber allen Gipfeln ist Ruh"* ("Over all summits there is rest").[2]

Buchenwald, April 20, 1939

Hitler's fiftieth birthday. Within forty-eight hours, 1,100 non-Jews were released. This was about every sixth non-Jew, every tenth man in the camp. It took hours to arrange for this mass release. They woke us up at two o'clock on both mornings. The camp was full of rumors; everybody expected to be released. A voice kept reading names over the loudspeaker. Hundreds of political old-timers were included—men who, after six years in camp, had given up all hope of release. Some of them suffered ner-

---

2. Editor's note: This is the first line of Goethe's "Wanderers Nachtlied" ("Wayfarer's Night Song").

vous breakdowns, wept, cried, "I don't want to get out of here, I don't want to leave my friends, where shall I go?" Of course, this was only momentary. An hour later they gladly marched off.

But even among those who kept calm, there was some serious talk. Today they were here as Communists, but tomorrow they would be regarded as converts, improved and returned to human (Nazi) society. They would have to raise their arms and say, "Heil Hitler," and get busy attending Nazi meetings if they didn't want to be sent back right away. Brrr."

The camp went crazy. Discipline fell to pieces. Everybody was exhilarated—prisoners, capos, officers, even the commanders. We were working inside the fence (otherwise it would have been difficult to find the people who were called) and that gave a touch of Sunday to the whole event. Nobody wanted to bother with daily drudgery. We marched around in groups and didn't even pretend to be busy.

I remember particularly one incident. Our working group was supposed to carry logs. And what did we do? In the wonderful spring sunshine we lay down on the logs and did not even bother to post a lookout. I do not know how it ever occurred to us. Two days before or two days afterward, the whole scene would have been so utterly impossible that even to suggest it would have been insanity. But there we lay in the sun.

Suddenly an officer stood among us. "Are you completely out of your minds?" Helplessly he shook his head. Who had gone crazier, him or us? On any other day he would have crashed down on us with his boots, his fists, with a stick or stones, or he would have dragged the whole gang to the "door," made us receive "twenty-five" each, and then hanged us on the "trees."

But today it was like fairyland. He only asked for the capo. There was no capo. We had simply strolled away from our bigger working group. Finally someone went up and presented himself as the capo. He received a single slap. "Get out of here." We went away and did not even bother to take the logs with us.

That was so unreal, so unnatural, that I am afraid the reader will not fully appreciate it. It was a prisoner's dream of wonderland—to be caught not working, and still not be hanged on a "tree"!

Dachau, April 1938

That year Easter Sunday marked the first holiday in camp for many years. On Saturday, the officers in charge of work got busy. They wanted to finish their jobs before the holiday. It was a turning point in the history of the camp.

We first 150 Austrians had almost finished our job, constructing a road where the old dungeon had stood before. One last gap had to be filled. All old rubbish had already been thrown in. All available gravel too. Still the hole was there. Suddenly the officer got an idea. For years old bricks had been piled up which the invalids had freed from concrete so that they could be used again. Thousands of bricks. He ordered the bricks thrown into the hole—by the wheelbarrow load and by the carload. He himself took a hand at it, to make it go fast, faster, fastest, so that the hole would be filled by noon, and the commander wouldn't notice that the bricks had been thrown in.

Dachau, May 1938

The commander played the same game with his superiors. Herr Himmler was coming to inspect the camp. Koegel wanted to demonstrate that Dachau really was the cleanest hell in all of Germany. He had 1,500 men swarm all over the roll-call square and gather up every tiniest bit of straw or wood. Then he sent them out again to gather the bigger pebbles (which hurt so much when you were ordered "Roll!" or "Maggot!"), so that Herr Himmler's aesthetic feelings would not be offended by irregularities.

When everything looked neat and clean, Kogel discovered an unpleasant sight. For years cement bags had been piled up, in order to be sent back to the factory to be used again. Hundreds of men had gotten their "twenty-five" during these years for having carelessly torn up such valuable bags. But now the pile looked unaesthetic.

Koegel ordered the wagons to carry the bags off to Sterzer's gravel pit. He himself commanded the destruction. Driven by his yelling, the five cars shuttled back and forth; thousands of bags were thrown into the pit. Then, in order to prevent Herr Himmler from discovering that valuable goods had been sacrificed to his sense of beauty, Koegel ordered the whole thing buried under a heavy layer of rubbish and gravel. Until nine o'clock that night, Sterzer's men were busy shoveling back the gravel, which they had dug out under the strokes of his rod and the clatter of the chain with which he beat them.

Dachau, June 1938

Two men were forced to stand face to face and beat each other. One was fat and sturdy, the other emaciated and worn. Both of them were bleeding, but the SS wanted to see more.

The thin man had been one of Austria's highest judges. During the time of Dollfuss and Schuschnigg's fascism he sent underground Social Democrats and Nazis to the gallows. The fat man was one of the hangmen who had executed his verdicts.

As this story got around, the political prisoners were disgusted. This was not their way of revenge. They had all this time refrained from the cheap satisfaction of beating up this man who had sent them and their brothers to prison and gallows. In camp he used to sit at my table, and I remember hearing him say, "The nicest people I have met in this camp are the Communists whom I imprisoned." They did him no harm in camp. But on the other hand there was no reason to use any special connections now that he was in trouble. He was just left alone.

And alone he died in Buchenwald on January 1, 1939.

Later it was discovered that the professional criminals whom he had sentenced had betrayed his identity to some guards.

Buchenwald, November 1938

The grapevine reported that an attempt against Hitler's life had been made.

No, not Hitler's, Göring's. No not Göring's, someone else's. It was the German ambassador to France, killed by a Jew.

At first nobody dared to believe it. But the rumor persisted. And terror struck the camp. This would be the end. *Das Schwarze Korps* (The Black Corps), the weekly magazine of the SS, had repeatedly published threats as to what would happen "the day after a Jewish weapon has been aimed at one of our beloved leaders." Nobody dared to talk about it. It surpassed our imagination. Would they shoot all Jews? The political ones only? Or every second, fifth, tenth, or perhaps a whole barrack? Mass executions were expected.

The non-Jews begin to segregate. The Nazi anti-Semites among them went about with expressive faces; the neutral ones preferred not to appear as "friends of the Jews," although privately many vowed to help their Jewish friends. Only the political men, the Social Democrats and Communists, showed ostentatiously that they intended to stick it out with their Jewish comrades. They demonstrated to the camp that to them a Jew was as good a man as a so-called Aryan, no matter whether some fool had shot an ambassador in Paris or not.

In the evening the truth came out. A young Polish Jew had shot a German attaché in Paris. It did not sound so ominous any more.

But the next day it began. Jews were brought in. Jews, Jews, Jews, by the dozen, by the carload, by the hundred, and by the thousand. In all stages of life—wounded, sick, crippled, with broken limbs, missing eyes, fractured skulls, half dead, and dead. They were of every age—youths of fifteen and sixteen and old men of eighty and over. A little boy was found among them. He had clung to his father's hand when the SS tore away his father, so they simply took the boy along.

Within three days, 11,000 Jews were brought in.

For awhile nothing happened to the Jews in the camp. Finally that came too, but it came in an unexpected form. First, every Jew had to send home a mimeographed slip, announcing, "Ich habe bis auf weiteres *Postsperre,* darf daher weder Briefe, Karten und Pakete empfangen und absenden. *Anfrage an die Kommandatur des Lagers sind verboten und verlängern* das Schreibverbot." ("Until further notice I am under *mail blockade* and therefore am not permitted to receive or mail letters, cards, or parcels. *Inquiries with the administration are forbidden and prolong the prohibition against writing.*") This mail blockade lasted for about two months.

Next the Jews' food ration was cut. A loaf of bread, ordinarily given to two men, had now to do for five. The scant ration of margarine—a couple of ounces daily—was cut out. The allowance of sausages and cheese was cut in half. The soup portions were decreased. Smoking was forbidden. No money was handed out.

Finally, the Jews were excluded from medical treatment, both clinical and in the infirmary. Men died or lost their limbs because of this regulation. Nevermind. They are all murderers anyway. Didn't a Polish Jew shoot a German attaché in Paris? Johnny Hackmann, second commander, went in person through the Jewish infirmary, and threw out about half of the sick. Next morning he came again, had everybody open his bandages, and again threw out about half of the rest. With their gangrenous wounds, the men were chased back to their barracks, and then had to crawl to work again. A Jew had shot a German. The guilty had to pay for it.

The non-Jews, with the politicals in the lead, came to the rescue. Illegal treatment was given in the infirmary, first primarily to political people, then to everybody who could get there. Medical supplies were smuggled out of the infirmary—bandages, pills, ointments, instruments. Under the direction of former Jewish physicians, first-aid stations and veritable hospitals were set up, with water jars and pocket knives as the most advanced instruments for cutting and even for amputating fingers. Capos helped conceal the treatment and gave warning when officers were around. Those capos who did not cooperate were put under pressure by the politicals and, if necessary, involved in some corruption and then handed over to the administration.

Camp food was smuggled, both to the pogrom Jews (who were kept behind a fence) and to the Jews in the camp.

Parallel with the political smuggling was a nonpolitical variety, led primarily by the professional criminals who wanted to make money. But others gave their food and other supplies for nothing. The most touching stories of undying friendship could be told. They cross race and group boundaries. The political people brought their help in organized form, and the nonpolitical prisoners did it on the basis of individual friendship, or personal acquaintance. "Asocials," the outcasts of the camp, brought half of their food to the Jews. So did professional criminals who were ordinarily so unreliable. So did Jehovah's Witnesses, glad of an opportunity to please the Lord.

It was the heroic time of Buchenwald, when ragged, emaciated, hungry, and exhausted prisoners fought the battle for the lives of hundreds and thousands of their Jewish fellow prisoners. In hundreds of cases the battle was lost and the number of deaths soared. It was the time of the bitter cold when lack of food and lack of treatment were particularly dangerous in case of infection. But in many hundreds of cases the battle was won, and men were saved and helped along, until finally, after two months, the terror let up and "normal" conditions returned.

Buchenwald, January 2, 1939

Commander Rödl over the loudspeaker: "It has repeatedly occurred, although it is forbidden, that prisoners during their free time have gone down to the forest and thrown snowballs. Because of this a wolf has perished. It is none of our business to keep a wolf for you, and yet through your stupidity the wolf perished. Some barracks have declared their willingness to contribute to a fund to buy a new wolf. After dinner, lists will be circulated and everybody who wants to contribute will have a chance to pledge any amount for that purpose."

This message left us exactly as baffled as it does the reader. Nobody had ever heard of a wolf in the camp, and still less of a wolf being killed by snowballs. All we understood was that after dinner they wanted some money, and that we had to pledge it, or else ...

The non-Jewish barracks pledged small amounts. The politicals sent caps full of copper and nickel. But the Jews, at whom the whole thing was directed, signed for bigger amounts. Before nightfall twelve thousand marks had been pledged. It need not be said that no wolf was bought. Even the existence and the death of the old one was doubted by most of us. Evidently the administration kept either a she-wolf or a wolf-dog for breeding purposes. It seems that the dogs got into a fight, and the prisoner in charge tried to separate them by beating them with an iron bar. While doing so, he happened to kill one of Commander Rödl's pets. To escape punishment, he claimed that prisoners had harassed the dogs by throwing snowballs at them, whereupon the dogs had started a fight during which the pet was bitten to death.

A wolf costs about three hundred marks in any zoo. Twelve thousand marks would have been enough for a sizable herd of forty wolves.

Buchenwald, December 1938

It was late after evening roll call. It was snowing heavily, still we had not been dismissed. The band played a new march. It was played again and again. It had a stirring melody. We began to stamp the rhythm. Nobody knew what it was all about.

Rödl took the microphone. He was drunk. "We have had a contest for the best camp song. Now we will listen to the winner. From now on this will be our camp song. Conductor, begin!" He sang it a few times.

The words were not too bad, considering the circumstances—what can you say in an official camp song? The last verse had its points:

...We shall not give up our courage!
Keep in step, comrade, here, and don't lose your spirit,
For the will to live on runs still through our blood
And faith in the heart we still carry.

Oh, Buchenwald I never shall forget you
Because you are my fate ...

Rödl himself was excited by the stirring rhythm. He thought up some more fun. "Let's have some riding games. Professional criminals against the work-shy." The men of two barracks jumped upon each other's backs and played horses and riders. The work-shy were not good and quickly lost the battle. The politicals, though not particularly interested in fighting Jehovah's crew, felt that their prestige was at stake—and soon the Jehovah's Witnesses were thrown off in the snow.

The band kept playing the new song. Next to the "door," the men whose "twenty-five" was due that night were lined up. They were strapped onto the stand one by one and got their whipping. Their cries intermingled with the blare of the band and the laughter of the horse fighters.

On the other side some newcomers were lined up, still in their civilian clothes. With wide eyes, they followed the spectacle. They seemed to believe that this was everyday life in camp.

No, it was not everyday life. It was an extraordinary conjuncture of cruelty and regimentation and the primitive thoughts and drunkenness of the commander, combined with snow and cold and hunger and craziness. Only the whipping was routine.

Rödl got a new idea. He ordered a parade. Ten thousand men began to march. As we passed Rödl, he divided the columns with his arms, bringing disorder into the masses. The band kept blaring the new song. It was snowing so heavily that we could not see more than half the square. Thousands and thousands marched out of the snow, came into the beams of the huge searchlights, passed Rödl, disappeared into the fog. We marched round and round, without purpose or meaning, feeling as if we were in a lunatic asylum where nobody knew when the devil would break loose. We were hungry; dinner had already been delayed for two hours. Deep darkness fell over the camp, but Rödl kept directing this grotesque parade.

A few barracks seniors with initiative simply marched their men home through the snow. Others followed. Within ten minutes the square was empty. Rödl kept waving orders with his arms, but nobody was there to follow them. The band beside him kept playing. Finally, he went home, and the band left; the Witches' Sabbath was over. The Buchenwald song had been born.

From then on it was sung thousands and thousands of times at the order of commanders and guards.

Two Viennese Jews, Hermann Leopoldi and Löhner-Beda, who had cooperated on many a popular song before, were its authors. The political prisoners did not like it particularly; its melody was too much like that of a popular song. They resented having their march through hell accompanied by a Viennese Waltz. Yet two months after the song's introduction, Free Radio Strasbourg broadcast the song all over Europe, as an example of the prisoners' unbroken spirit.

Rödl's superiors were furious. The song was forbidden. But Rödl ordered it sung again. He was a lover of songs.

Buchenwald, December 21, 1938

The state attorney read the verdict: the People's Court (*Volksgericht*) had sentenced Peter Forster to death for murder. In May 1938, he had killed an SS man and fled from Buchenwald. He had escaped over the Czechoslovakian border. But after the Munich Agreement, the Czechs had extradited him. Now he was brought back to the place of his deed. The attorney read a telegram from the Führer, announcing that there was no reason for clemency. Then: "Commander, herewith I hand over to you Peter Forster, to execute the verdict." Commander Koch ordered, "Bring him to the gallows!" We heard the man being led to the scaffold. Some noise arose, disturbing the quiet. Later we heard that Peter threw a few truths into Koch's teeth. They brought him back to the dungeon, gave him an injection, then led him out again. This time he walked over quietly. We heard the doomed man's feet stamp the ground for the last time. He was led up to the scaffold by two professional criminals, camp senior Richter and barrack senior Osterloh. They fitted the rope around his neck.

Again Koch's voice roared through the crystal winter night: "Puuush o-ooff!" One move—and Peter Forster was no longer our fellow prisoner, but a struggling something, dangling in the air—one minute, two minutes—time moved slowly while we 20,000 prisoners watched the soul fleeing the disgraced body.

PART TWO

THE SOCIETY

Chapter 11

The Task

Wherever a large number of people are thrown together, no matter under what circumstances and to what purpose, they will soon work out a system of routine and cooperation, to smooth friction and to perform whatever tasks the situation may require. If they are together long enough, a more or less structured society will develop, based on the social background and concepts which its members bring with them from their previous surroundings.

The prisoners in a concentration camp are no exception to this rule. Living together for months and years, they form, within the frame of administrative regulations, a well-structured society with its own group relations, its powerful leaders, its racketeers, its common man-in-the-street, its outsiders, its underdogs, and its outcasts. Individuals, groups, and whole categories of prisoners find their definite places on a social ranking scale, no less complicated and no less subject to prejudice than that beyond the fence, although the criteria by which a man is evaluated differ to some degree from those outside. Many a man who was highly esteemed in his civilian community may find himself on a deplorably low point of the scale, with people rated far above him of whose existence he had never dreamed or whom he had considered too inferior to be worth even his contempt. A highly educated ex-banker, with no previous conviction but known to his fellow prisoners as an egotist, may count for nothing in comparison to an uneducated laborer who has spent four years in a penitentiary because of illegal Communist propaganda, if the latter is known as a helpful and reliable comrade.

Group relations are more subject to social prejudices following closely those prevailing outside than are relations between individuals. Nonpolitical non-Jews are inclined to think that Jews are rich and corrupted, the vast majority of non-criminals consider the professional criminals unreliable, and almost everybody considers the gypsies treacherous fellows. Social prejudices vary from group to group, corresponding to their social background. It is the actual distribution of power which determines whose prejudices govern this society, and therefore take the form of social law, and whose are suppressed, persecuted, or ridiculed as "stupid prejudices."

In all this, the concentration camp society differs so little from any other agglomeration of people, that it would hardly need to be mentioned, were it not for the widespread belief that people behind the barbed wire *do* behave differently from those outside.

But there is one decisive difference that makes concentration camp society something greater than the almost automatic result of the fact that several thousand people are together behind a fence. When people meet voluntarily, say in a summer camp, the social life among them tends to support the purpose for which they have met. When people are thrown together involuntarily, say as prisoners of war, then the main purpose of their internment, namely to prevent them from continuing to fight, is already met by the mere existence of the camp itself; the society of the internees has no influence upon that, except in the rare event of preparation for general revolt and outbreak. But when people are thrown into a concentration camp, they are there not only to be segregated from the rest of the world, but also to be broken as individuals. The latter purpose is not achieved by the mere fact of internment. Rather it is a slow process, and the society of the prisoners tends to counteract this process.

A man is thrown into concentration camp as a means of cutting him out of human society like a rotten piece of flesh out of the living body. He shall have nobody to speak or listen to. His mouth shall be shut, his body mutilated, his spirit broken. His name shall be forgotten; he shall disappear as a number among numbers. His life, as long as it is left to him, shall be only a physical vegetating, with no memories about the past, no meaning to the present, and no goals for the future. He shall be only a cog in the huge mechanism of Nazi terror, pressed by other cogs and the weight of the whole machinery, seldom repaired, but used until worn out, when finally the late individual, now a number, will be written off the inventory.

But within his society a man finds a meaning again for his own existence. He finds tasks upon the performance of which he is evaluated, and judged and treated as a human being by his fellow men, perhaps not always as a valuable one—but even the outcast is the outcast of a human society and not the rubbish on a waste pile which the administration wants him to be.

For thousands of prisoners the task is only "to see it through," but this is in itself an important task when simple physical existence is a daily triumph over hell and terror. Others take part in the individual's daily struggle for survival, and in more spectacular cases, large groups take pleasure in his victory. When old man Lenk from the first Austrian transport, walking around more dead than alive, was finally released, we rejoiced that he had beaten the camp. And when we learned that he had died a few days afterwards, we added in grim irony, "But he beat them by a nose." The 81–year-old Katzenstein was a man whom nobody liked because he was a senile old crank, but when he was released, the whole camp drew courage from his survival of almost two years in the camp: "If that old bag of bones could do it, we will surely do it too!"

Hundreds of others deal successfully with the most difficult task—intellectual survival. They resent having their minds taken up by the paltry camp gossip about food and maltreatment and release. They discuss politics, economics, underground work, hair-splitting between political factions, and also the whole field of human knowledge from psychology to mathematics, from Egyptology to metallurgy, international highways, and the production of optical instruments. The whole realm of science is still open to the man who, with his companion, carries a hand-barrow full of gravel through the forest—as long as there is no SS man around.

Some use brain twisters. I remember a three-day argument over the queerest subject: a mathematical theory about the disappearance of the dinosaurs. If I understood its proponent correctly, they starved to death because–while eating up the leaves of one tree, their muscles shrank so much that they could not drag themselves to the next. We argued violently over this nonsense, but we enjoyed it because it led us away from the camp and helped to keep fresh our ability to argue. The recollection of treasures of art, plays, poems, is an important aid to survival. One morning in Buchenwald, I spent seven hours with a friend, dumping clay into a hole and reciting poems by Hans Christian Morgenstern. When we had dug up every line we remembered, we passed the treasure along to our friends, as an important contribution of something that did not smell of clay. For two days Morgenstern was in vogue at this working place.

People less interested in intellectual training try desperately to keep their personal style. There was a man who lived by the motto, "They can force me to eat from a trough, but they can't force me to be a swine." He would spend a whole evening cleaning two herrings and cutting them into nice filets. Another man decided that in this hell, where you couldn't speak or hear three sentences without two curses, he would not use profane language. And aside from a few occasional concessions to the devil, he succeeded fairly well.

Some men create for themselves much more complicated tasks, the performance of which would be counted among the highest ethical contributions in any society. People who considered themselves doomed never to leave the hell of the concentration camp except "feet first," made it their task to help as many of their comrades as possible.

One of the most outstanding personalities I ever met was Rudi Arndt. In 1939 he was about 28 years old and had already spent five years in penitentiary and concentration camp for Communist underground work against the Nazis. He was not a big party leader but one of those inconspicuous men who were brought to the camp by the hundreds to perish there. Over the course of years he had become one of the leaders of his comrades in the camp.

In the winter of 1938–39, my hand was frostbitten. The infirmary refused to treat it. When it became so bad that it seemed a question of hours whether the hand could be saved, I turned to Rudi, who then worked in the infirmary as an aide. When he did not succeed in getting me accepted for treatment, he began treating the hand himself. I told him not to do it, it might cost him his place in the infirmary, which was heaven itself. "I did not finagle this place for myself so that I'd have a warm spot during the winter. I came here to help my comrades. If I can't do that, what good is it for me to stay? I'm doomed anyway, I know that. But before they get me, I want to help along as many of you boys as possible. You will get out of here and help to finish off the Nazis. I will be dead then. But I will have done my share." I remember his words as though they had been spoken yesterday.

After two days, blood poisoning set in. Using all his political influence, he now obtained a bed for me in the infirmary. When after many weeks my hand was finally saved, I was incautious enough to say to Rudi, "And thank you for what you have done for me." "Oh shut up. I didn't do it for you personally. I did it to fight those guys up there. And I expect you to do the same."

After a few weeks of service in the infirmary, Rudi thought his job there did not provide enough opportunity to help his people. He quit his warm spot and voluntarily joined one of the dreaded working groups outside the chain of sentinels to encourage the men there.

The end of Rudi Arndt came after my release. It was told to me by a close friend of his and mine. He had become the head of a network through which the politicals placed their people in the better working places. One day he got wind of the fact that the administration was on his trail. He was not too strong physically and was afraid that under torture he might betray his comrades. To protect them from his possible confessions, he committed suicide. He ran into the chain of sentinels and was shot "on attempt to escape."

Rudi Arndt is one of the most outstanding, though by no means the only, example of a man who created his own meaningful task in a completely meaningless society.

All these attempts to keep alive intellectual existence and to create and perform meaningful tasks can occur only in a society that takes part in and recognizes victory and defeat. Only an infinitesimal number of men throughout history have been able to keep mentally alive as human beings when they were completely cut off from human society. Most men need a forum in which to display strength or weakness—be it only a guard they can defy or a bit of paper on which to leave their defiance to posterity.

The concentration camp as an institution does not provide the individual with such a forum. There is no judge into whose teeth he may throw the old challenge of the rebel: "You may put me into jail, but history will march on against you." When he dies in camp, there is no hangman to tell defiantly: "You may chop off my head but others will continue my work until we win." Most prisoners perish in the most unspectacular way, of some minor infection or disease, or from general exhaustion with no discernible cause.

The guards are a herd of slow-witted animals, with no understanding of moral strength; only physical toughness occasionally draws some respect from them, as the only virtue they themselves are able to display. They are not a forum for defiance—they are hardly personal enemies, nothing but parts of a machine that will have to be smashed piece by piece, when the time is ripe.

The commanders, brutal or refined killers, harbor no appreciation for moral strength either. Grünewald in Dachau had a friend of mine hanged by his wrists, because he had been incautious enough not to deny his knowledge of a certain disciplinary affair, but to say instead, "I won't tell you because I won't betray a friend." He said this when he was already hanging on the pole, but Grünewald, with no appreciation for such heroism, simply told him, "I will ask you again at intervals of an hour. But after evening roll call I won't come again, it is up to you how you manage to survive the night on the pole." For two-and-a-half hours the man stuck it out. Finally he decided that it was perhaps not worthwhile to sacrifice his life in order to spare his friend nothing worse than a thrashing of "twenty-five," which he would in all likelihood survive. And Grünewald was the only one of whom he might have expected some human reaction to this kind of heroism.

It is the society of the prisoners which fulfills this most important task for the individual: It provides him with the forum he needs; it approves and disapproves of his behavior, thus lending meaning to his actions and reactions. The man who is being whipped on the stand knows that his friends will consider him a good man if he does not scream. There is more chance of his screaming when nobody is around to hear it, not only because it hurts, but also because nobody cares and nobody appreciates it if he keeps silent.

The society not only provides the man with a forum, it also exerts itself on his behalf, thus giving him the feeling that he is not completely lost, that he belongs somewhere, that he can find a minimum of shelter at least occasionally. A man who belongs to any group in the camp, and who has received a heavy beating or is otherwise incapacitated, will find help when he comes home at night. Others will help him wash his bruises, clean his clothes and shoes and give him extra food if there is any. They will take over his part in cleaning the barrack and carrying the food; they will encourage him and perhaps try to get him transferred from his place of work. In very bad cases, even the man who has no friends will be taken care of.

In all this, the help a man can give is at least as important to him as the help he receives. To do something for someone else is encouraging proof that the Nazis have not yet been able to turn him into an apathetic creature that vegetates without any initiative of its own. His consciousness of himself as a human being is strengthened still more when the help he gives or receives is part of an organized action. My hand and probably my life were saved through political action, and so were the lives of many men. When lives were lost, it was often after a long struggle to save them. The political prisoners, in appreciation of Oswald Richter's past, tried all possible means to save his life; he spent perhaps more time in the infirmary than out of it. He finally died of an ailment for which there was no cure in the camp.

Organized help becomes more important and more inspiring for the whole camp when it is carried out on behalf not just of individuals but of large groups simultaneously. The smuggling of food and medical supplies to help the pogrom Jews in November, and then all the Jews when medical treatment was forbidden to them, was organized on such a large scale that it was no longer only an action to save lives. By its size it became a political action of the first order; it was a direct counterblow against the intention of the pogroms.

All this does not mean that the prisoners are one united mass of determined resistance; it does not mean that common suffering makes them all good and helpful. They do to each other, both individually and in groups, as much good and as much evil as they would do outside, but the form of action is different. The society does not make its members "good," but it helps them preserve their own standards of evaluation, thus frustrating the attempts of the administration to set standards of good and bad. The administration tries to establish the concept that a man is "good" when he is a useful prisoner, obedient, subservient, and hard-working, when he constructs his bed according to regulation, and so forth. The prisoners' society evaluates the man according to ethical standards, though these standards may vary from group to group. A political prisoner, when describing a man as "reliable," may mean something different from what a professional criminal means by the same word. But both allow for the expression of individuality within their respective spheres of human society, while the concept of the administration distinguishes only between more or less well-polished cogs in the machinery.

The society of the prisoners thus provides the frame within which individuals and groups find their place and their functions in cooperation and conflict. It opposes the terror of the camp, the attack upon the individuality of its members, and the attempt of the administration to enforce upon the prisoners its concepts of classification by race and crime and servility.

This society fulfills one more important task, beyond the immediate struggle against the particular administration of a particular camp. That is its political task.

In the minds of its creators, the concentration camp is the political instrument by the help of which they intend to stamp out the last spark of resistance against their system of tyranny. The Gestapo tries by all means to get hold of leaders and members of the anti-fascist movement that is moldering underground. By the dozens and by the hundreds, they arrest these men and women, execute the leaders and throw the rest into the dark hole of the concentration camp to rot away and perish there. They uproot them from their political and social relations in order to shut their mouths, to deprive the speakers of their forums and the forums of their speakers. They throw them together with ordinary criminals, vagabonds, and nonpolitical people—those who do not see any meaning in the underground worker's activity, or who are afraid to join with him even though they may be sympathetic. In this vast ocean of people, they expect the political fighter to disappear, to lose all self-respect, every ideal, every hope ever to change the fascist order against whose very existence he is rebelling.

And in these concentration camps the rebels find each other. The consciousness that they are members of the same persecuted group, a group of activists at that, and that they are fighting for the same political goal, welds them together in political resistance and political hope.

Within the camp they form an absolutely invisible political organization—invisible not because it is so well hidden but because it does not consist of anything that an SS man could observe. There are no secret meetings and no secret officers. Its leaders are not appointed by anybody, nor are they formally elected or listed on a piece of paper. They are distinguished from other men only by the fact that others perhaps speak more often to them and do what they advise, or take courage from what they say. The "meetings" that occur consist only of a few people singing together (when an SS man happens along, they sing the harmless romantic songs of any youth club) or sitting together on a door step, exactly as hundreds of other little groups are doing at the same moment all over the camp. Nobody calls another a "comrade" in the political sense of the word.[1]

---

1. The two meanings of the word "comrade" in English are represented in German by two words: *Kamerad,* meaning companion, and *Genosse,* meaning a member of a leftist political party. In the camp the latter is replaced by the less conspicuous word *Kumpel,* which itself has several meanings. Originally it designated minors, later it meant fellow worker, and then generally "fellow" man in any activity. The leftist political prisoners in the camp use the word *Kumpel* almost exclusively to designate their political comrades.

But it is primarily this invisible political organization that balks the administration in its attempt to break men's minds and spirits. Instead of being atoms, lost in the vast sea of nonpolitical prisoners, the political men become the nucleus and most active part of the society of the camp. They are its real leaders, the only ones who are able at times to do something, not only behind the back but right in the face of the administration. The "Pirate Song" of the second-termers was but the most spectacular demonstration I ever experienced, and the concerted action to aid the "November Jews" but the most far-reaching of its many political actions.

The political prisoners are the ones who transform into its very opposite the official function of the concentration camp—to destroy not only all actual political resistance but also the very idea of it. The mere fact that the Nazis threw these men into such large concentration camps created the most powerful contradiction to the goal they served. They killed thousands and thousands of men in these camps, but among those who survived, the spirit was kept alive just because of the fact that there were so many thousands of witnesses.

Chapter 12

Power

The administration, by means of differential treatment, tried to establish its own ranking scale according to race and crime and discipline. This scale placed non-Jews above Jews and therefore gave the former all the official appointments as capos and seniors, and, where possible, the better jobs. The asocials or "work-shy" were considered despicable because of their "laziness," and gypsies were an "uncivilized" pack. Professional criminals were subhuman creatures except for those worthy gangsters who were used as slave drivers. Jehovah's Witnesses were a bunch of fools, but there was no harm in giving them reasonably good jobs. Homosexuals were occasionally made the subject of special "jokes," but were otherwise ignored. The only group one could really deal with were the political prisoners. They were at least disciplined; there were many able men among them to be chosen as seniors to keep order in the barracks and as trained craftsmen for special job assignments. They were less corrupt than other groups, and generally less of a nuisance. But they weren't much use as real slave drivers, because they wouldn't beat their subordinates enough to keep things on the move.

And thus in a strange way, by different methods of reasoning, the administration came to a ranking scale which, except for the anti-Semitism and the strong position of some of the professional criminals, differed little from that of the prisoners themselves. Among the prisoners it was the actual distribution of power that determined the ranking scale. The distribution of power was determined by official appointments and by the unofficial influence which each category of prisoners was able to wield—through its ability to cooperate within its own barracks and to organize a network of relations throughout the barracks and working grounds. This unofficial influence affected the distribution of jobs and the treatment of the prisoners by capos and seniors.

Power in a concentration camp was represented by:

Official appointments as capos, seniors, barracks clerks, canteen men, barbers, etc.

Official assignments to special jobs in the clothing department, machine shops, shoe- and stocking-repair shops, and administrative offices.

Official work assignments in all these shops, as well as the bulk of all other skilled or sheltered or otherwise desirable jobs.

Unofficial positions as sub-capos, capos' aids, vice-seniors, etc.

A share in the network of relations which influenced job assignments, transfers between jobs and barracks, the ability to obtain new tools, shoes, clothes, extra supplies of towels, caps, mugs, etc.

Access to or domination of smuggling and trading routes inside and into the camp, especially for food and tobacco.

A share in the organized corruption and racketeering with which the camp was honeycombed.

Informal connections with guards and officers to obtain news concerning affairs both inside and outside the camp, to negotiate with them about withdrawal of written reports against individuals or whole barracks, or to make use of them in the smuggling routes.

The possibility of having people treated in the infirmary, when an SS officer or attendant refused treatment, which in turn led to an illegal but occasionally decisive influence upon life and death.

In extreme cases, the possibility of killing a man or handing him over to the administration, which may have had a similar result.

Finally, and above all, the ability to put up organized moral resistance against the terror of the camp, with occasional demonstrations before the very eyes of the administration.

Because of their social background and their previous training in cooperation, the political prisoners were the ones who were best able to constitute themselves as an organized group in the camp. Invariably they took over the leadership of their fellow prisoners.[1] Usually they were given those official assignments which are primarily of a coordinative nature, that is, seniors in the barracks and capos for skilled work.

The group that came closest to them in cooperative ability, the Jehovah's Witnesses, showed no bent for leadership or organization outside of their own barracks. They were practically never appointed to any positions except those of seniors and capos within their own category. In Buchenwald they held a great number of kitchen jobs and assignments as personal servants for the SS officers.

The professional criminals were quite capable of organizing rackets, but because of their highly uncooperative background, they were unable to organize smooth, routine cooperation on a large scale. When left to themselves, as in Dachau, they had to submit to the domination of the politicals, because they could not win enough respect from the other groups to establish key points for a campwide network of relations. That held true even though some of them were appointed as capos, as they usually mistreated their subordinates in a most horrible manner.

Because Buchenwald originally started as a camp for professional criminals, they were of course given all assignments in the beginning, and later on, when political prisoners were brought in, they still held a great number of positions as capos and seniors. When the struggle for power between the two groups began, the administration backed the professional criminals for about a year, and in this way they were able to retain a great deal of power and influence long after the politicals had taken over leadership among the prisoners themselves.

The asocials never had any sort of influence. They were always treated as second-class beings, by the administration because of their alleged laziness, and by their fellow prisoners because of their general lack of ability to cooperate and organize; also because of the fact that the bulk of the "asocials" were more slow-minded and personally less reliable than the rest of the camp.

The Jews ordinarily had no official assignments, although at times there were Jewish capos and seniors appointed for Jewish working groups and barracks. That was the case in Dachau for some time previous to January 1938, and in Buchenwald after January 1939. They never had any leadership power outside their own racial group. But within their

---

1. This held true not only for Dachau and Buchenwald but for concentration camps all over Germany, as was told to me in detail by former inmates of a great number of other camps.

group, which in the larger camps always amounted to about half the population, the politicals were the leaders and holders of all unofficial power, even if they had to obey non-Jewish capos and seniors. Usually the latter were politicals anyway and therefore appointed their brothers-in-creed to the unofficial positions, such as vice-seniors and sub-capos.

The Jews' share in the unofficial network of relations depended upon their relationship to the dominating group. Within the administrative limitations, the political Jews had access to practically everything that was open to the political non-Jews. Non-political Jews, if they had money, usually had easy access to the rackets which the professional criminals established, or they created large rackets and black markets of their own.

The gypsies were treated as outcasts both by the administration and by the prisoners. The general social prejudice against the "uncivilized" was strengthened in the camp by the sad experience that not only was it impossible to organize the gypsies to any degree of cooperation but also that a great number of them proved utterly unreliable personally. There were exceptions, of course, but in general the gypsies were left out of any group that did something which was not strictly legal. It had happened too often that gypsies had betrayed others to the administration, not because they wanted to cooperate in any way with the Nazis, but because they were short-sighted enough to enjoy the momentary advantages of such betrayals.

Each category of prisoners tended to rank the others according to its own social concepts and prejudices, the ranking scales being modified by the system of power that actually existed. The ranking scale that finally prevailed throughout the camp was the one of the dominating group, which was strong enough to distribute favors and exert pressure according to its own concepts and predilections. The others may not have liked their place on the scale and thought themselves worthy of better treatment, yet they had to accept it and could only grumble about favoritism and injustice on the part of the leading group.

In Dachau practically all the power positions, except most of the assignments as unskilled labor capos, were in the hands of Social Democrats and Communists. Hence they were the ones who set the standards and decided what was right and wrong. They ranked their fellow prisoners primarily according to political reliability and merit, ability to cooperate with others, and group responsibility. They punished egotism and corruption not only because they disliked them, but also because they meant "lack of comradeship" (*Unkameradschaftliches Verhalten*), which threatened the existence of the groups.

They considered discipline a virtue, not because they were servile toward the administration, but because discipline served their own purposes. It kept the groups intact while reducing to a minimum the friction among themselves and the number of spots vulnerable to attack by the administration.

Using these criteria, the politicals in Dachau gave top ranking to the non-Jewish politicals, who had the power positions in their hands, and the political Jews, whom they treated absolutely as their equals. Next in rank were certain nonpolitical people whom they accepted as their comrades on an equal level. This included most of the liberals and also a great number of businessmen, workers, craftsmen, a number of selected men from the asocials, a few selected professional criminals, and so forth.

Further down the scale came the great mass of nonpolitical people, who could, with more or less effort, be forced to cooperate to some degree: that is, Jews and non-Jews with the red badge, the homosexuals, the race-polluters, and so forth. Below these were the professional criminals, then the bulk of the asocials—the underdogs—and the gypsies—the outcasts.

Second-termers and Jehovah's Witnesses, both held in high esteem, didn't enter the scale because they were locked up in the isolation of the punitive company.

In Buchenwald the ranking of the politicals was similar to that in Dachau, with the difference that the professional criminals ranked higher. Backed by the administration, they held such a tremendous amount of power in their hands that they commanded a certain amount of respect even from the politicals, who would otherwise have treated them as second- or third-rate beings.

In Buchenwald, second-termers and Jehovah's Witnesses lived among the other prisoners, and therefore were given the high ranking that was due to them, as two of the most reliable and cooperative groups in the camp. The second-termers especially held the most desirable jobs.

The professional criminals in Buchenwald, with their vast share of power, treated the camp according to their own ranking scale, following criteria of power, influence, money, and individual ability in shirking, smuggling, racketeering. By these criteria capos and seniors were big shots. So were their personal friends. So were people with money that could not be squeezed out of them. So were people who had at their disposal favors that ordinarily could not be obtained by blackmail or bribery, such as treatment in the infirmary or transfer between jobs and barracks.

Men who did not belong to any of these categories were underdogs with various degrees of inferiority. At the highest of these levels were those who couldn't hurt the criminals, but whom they couldn't hurt either, such as Jehovah's Witnesses and nonpolitical reds (non-Jews), over whom professional criminals were seldom set as capos. A man with money that could be blackmailed out of him was not a big shot but a useful underdog.

The professional criminals ranked themselves highest on their scale, and they considered the politicals, especially the second-termers, as about their equals. Then came the political Jews who were backed by the non-Jewish politicals, then Jehovah's Witnesses and the nonpolitical reds, followed by the more alert part of the asocials, with whom the professional criminals associated in smuggling and trading. Several non-Jewish groups took the next ranks, followed by the great mass of the nonpolitical Jews, many of whom on the working grounds and in many barracks were left at the mercy of their professional-criminal overlords. Finally came the great bulk of the asocials; the gypsies ranked as the outcast.

The virtues in addition to power which ranked a man high on this scale—daredeviltry, toughness, shrewdness—were found mostly among the professional criminals themselves and the most alert asocials, but could be exhibited by individual members of any group. Hence the individual friendships of the professional criminals had a greater tendency to cover the whole range of categories than did the friendships of, for example, the political prisoners, who kept more to themselves.

Thus in Buchenwald, where there was a struggle for power between two dominating groups, the society was more highly differentiated than in Dachau. In Dachau the politicals set the standards, and the hundreds of personal relationships between groups of unequal ranking were exceptions to the rule. For example, the dozens of personal friendships between politicals and professional criminals were exceptions to the general position of the latter as a group. In Buchenwald the standards were considerably less rigid. The two dominating groups themselves were numerically small, and they tried to find allies or spheres of influence among the larger categories. The politicals linked up more closely with the Jews, because among them they found a large group of their own brothers-in-creed and, in addition, many men who, on the basis of their social background, were acceptable to them. The professional criminals had closer relations with the more alert members of the asocials, many of whom had the same social background as the criminals. Many asocials were employed in the SS kitchen and the camp kitchen, and in shoe and clothing repair shops, all of which were important sources and centers of illegal trade and smuggling, and therefore decisive key points in the racket system. This made for close contact with the professional criminals who dominated the rackets.

The professional criminals, particularly the anti-Semites among them, were in close touch with those former SS men who wore a red badge. (Some of them wear a green badge anyway). This was partly because they had the same social background, partly because they cooperated in smuggling, and particularly because they were both rejected by large numbers of their fellow prisoners, especially the politicals and some of the nonpolitical reds.

As a result, the nonpolitical prisoners in Buchenwald had an organized social life of their own and were actively allied with other groups, in contrast to their position in Dachau. This difference was greatly emphasized by the difference in the layout of the two camps. In Dachau all groups could easily communicate with each other along the main street, which separated Jews and non-Jews, but from which every individual barrack was accessible. In Buchenwald the various groups were more widely separated from each other by the very nature of the layout. The Jews occupied the four top rows of barracks. The non-Jewish politicals and the professional criminals, together with Jehovah's Witnesses, homosexuals and others, were housed in the lowest two rows. In between there was a "black belt" (so called because of the black badges) of two rows of non-Jewish asocials. The distance from the top to the bottom rows was great, and men seldom strolled all the way up or down the hill, unless it was to visit a particular friend. Thus haphazard contacts with acquaintances took place only on the working grounds. Neither the top nor the bottom rows, except for some of the professional criminals, were particularly eager to make close contact with the black belt. And so, during the leisure time, the major categories formed what were practically communities of their own within the society of the camp; contact was established primarily through the red and green seniors and officials in the Jewish and asocial barracks.

The bulk of the prisoners in Buchenwald were not lined up directly group by group with the two rival groups, but managed their relations individually by haphazard acquaintance or necessity. On the working grounds, prisoners tried to win the friendship of the group that had both capos and sub-capos there, and if that did not work and they were mistreated, they would try to get transferred. Political people found softer jobs by taking advantage of political relations. Nonpoliticals had to rely on money and bribes, which tended to make them approach the professional criminals. The important clothing department and infirmary could be reached best through political channels, while the black market was primarily accessible through professional criminals or asocials.

The ranking scales as described here applied more to whole groups than to individuals. The individual man was always treated on his own merits. A stupid political might be looked down upon by an intelligent asocial, a professional criminal might be the trusted friend of a political senior, a former SS officer might be on good terms with a former Communist member of the Reichstag, perhaps a Jew. But the forming of friendships outside one's own group was made easy or difficult by the prejudices and experiences regarding the other group. A political might have accepted a professional criminal as a trusted friend after the man had proved himself trustworthy, but he would give a blank check of trust to another political, and not withdraw it until the other had proven untrustworthy.

In times of stress and need, the ranking scales of the dominating groups gain in importance. One group may exclude all members of another group from favors at its disposal, and the individual man from the other group may not get a chance to prove that he is worthy of better treatment than his group as a whole. When the administration temporarily refused treatment for Jews in the infirmary, then the little treatment that could be given illegally was accessible chiefly to political Jews, because it was the political non-Jews who were able to give it. This may sound like horrible inhumanity, or even murder, to a man who learns that some man's life could have been saved by illegal treatment which was refused, but the politicals in the infirmary had to weigh the risk they themselves took in giving such treatment. They often did it at the risk of their own lives, always at the risk of their own position, and they were not willing to take this risk for everybody who wanted them to take it; they wanted to make their own selection. From a more objective point of view, however, it seems that the total number of lives saved by illegal action was certainly not smaller than what it would have been if the individuals who were saved were more indiscriminately spread out among all categories of prisoners.

Less dramatic, but almost more important for the everyday life of the camp, was the fact that professional criminals dominated the smuggling and trade routes. When the administration forbade the sale of tobacco at the canteen, it was available only to those whom the "greens" considered worthy of it, and that was not exclusively the highest bidder in money, but often the closest man in the ranking scale. When the scarcity got worse, black market tobacco was restricted more and more to the mighty—that is, the professional criminals themselves and a few of the political capos. The same thing happened with food when the canteen was closed for weeks. But money played a larger role in food distribution, because much of the smuggling went through the hands of the asocials, and they certainly sold to the highest bidder. That, incidentally, excluded a large number of the politicals, who had very little money.

In the everyday life of the camp, the ranking scales were most important in the distribution of soft jobs and transfers, particularly when certain groups were at odds. For instance, on a large working ground that was in the hands of the "greens," Jews could be out of luck for a long time, because in another work place, the politicals had used their influence to remove a "green" capo who had mistreated some Jews. In such cases money and personal relations were less powerful than group attachment and group prejudice. In general it was easier for a man to get help from a powerful group if he belonged to a category that stood in high esteem with the helping group, than if he was valuable as an individual. An impersonal relation to a strong group was usually more helpful than personal relations with a strong man.

The power of the officially appointed capos and seniors was almost unlimited. They could drive and beat their men, punish them with unusually hard jobs, report them for punishment to the administration, and mistreat them in any way they could think of. The administration backed every violent act of these men, including severe injuries. If a man was killed by a capo, not much fuss was made about it.

Capos and seniors were usually appointed for an indefinite length of time. Ordinarily they were removed only as a punishment for graft. Occasionally, when corruption became too widespread or discipline too low, there would be a big shake-up, and many might be replaced. But most of them were in power for years, and were often reappointed after they had been removed temporarily. Thus a fairly stable, official ruling class arose, which, in the course of time, developed a certain *esprit de corps,* in spite of conflicts that might have gone on inside the corps.

The tasks and functions of the various officials differed widely, hence the principles by which they were selected also differed.

The senior supervised the daily routine in the barrack. He saw to it that the rooms were clean and the beds and lockers in order, and that the men marched to and from roll call in good order, on time, and with their ranks complete. He organized the turns of the food carriers and of the

149

men who cleaned up the rooms during spare time. It was his responsibility to see that men appeared on time when the administration called for them for punishment or anything else. He kept discipline in the barracks during spare time. Often he had to direct a punitive drill for his own men, upon order of the commander—it was very seldom that a senior ordered one on his own initiative.

These duties made the senior's function primarily coordinative. If he was an able organizer and his group was cooperative, the barrack ran smoothly, with a minimum of violence. This was particularly the case in political barracks and those of the Jehovah's Witnesses. If the prisoners were an agglomeration of unorganized people, as was the case in the asocial and many of the nonpolitical Jewish barracks, there was much brawling and shouting. If in addition, the senior was a bad organizer and perhaps enjoyed exercising his personal power, he would beat and punish his subordinates.

A quiet and smoothly running routine was part of the administration's concept of a good concentration camp. This did not cause them to improve the overcrowded living conditions, but it induced them at least to appoint as seniors those men who were most capable of running the barracks smoothly. They chose good organizers who had been in camp for a long time—and in most cases this meant the politicals. Furthermore, the officers who suggested new appointments to the commander were usually informally in touch with those who were already acting as seniors, and took their informal advice about whom to appoint as seniors. The Socialist and Communist seniors saw to it for the most part that only their brothers-in-creed got in.

The capo's task required much less coordinative ability; he needed to be a good slave driver, particularly when he was in charge of unskilled labor. When hundreds of men did nothing but dig up gravel from a pit and carry it away in wheelbarrows, there was not much to be coordinated. Neither was any coordination required when workers carried stones on their shoulders over a distance of a few hundred feet, or bricks on their arms, or loaded and unloaded tip carts with gravel. All the capo had to do was keep things going, and fast, and occasionally see to it that the men didn't dig on the wrong side of the pit.

A good senior could demonstrate his ability by showing well-made beds, and usually he would not be asked whether he achieved them by beating or by imploring, or whether his men did the job voluntarily. A good capo of unskilled labor had nothing to demonstrate his ability, except the speed with which his men moved and the size of the loads they carried. Nobody counted the shovelfuls of gravel thrown up, nor the number of tip carts or wheelbarrows loaded and carried off. The inspecting officer was interested only in speed and full loads. Thus the capo ran around and beat and kicked his men, yelled, threw stones at them, reported them for laziness, kicked them over their wheelbarrows and back to their feet, slapped them or threw them down a gravel pit. These things he had to do as long as the officer was around, whether he wanted to or not. In Buchenwald, where the capo had considerably less supervision, only the sadists among them kept driving all the time. The others inserted occasional periods of letup.

For this work as slave drivers, only the most brutal and sadistic specimens were chosen, those who had a reputation for being able to drive their men faster, faster, still faster, and always filled with fear of what might happen next. In Buchenwald most of these men were chosen from the professional criminals. In Dachau most of them had the red badge but were nonpoliticals. Among them were the most famous killers— Sterzer and Zock in Dachau, Azzoni and Berg in Buchenwald, to name a few. Sterzer had a red badge but was a horse driver, incarcerated for incest with his daughter. Zock had a red badge but was in camp for being a pimp. Azzoni, also with a red badge, was a former SS man; Berg had a green badge and was an alcoholic, and formerly a ship's captain.

It was seldom that an honest man slipped in as an unskilled-labor capo. It happened very occasionally when a skilled-labor capo finished one job and there was no other skilled job available. Then he was put in charge of the next unskilled labor ground.

Capos in charge of skilled work had much more of a coordinating task, similar to that of the senior. In the furniture shop, the sawmill, and at construction work such as plumbing, tiling, and carpentry, speed was less important. Here the administration was interested in quality, and therefore selected men according to their technical ability. Often they gave men the kind of work they had done in civilian life. This led to a selection primarily of industrial workers, which again caused them to select Social Democrats and Communists. In Buchenwald a few Jehovah's Witnesses were also made capos in skilled labor work areas.

There was not much noise and violence in skilled labor places, for the same reasons as in the barracks with political seniors, and jobs in such places were very desirable. However, there were only a few of them.

Semi-skilled labor, such as concrete-mixing, took an intermediate position. Usually it required a high enough degree of skill so that the men could not be hurried too much if the work was to be done well, but not so much skill that the man in charge necessarily had to have been trained in the trade. It was more a matter of chance then, what sort of man was put in charge; but even a bad one was restricted by the nature of the work.

There were several other official appointees. One of them was the barrack clerk, who kept the records of the prisoners in his barrack, the mail list, the list of men who were on punitive extra time or "door" duty, and similar records. In Buchenwald each barrack also had a barber and a canteener.

All of these men belonged to the "barrack detail," that is, they helped clean up the barrack during the day. Their appointments were usually strongly (though informally) influenced by the barrack seniors; hence in Dachau they were almost exclusively politicals, and in Buchenwald they were either politicals or professional criminals.

At the peak of the whole official structure in Dachau was a camp senior. However, his was not a very strong position, his function being mainly to supervise the technical part of the work. He was more or less a technical aid to the officer in charge of construction.

In Buchenwald there was one camp senior and two deputies. The camp senior had power over life and death to a greater degree than any other prisoner, and his influence upon the general situation in the camp was probably greater than that of any SS officers except for the commanders and the *"Rapport Führer"* (the highest noncommissioned officer in charge). He had a tremendous influence on the general attitude of capos and seniors and upon their appointments. He had to make frequent reports to the commander and the officers in charge of work and special departments, and in this way he had a strong influence upon regulations and general policy. The two deputies did not have a great deal of influence, although they took part in the supervision of discipline in the whole camp.

Not much can be said about the selection of these camp seniors, since there were too few of them to discern any trends.[2]

There was one office in Buchenwald that did not exist in Dachau: the "Control" (*Kontrolle*). Originally its members were stool pigeons kept by the administration to spy on their fellow prisoners, as was done frequently in ordinary prisons. But in the course of time their function changed. They were no longer used to spy on secret conversations and

---

2. Descriptions of the first two camp seniors that were in power during my time are found in the chapter on the struggle between political prisoners and professional criminals.

activities, but to sneak around like the officers and report people for "laziness." In order to keep themselves in power, they had to file a great number of reports.

The fact that some men were allowed to stroll about the camp without getting punished could not be kept a secret forever. The camp found out who they were, their prison numbers were passed along, and everyone watched out for them just as for SS officers. Originally they were not easy to recognize, but when they assumed the privilege of wearing high boots—of which there was a small supply in the clothing department— their boots betrayed them.

The more they became known, the more they lost their usefulness as a secret institution. At first the administration replaced them occasionally by new men, but at length they became well known and were regarded as capos without working groups. When finally the capos received armbands with the word "capo" printed on them, the former stool pigeons also received armbands with the word "Control."

The "Control" developed into the most corrupt institution in the whole camp. They wrote reports against people and held them under the victim's nose: pay or else... They covered up all sorts of smuggling in return for high payments. They closed their eyes to irregularities when they saw fit, but invented some if they so preferred. They puffed away on cigarettes in the tool shed and went out to report others for smoking. They took naps in a hideout and then went out to get their daily quota of reports for laziness.

From time to time these things came out, and the culprits were terribly punished and either replaced or left in power if the commander thought they would be frightened and more useful.

There were usually five "controllers," most of them professional criminals, with occasionally a nonpolitical among them.

One peculiar case of a "controller" may be mentioned for its strangeness. A newcomer was rumored to be a high-ranking SS officer, close companion of commander Rödl, the old friend of Hitler's. Rumor had it that he was to stay in camp for a few months in order to teach him not to squander in drink everything the party gave to him as a reward for his excellent Nazism. Whatever the truth about this man, suddenly the number of reports against Jews rose. The man was observed beating up Jews, doing no other work, and his number was passed along. Conveniently enough, it was the number 1,000.

After a short time he was transferred to a small subsidiary of Buchenwald, a temporary camp near a housing project. He was installed there immediately as a camp senior, which seemed to corroborate the rumors about him.[3]

In Dachau each barrack had one barrack senior, four room seniors, and one clerk, which added up to 162 men in twenty-seven barracks.[4]

In addition each working group had one officially appointed capo, and, when it was very large, occasionally one or two sub-capos in fairly official positions (i.e., appointed by the capo but recognized by the officer in charge). Working groups varied in size from a few men on a special job to about 100 in the larger, with groups up to 300 in rare cases. On the average there was about one officially recognized capo for every sixty men, or about ninety capos all told, including the leading men in the infirmary and so forth.

In Buchenwald each of the wooden barracks (with two rooms) had one barrack senior, two room seniors, one clerk, one barber, and one canteener. In the brick barracks (with four rooms), there were two more room seniors and one more barber. That made about 240 men in thirty-seven barracks.[5]

Again, each working group had one officially appointed capo and some semi-official sub-capos. The size of the working groups varied considerably more than in Dachau; groups up to 300 were no rarity, and groups of 500 occurred. Yet one capo per seventy men may be a good estimate, and there seemed to be fewer officially recognized capos and sub-capos than in Dachau. That makes about 140 capos, again including those in the special departments.

Thus the officially appointed ruling class in Dachau added up to about 250 out of 5,500 prisoners, or about 4.5 percent; in Buchenwald there were about 380 out of 10,000 prisoners, or 3.8 percent. In Buchenwald there might be added a great number of sub-capos who had less official standing and yet had almost as much power on their working grounds as the capo himself.

---

3. Bruno Heilig in *Men Crucified* reported about this man, Toni Lehner, that he was quite a reasonable fellow, with whom he had smoked many a cigarette during working hours. However, I know people who had seen him beating Jews, and I myself know "controllers" who smoked a cigarette with one Jew, and then reported another Jew for smoking.

4. Three of the thirty barracks were taken up by the infirmary and the canteen.

5. Seven of the reported forty-eight barracks were taken up by the kitchen, infirmary, bath, clothing department, etc., and four barracks were under construction.

This official power structure was connected with the unofficial power structure of the prisoners themselves, some of whose top figures had more power and influence than some of the men with resounding official titles.

Each man in the infirmary had a higher social status than almost any capo in the camp, and within his own barrack or room an unofficially appointed vice-senior, when backed up by the senior, had practically the same power as the senior himself.

Chapter 13

Cooperation

The amazing punctuality and exactness with which the thousands of prisoners perform their daily routine almost demand the metaphor, "Co-operating like a well-oiled machine." For the majority of the prisoners, this comparison is even more true than might be expected. A machine part, properly shaped and placed, cannot help but cooperate smoothly with the rest, once the machine is set in motion. The routine cooperation of cogwheels is exactly what the administration wants. The degree to which they achieve it varies somewhat with the various categories of prisoners. The cooperative training of the politicals seems at first sight to play into the hands of the administration, while the individualistic attitude of the professional criminals and the indolence of the asocials appear as serious obstacles.

Yet the latter prove quite susceptible to the influence of threat and terror. Beaten and pushed around by capos and seniors, heavily punished in large groups for minor violations of rules on the part of individual members, not even the most atomized agglomeration of "ascocials" remains the same amorphous mass after a few weeks of life together in the same barracks. The same applies to the professional criminals and other groups. After some time they acquire the necessary routine cooperation that alone enables a barrack to pass an inspection unpunished.

In the long run, of course, the solidarity of fear is not a very reliable basis for cooperation. As long as the individual men see a choice between being afraid and making their beds carefully, or taking a chance instead, there will always be enough of them who make their beds badly, or who are careless about their dishes. Pleading speeches by the senior become a useless bore, violence appears as meaningless sadism, and the barrack gets caught at fairly regular intervals.

The politicals, because of their previous training, fare better in their attempts to cope with the requirements of meticulous order.

In the ordinary camp routine, differences between the politicals—and, incidentally, the Jehovah's Witnesses—as compared with other groups, lie less in the effect than in the amount of violence necessary to achieve it. After all, every barrack has to be at roll call on time, cooperation or no cooperation. But political barracks fall in line quietly, with not more than an occasional, "Come on, come on, hurry up" being heard. But in an asocial or nonpolitical Jewish barrack, the senior may have to push the men around, because they are fighting for the "good" places—not in front, not as wing-men—and to shout at the latecomers. The first rows may already be marching, while the last rows are still being formed. A passing officer may report the whole "pigsty" for punishment.

At mealtimes the food carriers of a political barrack are usually ready before the whistle blows, while in other places the senior has to shout for his men. If they aren't ready, he has to send others. If they protest that it is not their turn, he may slap them to cut short the discussion—no time can be lost, or the barrack will be without food.

It is similar on the working grounds. Where asocials or other nonpoliticals work in great masses, more violence is required to keep the work going at average speed—not because the men are actively resisting, but because of their general inability to cope with a situation in which cooperation is the best way to keep out of trouble.

If a well-cooperating barrack gets caught because of some disorder, the senior may make a little speech: "Those among us who are careless endanger the whole group. You have to remember your responsibility to the group. We have to preserve our solidarity, now more than ever." The words may have different meanings to different people, yet all of them realize that this is essentially a political speech, an appeal to their political solidarity. If the barrack gets punished for no avoidable reason, the senior may tell the men: "Well, they've got us this time. For nothing that was our fault. All I can tell you is, stick together, don't give them a chance. They are after us."

In a badly cooperating barrack, the senior may scream: "Haven't I told you repeatedly? Now it serves you right to have your drill. From now on I am going to report every man who does not make his bed with extreme care. I am not going to take 'twenty-five' because I let you make a pigsty of your barrack." And he may order his men to construct beds throughout their spare time, have them sweep and clean and brush the floor and the toilet and clean their dishes all Sunday morning, and always under the threat: "I'll report you! I am not going to go over the stand for you."

Yet if all the superior cooperation of the politicals were based on nothing but their better training and the same fear of punishment, they would soon be in the same spot as the asocials: They would be caught time and again because someone thought that this was the time to take a chance with a badly made bed.

Voluntary cooperation over long periods of time is only possible where the men draw satisfaction from it, beyond the immediate purpose which it serves. The minutest routine training of unwilling men cannot measure up to the smooth cooperation of those who consider their working together a triumph over the situation. This voluntary cooperation arises only between men who share a common ideology, with common goals that are independent of the situation and therefore safely outside the grasp of the administration. Only where men feel themselves outposts of a fighting army, will they be able to cooperate even if the administration strikes at them again and again. Yet cooperation will break down immediately among people with no common ideology, as soon as the administration mistreats and punishes them in spite of their well-made beds. It is more or less incidental for the men who cooperate well that the administration, caught by its own concepts of a smoothly running hell, leaves them more in peace than the others.

Only two categories of prisoners developed this voluntary cooperation to any high degree: the political people from the left—Social Democrats and Communists and their splinter groups—and Jehovah's Witnesses. Both were groups with strongly developed ideologies, both considered themselves outposts of an army that had been beaten but not permanently defeated.

People with a common ideology who do not think of themselves as the outposts of a fighting group—such as most of the conservatives—

show hardly any tendency to form large cooperative groups. They keep together in small circles of friends, either submitting to the cooperation of the politicals from the left or living a life as outsiders.[1]

The greatest differences appear where cooperation beyond the minimum necessity to avoid punishment is required. "Ideological" barracks, such as those of the politicals and Jehovah's Witnesses, organize their free time so that they get through with the minimum amount of noise and strain on the nerves. Distributing the food follows a quiet routine, people don't push one another to get there first; they sit down at the tables quietly, and if there are not enough seats for everyone, then each table has a well-established order in which people eat. In other barracks the men fight for places in the line and for places at the table, yelling at one another, cursing, and even hitting each other. During the first weeks in Buchenwald, the barracks were terribly overcrowded, with almost twice as many men as beds. In spite of the fact that the double-layer bunks had been replaced by triple layers, every night terrific battles were fought over the bunks or even for a share of a bunk, and when finally the lights went out, dozens of men had to lie on the floor, fortunate if they could at least find a straw bag or a blanket. But the barrack containing the German political Jews solved the problem in a way that forced admiration even from those who had become accustomed to their smooth cooperation in Dachau. First they moved the beds together, so that they stood three in a row, then they assigned sleeping places, not to be changed, so that five men shared three beds. In this way nobody had to sleep on the floor, and at the same time enough space was created so that they could move between the beds and keep the room clean.

In many barracks semi-official deputy room seniors were appointed. In nonpolitical barracks, they were nothing but adjutants to the senior, helping him keep order by yelling at the men. But in political barracks they were appointed with the tacit consent of the men in such a way that they acted almost as selected representatives of the room to negotiate with the senior. In these cases their personal authority was quite far-

---

1. This refers to the situation up to the time of my release in May 1939. Afterwards, conservatives from conquered countries felt themselves not so much the sold-out part of a political party—as was the case with the Austrian conservatives—but rather the martyred representatives of a subjugated nation that was still fighting on for its liberty. From my experience in the camp it seems that Catholics, if persecuted for their religion, would probably develop the same cooperation in large groups as the Leftists and the Jehovah's Witnesses. But up to 1939 no large groups of Catholics were brought to camp for their religion or the political attitude of their church.

reaching, since it was based primarily on their popularity and on the usefulness of their services. In contrast, the authority of such a deputy in nonpolitical barracks reached only as far as the senior's stick, that is, all the way across the room, but only on the surface. Voluntary cooperation among the men could not be created by shouting or beating.

In most rooms, table seniors were appointed for the purpose of keeping order and discipline, and to keep the tables clean. In Dachau, where there was relatively a good deal of space at and between the tables, and everybody had his individual locker, it was not too difficult to keep order, and these table seniors were not very important. In Buchenwald, where the tables were overcrowded and there were no lockers, the senior had to see to it that everybody somehow got his food and that the dishes were cleaned and put on the shelves. In addition he had to distribute the weekly change of clothes, and every evening the so-called "rations"—the small allotment of cheese or sausage, etc., for the next morning. The change of clothes in particular often developed into a source of favoritism, since most stockings were torn when they were distributed, shirts were too small, and there were only a few fairly acceptable pieces.

In Buchenwald each table also had its own canteener, who transmitted orders to the barrack canteener and distributed the food that came in. Since, invariably, less food arrived than had been ordered, much fighting went on about the proper allocation.

Both table seniors and table canteeners were appointed either by the room senior, or by agreement among the men. Sometimes they were the heads of little cliques who simply usurped what little power lay in these positions. Most fights among prisoners during dinnertime centered around the claim that somebody had received too much or too little of something of which there was not enough.

In political barracks these appointees had a strictly coordinating function, which they fulfilled with a very minimum of favoritism. And because they were working with men who wouldn't blame them unless there happened to be a serious grievance, the whole organization reduced substantially the friction between the men, which in turn contributed to the quietness that was typical for political barracks. Lack of friction enabled the men to give more attention to the way they behaved toward one another. They lowered their voices, and if they wanted to call somebody across the room, they would either go to him or have somebody else get his attention. Badly cooperating barracks were noisy, and most of the men were inconsiderate of each other—pushing, shouting, yelling across the room, trying to out-shout one another—until the din rose too high, and the senior would out-shout them all, bellowing, "Why don't you all shut up!"

The difference was particularly striking on Sundays. In cooperating barracks there was much reading, playing of games—chess or checkers, homemade of cardboard or wood, sometimes of bread—and quiet conversation in little groups. In non-cooperating barracks where the people had a high educational level, such as some of the Viennese Jews possessed, there would also be some reading and intellectual conversation. But considerably less than in the political barracks.

In the asocial and professional criminal barracks, there was much less conversation except for camp gossip. As a result the men were not so likely to sit together quietly, but interrupted their talks frequently or changed partners, or shouted for other people, and so forth.

There were little libraries in the two camps. Service was free. The one in Dachau worked fairly well and had a stock of readable books, such as German classics, fiction, history, travel, and so forth. Prisoners made their choices from a typewritten catalog, advised by the librarian who was a political prisoner. The time spent in the line was about fifteen minutes on an average day and about half an hour on Sunday. This was not prohibitive after the work-free weekend was introduced.

The library in Buchenwald functioned badly. Books had to be ordered through the senior; it took days for a book to be delivered, and then it was usually not the one that was desired. Since there was practically no spare time, reading a book was not so much recreation as a tremendous expenditure of energy. It was impossible to read in the overcrowded rooms, and the sleeping room, the only place where one could read, could not be entered more than half an hour before official bed time. Then, in the half-darkness of his bunk, perhaps with his back aching, and disturbed by the noise from the adjoining day room, the prisoner tried to get away from the concentration camp. Fifteen or twenty pages in one evening were, under these circumstances, a great achievement. Most people did not have enough energy or desire left for reading in these conditions. Most of the reading was done by political prisoners, who considered it one of the weapons in the struggle for political and intellectual survival.

Newspapers were read much more extensively than books. In Dachau practically all German newspapers and magazines were permitted, in Buchenwald only a small selection. The prisoners subscribed to the publications with money from their accounts. Subscriptions could only be made by individual prisoners, not by groups. In Dachau there were a good many more subscriptions in the political than in the nonpolitical barracks, and they were of a greater variety.

In Buchenwald the local Nazi daily *Thüringer Gauzeitung* and two or three editions of the *Völkischer Beobachter*[2] were available, together with the weekly magazine of the SS, *Das Schwarze Korps.* In Dachau the nonpolitical barracks usually subscribed to the *Völkischer Beobachter* and one or another illustrated weekly. Occasionally an intellectual subscribed to a popular science magazine.

In political barracks the variety of magazines and papers was surprising. I remember having seen in one room the following papers: *Völkischer Beobachter*; the *Frankfurter Zeitung,* which was less Nazified than the official party papers and more reliable in reporting on political and economic developments; the *Kölnische Zeitung*; a few weekly magazines such as *Hackebeil's, Kölnische,* and the *Berliner Illustrierte*; a few nonfiction weeklies such as *Das Schwarze Korps, Deutsche Wehrzeitung,* published by the Army, *Die Koralle,* a popular science magazine; a few monthlies—*Atlantis* and *Wissenschaft und Technik,* both representing the highest level of popular science magazine in Germany; and *Westermanns Monatshefte,* a literary magazine.

One reason for this striking difference was the greater interest in world affairs and matters of science among the politicals, together with the ideological attitude that to keep the mind in training was a political duty. In nonpolitical barracks, people who discussed science, philosophy, and mathematics were considered queer birds and might be asked, "Have you nothing more important to talk about?" In political barracks, the opposite attitude was taken; the man who did not show a vital interest in world affairs or other non-camp subjects was considered beaten by the camp. A splendid chess player, a good mathematician, an expert on literature, a technical expert who talked about his subject was welcome and respected. And still more so was one who was able to transform the gossip of the *Völkischer Beobachter* and the restricted news of the *Frankfurter Zeitung* into a comprehensive analysis of political and economic affairs. But a man who kept talking about the camp, the work, the food, or perhaps the "twenty-five" he had received recently, was considered a nuisance and hushed up: "Don't you have anything more important to talk about?"

The main reason, however, for the difference in variety was the difference in the ability to raise funds. Subscriptions were expensive, and

---

2. The central party daily of the Nazis, which came out in Austrian, Munich, Berlin, West German, and other editions.

those who could afford them, never could afford more that one newspaper and perhaps one magazine. In these cases the *Völkischer Beobachter* or the *Frankfurter Zeitung* was the usual choice. Occasionally a few friends cooperated and shared their subscriptions, thus creating a little variety.

In political barracks the resources of a whole room were pooled. An advisory committee selected the papers, and the political leaders distributed the subscriptions so that the people with more money took the expensive ones. When the papers arrived, they were considered the property not of the individual subscribers but of the whole room. This of course worked only as long as the men were convinced that everybody was contributing as much as he possibly could. The leaders saw to it that this was the case. Those who tried to shirk their duty, particularly nonpoliticals in a political room, were forced by private persuasion, social pressure, and by ostracism, as if the whole thing were a common racket. The prisoners enjoyed not only the interesting content of their papers, but the political implications of the whole action.

Fundraising was also important for the direct support of men who did not receive any money from home. While subscriptions were paid from a prisoner's account and were therefore, in the case of someone receiving 15 marks, more of a burden for his relatives who sent the money, support money had to be paid from the supporter's pocket, and it was thus more keenly felt. It actually decreased his own weekly spending money.

In nonpolitical barracks, funds for this purpose were raised at irregular intervals, with appeals not to forget the "poor" and the "have-nots" who were fellow sufferers. Attempts to transform this into more regular payments always bogged down or often turned into rackets.

Human charity does not seem to provide a lasting basis for solidarity as long as the group does not exert any pressure upon those who don't exhibit charity. And charity is doomed to be too weak an appeal, especially when what is asked is not part of the rich man's money to be given to the poor, but a man's next-to-the-last penny to be given to those who have no penny at all—particularly when asked of people who have never before had to make decisions about their next-to-the-last penny. But it was these very people, those who received ten or fifteen marks, toward whom the appeal was directed, most of whom had previously been fairly well-to-do or even wealthy.

In political barracks fundraising was done using absolutely political concepts. The appeal was directed not to the men's sympathy for the "poor," but to their solidarity with their "comrades" who happened to have no money. To make a contribution was not considered an act of individual human kindness but a political duty. The payment was not so much a gift from man to man as a tax on the members of the group. Whoever regularly drew money above a certain amount paid dues to the fund, usually two marks out of fifteen, or one mark out of ten. Informally elected or appointed administrators of the fund distributed the allotments. Rackets were practically unknown.

From time to time the administration forbade fundraising. In these cases, nothing more was done in nonpolitical barracks. In political barracks, a system of direct payments to the ultimate recipient usually replaced payment to the fund. This method was less popular of course, and at times embarrassing, but in the end the solidarity of the group overcame the embarrassment.

Nonpoliticals and conservatives in the political barracks, who didn't see why, merely because they were in a concentration camp, they should have had to exhibit solidarity with Socialists and Communists, were put under social pressure. After all they enjoyed the advantages of living in a political barrack which took care of them in need without asking them about their past. Nazis, of course, were not forced to make contributions.

Where people had the necessary ideological basis for solidarity, it was reinforced by the fact that they lived together in the same room for months and often years. There was not much transfer between barracks. However, utilizing all their relations and power positions, the politicals always contrived to concentrate their brothers-in-creed into certain barracks and to remove from their midst those who didn't belong. Thus they got more homogeneous groups than were found in any other barracks. When we came to Buchenwald, we were assigned to our barracks alphabetically—names beginning with A and B in the first barrack, C and D in the second, and so forth. There was no chance to keep people together by their political creed. But lo and behold: After one week practically all the German and a great many of the Austrian political Jews were together in one barrack.

On the working grounds, similar observations could be made about the various categories of prisoners as in the barracks. In part this was perhaps less obvious, because working groups were less stable units than the barracks, but in part even more so, because in some cases the prisoners had a bigger influence upon the composition of the working groups than of the barracks.

In Dachau, a change from one working group to another was difficult to arrange, because officially every single case required the permission of the officer in charge of construction. Although most transfers were arranged without this permission, the threat of punishment was great, and therefore ordinarily, at least the permission of the capos involved was necessary. Most of the working groups were small enough that the capo would know a new face, or notice if someone was missing. (This changed when the masses of Austrians came to the camp, and working groups increased considerably in size.)

In Buchenwald it was much easier to change jobs. Officially, permission was required from the bureau of construction, which actually meant that one of the capos involved spoke to one of the prisoners in the bureau of construction and had the transfer registered. However, this procedure became much too complicated as time went on and as the number of prisoners increased. It was actually kept up only for a few special working groups, especially those who worked outside the chain of sentinels. For the rest, only the permission of the capos was necessary—and most of the working groups (particularly those between which men would want to switch) were so large that the capos never got to know all of their men. The switches were effected either with the agreement of one of the numerous sub-capos, which frequently involved a little bribe, or by simply taking a chance on joining a group without asking anybody. Although a man could get "twenty-five" for such a switch, there were too many reasons for changing groups and too many occasions to do it for the threat to be effective. Hundreds of transfers occurred every week. Some of the capos tried to prevent it by keeping their own lists and calling their own roll every morning. This kept the number of changes down, of course, but did not make them impossible. If a group had five hundred workers, there were so many who had a legal reason to be absent on any particular day that it was difficult to ferret out those who had invented their reasons. (Legal or trumped-up reasons for not being with one's outfit might include, "ordered to appear before the commander," "ordered to the infirmary for treatment of an injury," "ordered to stay inside the camp by the mail office," or one of the most difficult to disprove, "grabbed by another capo," or "ordered by an officer to join another group.") The capo would have had to spend all his spare time keeping track of his crowd.

In addition to the individual's initiative to switch from one group to the other, there were organized channels to arrange transfers—political relations, relations to the professional criminals, and so forth. Group relations were used primarily to secure the bulk of the soft jobs in every working ground or to bring together in one working ground men of the same category. In Dachau, almost all organized transfers went through political channels. In Buchenwald, the two big rival groups used their networks to get their own people out of some places and into others. The politicals used this power primarily to establish working groups made up mostly of political prisoners. The professional criminals used it chiefly to transfer individuals, usually for good cash, with little regard for the composition of the crew, but rather only on the basis of the difficulty of the working conditions.

The more skilled the work, the greater was the influence of the crew upon the selection of additional members. For completely unskilled digging or carrying work, men were detailed without any regard to their ability. For the more qualified jobs, ability was a factor, and the officer and capo usually didn't know any man's ability. New groups were established haphazardly, but soon a process of selection would set in. The capo would chase out people who were unfit for the work, as he could get punished if a concrete or brick wall broke down: "Don't you dare to show up again tomorrow." But usually he had his group help him find new men. If the capo was good and the work not too bad or dangerous, the men would bring in their friends who were in less desirable spots. If the permission of an officer was needed, the capo would usually get it, so that he could show up with a "good" man, instead of "that idiot I got yesterday who did not know how to lay a brick."

Really specialized working groups developed almost complete autonomy in selecting their new crew members, thereby establishing certain traditions about whom to select and how.

For unskilled labor projects, which offered few desirable spots, organized group influence played a lesser role in transfer—except for the rare case when a decent capo happened to be in charge. For example, when the heat shaft was built in Dachau, a Social Democrat who usually directed highly skilled mason work was in charge. Aside from his masons, he also supervised about 150 unskilled workers who dug the bed for the shaft. He appointed politicals as sub-capos. Soon word went around that political people might enter his group without difficulty, if they could only manage to get away from their previous jobs.

Originally this group, being detailed for unskilled labor, had been chosen at random from the gravel pits, and consisted primarily of non-political Jews. But after a few weeks the majority of the workers were politicals, with a proportion of non-Jews that was unusually high in an unskilled labor group.

In Buchenwald the problem of where to place the Jewish political prisoners from Dachau arose. Since they were barred from indoor and skilled work, the politicals selected a place with many mason jobs. The place was in the hands of "greens" then. The politicals first connived against the capo in charge, and eventually had him replaced by a "red." Then they took over the positions of sub-capos, and finally, after a few weeks, the place became a domain of the politicals. Then they brought in political non-Jews as masons, and political Jews as helpers, as the Jews were not allowed to be masons.

When men had been together in a working group for some time, the same structuring process set in that could be observed in the barracks; little groups were formed of friends who tried to stick together on the same spot. Where the working and guarding conditions permitted, a small leading clique would form, which assumed power by influencing the capo in the distribution of jobs. Then all of the men together, whether they liked or fought each other, would begin to consider themselves as "belonging" to the group. They went through common experiences about which they talked later on in the camp. They might be participants in some incident that would become known throughout the camp—and then they would be identified, not as individuals, but as part of the group involved: "*Kommando Häuschen* (working group under capo Häuschen) got caught yesterday, and Becker (the officer in charge of construction) had them do punitive drill." Or, "The stone knockers caught it this morning. Some racket was discovered." Or, "The filter beds (working group making filter beds) had a tough afternoon. The guards got mad at them. Three men were brought in on stretchers with bayonet wounds."

The individual man then identified himself with the group: "I belong to *Kommando Häuschen.* Oh boy, did Becker get at us," or "I am in the filter beds—you have heard that story, I guess."

The higher the skill level of the work, the stronger this "we"-feeling usually became. It was increased by pride in the skill, by the privileged position that went with it, and usually by the fact that skilled workers, as we have seen, were more likely to be of the same category of prisoners, in most cases politicals, so that they also had a common ideology.

Working groups made up from different categories exhibited the same differences that have already been noted in the barracks: A political working group could be distinguished from a nonpolitical one at a great distance, by the smoothness of their routine, the small amount of violence, the close cooperation between the workers. They tried much more than nonpolitical workers to help each other and to shield one another from danger. And of course, because of the well-developed cooperation, their warning system usually functioned better, so that they got caught less often than others.

When two situations were at all comparable, for example, when two unskilled groups were both digging under similar conditions, the difference was still big. But such comparisons could not be made as a rule, because the kind of men selected, the capos, and the type of work done, were all largely determined by the fact that one group was political and the other nonpolitical. Thus, whatever differences there were became even more emphasized on the working grounds if the groups were fairly homogeneous.

I found an example of well-developed "we"-feeling in a nonpolitical, unskilled labor group in Dachau when I worked in a gravel pit called "Kiesgrube Sturmbann."[3] It was distinguished from other gravel pits by nothing except the fact that it took forty-five minutes to get there. Every night at roll call, the camp had to wait because "Kiesgrube Sturmbann" was late. When work had begun there, gravel was needed urgently, and the men were driven and beaten frantically all day long. At night they would tell us proudly, "Perhaps you think you have been through something? You ought to see us work at Kiesgrube Sturmbann. That's the real thing."

At the time I worked there, the terror had already subsided to "normal" levels. The group of about 150 men had been together for six weeks and expected to be together for another two months perhaps. They felt that they were unique—because they had a special name and had been together for some time, because the camp had to wait for them, and because they had suffered more than others. (The latter was not even true; at that time there was hell to pay in many places. But that did not disturb their saga.)

This was characteristic. Men want to be members of a community from which they can derive importance. People who were nobody and nothing among their fellow prisoners, neither highly estimated nor looked down upon, just "in-between," tried to impress upon others their importance by introducing themselves with, "I work at Kiesgrube Sturmbann, you know."

But it was equally characteristic that they did not stay together during leisure time. And those who, for some reason, were taken out of this group forgot completely their relations with it, except for personal friends

---

3. *Kiesgrube* is German for gravel pit. *Sturmbann* is a battalion of SS.

they may have made there. To be beaten together and to have a few superficial things in common was not a strong enough basis for lasting fellowship.

The masons and their helpers in Buchenwald, on the other hand, stuck together during spare time, and tried to keep relations to the group alive even after they had been separated from it. They helped each other at work, which was by no means the case in the gravel pit (where there was not much chance for mutual help anyway), and they considered themselves, together with their capos, a big political family. "I work with the masons at Truppengarage"[4] was a sort of political identification, and served as notice that the man belonged to a group of high standing in the camp. These masons had fewer superficial things in common than the men of Kiesgrube Sturmbann, but they had their common ideology.

The administration was ordinarily opposed to the formation of stable groups, which, of course, counteracted the very purpose of the camp—to break the prisoners' ties to their former resistance movements. But the officers in charge of construction, responsible for the work, usually had different ideas. They knew that stable groups would work better, in part because they attracted and kept good workers, in part because of the absence of superfluous violence. Thus, particularly in Dachau, where the administration was much more concerned about not letting strong groups develop, there was a steady see-saw battle in which the more political part of the administration, headed by the commander, would break these groups up from time to time, while the construction officer would afterward permit them to get together again.

However, at one time a remarkable attempt was made in Dachau to raise output in the unskilled labor groups, especially in the gravel pits, by utilizing the "we"-feeling that a steady group develops.

When the masses of Austrians arrived, the turnover of prisoners in the working groups increased rapidly. Through an unskilled labor group of 200 men, 400 or 500 might pass within a week or two. The new men, untrained, produced too little gravel. The administration lost control over the transfers between jobs; people switched almost as they pleased. The only way out was to offer some inducement to stay at a job. A new category of workers was created—"steady workers" (*Stammarbeiter*). Each capo was to have a certain percentage of these "steady workers,"

---

4. *Truppengarage* means 'military garage' and was used both as the name for the whole working ground where the garages were built, and as the name for several of the working groups stationed there.

who would belong to the group and could not be removed by other capos nor by officers, except the one in charge of construction. It was understood, although of course not announced, that these "steady workers" would be treated better by the capo, perhaps also protected against the arbitrariness of the guards, and would get the better working places and so forth.

The capos began to recruit "steady workers" by individual invitation and persuasion. Those who accepted were listed in a little booklet, and their roll was called every morning. Even Sterzer, the killer from the punitive gravel pit, who at that time happened to be in charge of another job, went about offering good treatment.

The whole scheme soon petered out: The good capos did not need to recruit their men, and the bad capos could not get any volunteers. Protection against the guards was, of course, so much wishful thinking. The only advantage was that, while the thing was new, the bad capos beat their "steady workers" less—but it was not new for very long.

Man's urgent desire to belong to a stabilized group, where he has his fixed place and is recognized, was demonstrated very strongly when, at the same time as the "steady workers" were introduced, the "slave market" was created.

Because manpower had increased beyond the number of jobs available, a sort of reserve pool was established for all groups which might be in need of men. A few hundred men were thrown together, from which each capo could requisition whatever number he needed to fill up his quota or to replace men who had to be left in the camp for a day, for one reason or another.

The capo would ask the officer for so many men, and the officer would hand them over. If the officer grabbed a man who was bandaged up or had white hair, the capo might protest, "Herr Barrack Leader, how can this damned wretch mix concrete? The wall will fall in." And the officer might push the man back and get another one.

Slowly the manpower in the pool deteriorated. The able prisoners found themselves steady places, and only the older ones and the invalids were left. Capos, before accepting a man, would look him over, perhaps feel his muscles, and look at his injuries. The men themselves tried to enter the bargain; if the capo was known as a sadist, they would try to show their injuries. If he was a decent fellow, they tried to hide them. The whole thing was soon nicknamed "the slave market."

The slave market had two advantages. A man who wanted to jump his group simply joined the slave market. Among the hundreds of faces, he was almost sure not to be discovered by his former capo. All he had to do was wait until he landed with a better capo.

The other advantage was that those not selected on a given day worked inside the fence at easier work, because by that time there was no more excessively hard work left inside.

But in spite of these advantages, the slave market developed, for those who did not use it as a clearing house, into a horrible institution. Exposed to the hazards of two market hours daily (at morning and at noon roll call), they lived in even greater uncertainty than the rest of the camp. In addition, when selected for the dreaded *Aussenkommandos* (outside working groups), they were doomed to the worst working places, because they did not even enjoy the small advantages which came from slaving steadily in the same place. The men began to hate their position and preferred steady work, almost irrespective of how bad it was. Then they could have at least a certain place where they belonged, and be respected or at least be scorned by others—even contempt from others is better than no relation at all.

This slave market, although its origin was purely incidental to the surplus of manpower, perhaps came closest to the administration's aim for the camp as a whole: To throw a man into a completely atomized heap of numbers, from which he was selected for his slave work perfectly at random. And it demonstrated fairly well how this hell could have been made even more unbearable, if they had succeeded.

Chapter 14

The Moor Express

The man-drawn wagons, one of the most conspicuous features of Dachau, present one of the best examples of prisoners in complete cooperation. Peculiar working conditions and almost complete self-selection of the crews caused "the wagons" to be one of the most stable working groups in the camp, with traditions and relations and privileges all their own.

The wagons were known as the "moor express," a name introduced by prisoners who had been in the peat bog or moor camps in northwestern Germany, where the song of the "Peat Bog Solders" (*Moor Soldaten*) originated.

A moor express looked like a light truck trailer, and ran on discarded automobile tires. What these wagons were used for on the outside, I do not know. In the camp the wagon had a crew of seventeen: two pulled at the shaft, three pushed in the back, and twelve pulled on ropes fastened to the sides of the car. There were two men on each rope, who threw their chests against a wooden bar, similar to the way horses throw their weight against the harness. Two men on one bar represented a particular refinement: If one were to be lazy, and push too little, the whole weight would immediately fall upon the other, who would of course resent it. Also the bar would slant, which would be conspicuous even to a casual observer.

Compared to wheelbarrows or men's bare hands and shoulders, the moor express was a relatively effective vehicle for transporting big loads over great distances. Aside from ordinary loads such as gravel, sand, brick, rubbish, cement, or lime, the car was used for loads that could not be transported in any other way except by truck, which was out of question in the camp—large trees, tree roots, logs, timber, straw in bundles, heavy machinery such as boilers, potatoes in bags, herring in barrels, coal, great quantities of clothing, blankets, straw bags, furniture, empty tin cans from the kitchen, and other miscellaneous material.

When Dachau was still under construction, work on the moor expresses was terrifically hard. The main loads were trees and logs and heavy material for the construction of buildings and roads. When a wagon bogged down in the morass and mud of the unfinished roads, the guards considered it both their privilege and their duty to make it move again. With rifle butt and bayonet they attacked the crew, and when the car finally was pulled out of the hole, they considered that proof of the effectiveness of mistreatment and repeated it on the next occasion. The most horrible crimes were committed on those who manned the wagons; the death rate was staggering. People who survived this period and were still on the wagons during our time talked about it as the heroic age of the wagons.

Only Jews were used for this hard job.

By our time however, most of the roads were finished with hard surfaces, and the wagons seldom bogged down. Most of the heavy construction work was finished, tree roots and logs were seldom transported, and most gravel and sand was carted by wheelbarrow. Work at the wagons had developed into a desirable job with many advantages.

Frequently the car was loaded only one way and was empty on the return trip. Many materials, such as sand and gravel, could not be loaded or unloaded by all seventeen men simultaneously; they would be in each other's way. Usually they worked in revolving shifts of four or six, while the rest stood by.

The wagons moved over long distances, often coming into very different parts of the camp during the day. The world of the men on these wagons was considerably larger than that of the average prisoner. So the day was less dreary for them, and the time went faster. The man who was digging gravel could only count the number of shovelfuls he threw up, or observe the shadows—or observe the wagons. But the wagon crews were usually well informed about the time. On their way through the "door" they could see the clock, and even if they worked all day outside the fence, they knew that six or ten trips made a half-day.

But the main advantage of work on the moor express lay in the way the crew was selected and in their peculiar relations with capo and guards.

Loading ordinary material such as gravel into a high car is much more difficult than simply throwing it up out of a ditch. So is the loading of more unusual materials. If timber is loaded three yards high without the proper skill, the wagon will turn over. If tiles, slabs of slate, or other breakable goods are loaded by inexperienced hands, great losses will result. And if the men don't work together like a well-running machine when lifting up to shoulder height a heavy boiler or heavy beams or large roots, then the load will drop and bury some of them, breaking their arms and legs. The guards will get angry. In addition, because of the tradition that wagon work is harder work, the crew has to accelerate to breakneck speed as soon as a commander appears. It needs calm, imperturbable men with great physical ability to speed up while handling these kinds of materials, or even to load sand so that it falls exactly in the corner of the wagon where it belongs.

Before the arrival of the Austrians there were about 350 Jews in Dachau. The old-timers among them had been brought there in 1936 from the peat bog camps in Esterwegen and from Lichtenburg in Saxony. Of these about fifty were in the punitive company, the infirmary, or the dungeon. Thus to man five moor expresses with a crew of seventeen each, eighty-five able-bodied and well-trained men had to be selected from among 300, many of whom were old or invalid or otherwise incapacitated. The total number of men available to work on the wagons was perhaps 120. And the total number of men who had worked throughout the two years, between 1936 and 1938, was perhaps 160, counting those who had died or had been transferred to the punitive company. That meant that each of the 160 men had spent on average at least six months at the wagons. To give a more realistic estimate: In April 1938 there was a supply of about fifty to sixty men who had spent most of the past two years together on the wagons and about sixty to seventy who had each been at the wagons for a few months, up to about half a year. For most of them, this represented at least half of the time they had spent in Dachau. That constituted an amazing degree of stability in this society of instability—equaled only in part by the non-Jewish political prisoners who worked in the furniture shops.

No officer or capo ever took an individual man out of a moor express crew, because he would immediately have had to replace him—the wagon could not leave the camp without a complete crew of seventeen. Thus the man on the moor express, more than any other man in the camp, could make a fairly safe bet on what, with whom, and under which capo he was going to work the next day. This relative security distinguished the crew member of a moor express from the common gravel digger, who never knew whether he would be with the same capo, or whether he would dig or push a wheelbarrow, or whether he would see familiar faces and a familiar working ground to which he had already adjusted himself, or whether he would have to begin all over again.

Since the number of men able to meet the high requirements was so very small, the selection rested almost completely with the crew. They were the only ones who knew which good man was available. If the capo wanted to do it himself, he could only go and hunt for former crew members whom he knew. And if the officer in charge tried to pick a man at random, the capo would almost always have to fire him after a day or two as unable to do the job.

The crew, a very stable unit, was usually led by a small clique that developed around the two men on the shaft, of which one was the true leader of the wagon and the other his deputy. They were almost invariably the best men on the wagon, since handling the shaft was at times a very difficult job. They were not officially appointed or recognized. But the capo, no matter what his relation to the crew, would always try to be on good terms with the men on the shaft, because wagon work was teamwork. While yelling and beating might have speeded up an individual man, it did not help to make him cooperative in an intelligent way; only the leader of the team could achieve that.

A well-established leader on a wagon assumed a position similar to that of the capo. He gave orders to the men, in front of the guards; he ordered rest periods, arranged revolving shifts during loading and unloading, and he had the decisive word in the selection of new men. Both capo and guards practically never touched the men on the shaft, even if they felt like teasing or beating the rest. Although outwardly in no way distinguished from the other Jews who slaved around the camp, these men were the uncrowned kings of the wagons.

The moor express was the only detail in which the crew was more stable than the capo. Other work places were identified among the prisoners primarily by the name of the capo. "I work under Zock" was a more adequate description of a man's situation than "I work on the barrack yard," or even " I carry gravel in a wheelbarrow over a distance of seventy yards." But the man who worked on a wagon would say, "I work on moor express number 3," and then for more detail, he might add the name of the capo at the time.

The leaders on the moor expresses were, with almost no exceptions, leading political prisoners. And so were the cliques around them. Consequently in selecting new men, they applied the standards of the politicals and preferred to take those of their own creed, or at least men who were good comrades, reliable, cooperative, willing to take orders from the man on the shaft, and friendly with others. If a new man disappointed them, they got rid of him again.

Such selection often took place only after careful scrutiny of the available men. For example, when the first Austrians arrived in April 1938, the leaders of the cars went systematically through the ranks of the newcomers, watched them, spoke to them, finally selected a few of them. They tried them out on two successive Sundays (when the cars worked primarily inside the fence) and after that adopted them as steady crew members.

At roll call, when the guards were detached for the working groups, each moor express got two guards. Whenever a car worked outside the fence, the guards were with it. But when a car entered the camp, the guards stayed in the waiting room, until it left again. When a car worked in more distant parts, perhaps carrying a load of cement from the storehouse to the camp, then the two guards were often for hours the only supervision except for the capo.

All this formed the basis for peculiar relations between prisoners and guards very different from those on the regular working grounds, where there was always a chain of sentinels who could observe one another.

Much depended on the personalities and the momentary moods of the two guards. If they were devils, they would drive the crew, make them run at top speed with the fully loaded car, forbid them to speak while pulling, have them stand at rigid attention or perhaps face the wall while four of them loaded gravel, or make them do some sort of exercise. If they were good-natured, they would let the crew stand at ease or let them converse in low voices. Conversations might develop between capo and guard, which almost took the form of a talk between man and man. They might have reasonable conversations with the crew members, ask about former professions, home cities, relations, and experiences.

There was evidently some old rule that the guards had to keep at a certain distance from the wagon and the crew. Capos with good nerves occasionally relied upon this rule when the guards teased or mistreated the crew. I remember the amazing sight of a capo—quite a devil himself, incidentally—who got angry with a young guard of about 18 years, and with his hoary voice shouted at him, "Over there is your place, Herr Wachtmeister. You know yourself that you have to keep ten yards away from the car. If you want to report the prisoners for bad work, you may do so, but while they are at work, I am responsible for the car and its crew. You can complain about me if you want, and we will meet at the commander's office. But you know that it is your duty to leave the crew alone." The young boy grew frightened and let us alone. Lutz, the capo, was known as a dangerous fellow, esteemed by the commander because, when he happened to turn against the prisoners, he drove them at a speed which the guards would never have thought possible

Even a prisoner could occasionally get in a firm word. Once a guard teased our crew, made us do all sorts of exercises—bend knees, fall flat on our bellies, and so forth. When one man asked for permission to step out to comply with nature's need, the guard had him run around the car a few times instead. When he finally wanted him to crawl under the car on his belly, the prisoner, who had been a flier in the German army in the First World War, and had been wounded and decorated, snapped to attention: "Herr Wachtmeister, when I was as old as you are now, I already had the Iron Cross, First Class!" And the guard left the man alone.

When the guards left the prisoners alone, the latter repaid kindness with kindness and warned them when an officer was approaching. This enabled the guards to stand together and chat while the prisoners were at work, instead of standing alone at a distance, and it allowed them to smoke a cigarette. If an officer found them smoking, they might wind up in the guard house. The guards in turn let odd pass for even on such occasions and let the prisoners shirk and loaf as much as possible with due regard for the possibility of a superior suddenly appearing. There were certain places, in our time for instance, the cement storehouse, where the prisoners were almost sure in advance that the guards would want to smoke, because the place was almost safe against surprises. So a trip to the cement house usually meant one long trip with an empty car, half an hour's shirking, slow loading work, and peace with the guards.

So desirable did the trip to the cement house become that the crews of the various wagons used to try to snatch it from one another.

Sometimes the guard, in his grace and mercy, left the stub of his cigarette for the capo. But not many capos would take it. No political man would touch it, much as he would like a puff; the capo who took it was despised by his crew.

When it was raining hard, the guards might tell the capo when a load arrived at camp, "Don't show up for an hour or so!" The capo would carry his gravel about the camp, unload as slowly as possible, perhaps drag around on fake business. When finally he had to leave the camp for a new load, the guards might be grateful for the hour they spent in the waiting room, and permit the prisoners to take cover under a roof.

This situation, with prisoners and guards both breaking their respective rules and orders, was somewhat grotesque. The political prisoners, while enjoying the letup in the work tempo, despised the guards for not doing their duty. The nonpoliticals, less concerned about dignity and duty, simply enjoyed the human traits of the guards that enabled them to take it easy for a couple of hours. (These human traits did not hinder the same guards next morning from beating and harrying other prisoners who could not offer such favors as guarding his smoking pleasure.)

The prisoners very often knew their working grounds better than the guards. They used all kinds of ruses to prolong the trips with the empty cars and shorten the trips with the loads. Sometimes the guards even helped in the game, because they preferred to talk in the sunshine behind an empty car, instead of watching the wretches loading gravel. The prisoners often knew which SS man could be placated by a nice song. They sang less stupid ones than other groups did on their way to work; they even practiced new ones from time to time, because it proved a good policy to surprise the guards occasionally with a new tune.

But of course bad guards could make hell of everything. It was bad enough when the car was loaded three yards high with timber or with several tons of gravel, and the guard kept shouting, "Faster, faster, lazy swine, lazy!" It became worse, when he ordered, "Run, run, will you!" But the worst was when on top of all the rest would come the familiar call, "a song!" Yapping for breath, the men would begin to tear out of their throats something that might pass for a song, and run as fast as they could, not so much to obey the guard as to get rid of him by reaching the camp soon.

They had only one slight chance for revenge. When the car left the camp empty, the capo might pretend to be furious at the lazy swine, and drive them at breakneck speed over the hard-surfaced roads. The car would run practically by itself, the capo would keep cursing and yelling, the prisoners, realizing what was happening, would run like mad, and the guards, with their heavy uniforms and weapons, would be sweating and lagging behind, usually not daring to order the thing to stop, afraid that it might look as if the prisoners had gotten them out of breath.

The prisoners enjoyed it with a sour smile, knowing that they themselves or their brothers would have to pay for the little joke. But the smallest chance to do something against the guards was worth a dear price in a situation where the men could practically never take any action of their own choosing.

One other mutual bargaining situation between prisoners and guards might be mentioned. The capo (or the man on the shaft) had to calculate the loads so that they would be back in time for evening roll call, which took place right after work, at six o'clock. If he calculated carefully, he could almost always spend the last twenty minutes or half-hour inside the fence by claiming that an additional round trip might take, say, an hour. In this case the guards were also free half an hour earlier.

This system worked out so well that finally Commander Koegel tried to break it up. He threatened every man, including the capos, with "twenty-five" if any wagon came home earlier than ten minutes before six. But the guards enjoyed these ten minutes too, and since time could not always be calculated so exactly, the guards, when in the game, let the men shirk through the last one or two trips, so they would not have to make a third one and be late.

Guards who did not play this game or who mistreated the prisoners, very often had to pay for it. The prisoners, sacrificing their own time, made the guards do overtime, until ten or twenty minutes after six. When a capo told a guard, "That is right, Herr Wachtmeister, just hurry them up a little. I was thinking myself of making these lazy swine work until … errr … six twenty"—this was understood as a threat, and the guards had no alternative but to be late or leave the men alone.

If the wagon came back to camp early, the men did not have the time off, but as they were under no special supervision, they would go about on fake business. They would take the car "for a little walk," so that "it could see for itself what the camp was like." If questioned by an officer, the capo would always have a good excuse, and if need be, he would load any material that happened to be around.

But at ten minutes before six, the crew would put the wagon in its place, and right under the nose of the guards on the watch tower, they would begin to wash the old car (and hastily their own shoes) with water from the nearest puddle, and perhaps clean the tools. A few minutes before official quitting time, the capo would march his crew to their barracks, and if nobody was around, he would release them. In the greatest haste they would get washed and cleaned up and appear already clean at roll call. Thus they didn't have to fight for a place in the washroom with the others. These were great privileges in a concentration camp. Of course things could go wrong and a whole crew might receive "twenty-five" if caught on such an occasion. Once, just as we were washing in a hurry, Commander Schneider appeared, and the only thing that saved us was a warning whistle, so that, half naked or naked as we were, we jumped out of the washroom window in the nick of time.

It should not be assumed from the description above, that life on the wagons was all idle shirking and paradise. It was not. Many guards were not in the least susceptible to all these ruses and bargains. They just drove their charges like the guards in other working places, and wrote reports for punishment. But it was true in general that there was considerably less beating and the work was easier on the wagons than at any other place except the workshops. And even a written report against a prisoner could sometimes be withdrawn before the return to camp, if the capo was able to placate the guard again.

The exceptional position of the men on the wagons, together with the way they selected themselves, created a group spirit, hardly surpassed anywhere else in the camp. Cooperation on a moor express was something near perfection. Unspoken laws regulated the work and the private relations of the men. The only spoken word was "comradeship," the only blame leveled against a man was "uncomrade-like behavior." Feuds, which sometimes occurred as they do among any group of men, were not fought out on the wagon. Long tradition and common experience made it possible to give orders with a minimum of words, even with fake words. The capo might yell at a man, or the man on the shaft might drop a word or two, which, incomprehensible to the guards, might contain a warning, a hint to hurry up or to slow down. One of the few funny incidents in camp life was the case of a guard who had picked up a word that he had often heard a capo shouting at his crew. Of course, it did not make much difference what he yelled, as long as he yelled. But the word he had picked up was a Jewish idiom, and what he yelled meant, "Lazy swine, lazy, will you slow down!"

On days when all the merry shirking games were out and the general hunt was on, when the guards drove and harried the men, it proved almost impossible to exhaust the crew of a moor express. The prisoners would look at the man at the shaft, and as long as he gave orders calmly, they wouldn't let guards or capo bring confusion into their ranks. They would grit their teeth and outlast whatever was asked of them. And on return to their barracks they would say, "Now we have shown them once more! These fools can't exhaust a moor express!"

What perhaps distinguished the moor expresses most from the camp was the degree to which the men could influence their own fate. With their smooth cooperation, the reliability of the carefully selected crews, and the particularly favorable circumstances under which they worked, they were able occasionally to outsmart the guards, and if need be even the capo. They could unite, on occasion, in a sort of passive resistance by being busy and yet not accomplishing anything. They could ostracize their own capo, who had nobody but them and the two guards to talk to. (In other places there might be several capos, or groups large enough so that the capo could beat most of the men and yet find somebody to converse with.) Every now and then, they could perform a stunt together, which the whole camp would speak of with respect.

One Saturday afternoon for example, a moor express crew of which I was a member was sent to do punitive work under Sterzer in the gravel pit. The occasion arose because when we were called to some special work during the noon rest, we had not been quick enough about dropping our food and gathering at the "door." Moor expresses ordinarily didn't run into this type of punishment, and it was anybody's guess how the vaunted moor-expressers would behave under Sterzer's chain.

We came to the gravel pit in full marching order, singing a fresh song, our man at the shaft posing as capo (the capo was not involved). At the pit he ordered, *"Kommando halt!"* and called to Sterzer, "Hello, old man, here we are, helpers of yours for an afternoon. What 'ya want us to do? Want us to empty your ole gravel pit? Oh gee, what an idea! All that in one afternoon?"

Sterzer stood befuddled. He was used to wretches who were frightened at the mere sight of him, and here came a glee club! (Of course we felt slightly on edge too, but we had decided on the stunt and now stuck it out.) Our leader did not wait for Sterzer to gather his wits. He gave orders: "Pick up wheelbarrows, shovels, on the double, will you!" In military order we picked up the tools. "And now fill 'em up, fast as hell, I tell you!" We filled them up "fast as hell," put an additional heap of gravel on top of each wheelbarrow, stuck the shovel into it like a sailing mast, and in military order marched off with gravel and all.

And we were gone for the afternoon. First we idled around the big mountain of gravel, with half-filled wheelbarrows, and when we were bored with that, we took to our barracks, leaving a few men behind (and relieving them every hour) just in case. When the afternoon was over, the punitive workers were released. We marched again in full formation to the pit, and the leader reported, "Order executed." Then off we went again. Sterzer did not go after us during the whole afternoon. He preferred to deal with his more familiar type of victims.

Of course he might have gone after us. The whole stunt might have ended on the stand or the "tree" or in the bunker. But since we were successful, we received all the credit due, were respected by all who heard the story, and felt a special pride in it.

From time to time, the moor expresses were sent to the heating plant to carry away the ashes. This meant a long trip, with an empty car in one direction and a very light load in the other. Usually all five cars went together, which was in itself a rare sight. Then a sort of competition would develop, in which crews would try to out-sing and outrun each other. Cheerful shouts would go from car to car. The SS men would get infected by the hilarious atmosphere and spur their respective crews to greater speed, not with bad intent this time, but because they were caught by the racing fever. The crews would feel that they were on parade, and proudly show off before the other crews and before any working groups that passed on their way.

This strange parade did not occur often, and when it was over, the men would go back to camp with a bitter taste in their mouths. They would feel that they had made fools of themselves, having shown joy in the presence of SS men and having behaved like schoolboys, instead of wretched prisoners in the hands of their enemies. But apparently this outbreak of spirits met a desperately felt need or it would not have occurred every time this curious parade took place.

The administration, of course, did not like the development of well-organized groups. From time to time they broke up a wagon crew, usually by charging corruption of the capo by the men. They actually could not find much of it. Relations were too intimate for rackets to arise. Whatever "corruption" there was took the form of occasional gifts to the capo from the crew, for no particular purpose but general good relations. Most of the capos were politicals and didn't take bribes, but of course they wouldn't decline a share of food that the crew might have. I remember one case where a capo and five men from a moor express were sent to the punitive company for "corruption," because one of the men had admitted to giving a postage stamp, worth three pennies, to the capo when he was out of stamps on mail day. The rest of the crew were dispersed to various working grounds. A new crew was formed. But after a few days most of the original men were back at their old places.

Another, more conspicuous case occurred once when our complete crew of seventeen men was sent to Sterzer, this time not for the afternoon, but for good. It was because Commander Koegel wanted to break up the moor express crowd. That happened at noon. Next morning some of the crew were missing from Sterzer's company. We were back at the wagon. Next afternoon a few more were missing. They too were back at the wagon. Within forty-eight hours not a single one of us was left with Sterzer, and most of us were back at the wagon.

In the early summer of 1938, when several thousand Austrians had already arrived, the administration thought the time ripe for a decisive blow against the wagons. One day all working groups in the camp were completely reorganized. In the case of the moor expresses, an officer went from crew to crew and took with him every man who had been in the camp for more than three months, which meant about seventy of the eighty-five men.[1] They were dispersed all over the place, to work at road construction and digging gravel. Completely new crews, most of them nonpolitical Austrians, were picked by the officers, at random.

The fifteen men left over from the old crews, now the most experienced men on the wagons, took over the shafts. As a result, something of the political tradition was kept alive, since these men had been selected by the former crews because they were political prisoners.

Now the wagons were no longer the elite. They had almost as many old and weak men as any other working group. In consideration of their lack of experience and of the fact that there was not much work left in the camp to keep the men busy, the size of the crews was increased to twenty-one per wagon, and two new wagons were added, so that there were now 147 men on seven wagons. The capos sighed and pleaded with the construction officer for their old men. The new wretches broke the slabs and tore the cement bags and did this and did that and were not good at all. It was actually not quite so bad, especially after the weakest had been replaced by more able men, but the capos wanted their old crews back. And the construction officer, who also wanted them back, closed his eyes when a capo threw out a few of his new acquisitions and put back a few of the old guard. After several weeks at least sixty of the seventy men were back. They were no longer such a conspicuous elite, since now they comprised less than half of the total of 147. But they managed to get together on certain wagons, and soon there were "German" wagons, with predominantly political crews, and "Austrian" ones with more nonpolitical men.

---

1. By this time, due to the great supply of men, there had already been a certain influx of new members to the wagons, which primarily replaced nonpolitical Germans with political Austrians. But the officers too were then less careful about leaving the crew together, since the men could be replaced more easily.

When the Jews were transported to Buchenwald, the tradition of the wagon crews among them came to an end. In Buchenwald, with its steep and muddy hills, wagons were practically useless. Only two wagons were used, with small wheels that sank deep into the soft mud and clay. One of the wagons was operated steadily by the punitive company, almost exclusively for the transport of logs. The second was used only occasionally, and then a temporary crew was gathered for the purpose.

Chapter 15

Justice

The society of the prisoners developed its own concepts of right and wrong, its own concepts of justice. Ordinarily these concepts found their expression only in terms of approval and disapproval, social pressure and ostracism, but at times the society acted and punished, occasionally with terrible severity, and then the concepts were immediately revealed through the attitude of the other prisoners toward the incident.

There was an extreme case of a stool pigeon who had betrayed prisoners to the administration for bribery and various other activities, both in Dachau and in Buchenwald. Finally, in Buchenwald the prisoners caught up with him. Camp senior Richter and the man's own barrack senior, both of them professional criminals, killed him by slowly beating him to death. They took three days to do it, during which the man tried to kill himself to escape the torture. He tried to run into the barbed wire, but the SS did not shoot. He tried to drown himself in a latrine, but they dragged him away. When it finally was over, most prisoners spoke with horror of the way it had been done. They protested that those who had killed him had no moral right to do so because they themselves were gangsters—Richter had killed and severely injured others for no good reason. Yet the great majority of the prisoners apparently thought it was right that the man had been killed. The information he gave to the camp commander in Dachau had led to suicides and to the transfer of men to the punitive company.

The concepts of justice varied among the different categories of prisoners. The man who broke a gold tooth out of a dead prisoner's mouth would have been completely ostracized among his comrades, had he been a political prisoner. But he was a nonpolitical, and the men around him, after overcoming their initial disgust, reasoned that after all he had not hurt anybody. And there are worse crimes than that, so let's forget about it, he won't do it again. They thought the man was punished enough with the "twenty-five" he got from the SS.

Most cases where the prisoners took some sort of justice into their own hands were thefts, occasionally usury, and informing. Only spectacular and very clear-cut cases were treated in ways that became known, because in less clear-cut cases, which would require extensive investigation, the seniors usually were unwilling to lend their authority. If the men started on their own, and a brawl resulted, the seniors frequently beat everyone involved without bothering to look into the merits of the case.

Property had two functions for the prisoner. One was to serve physical needs; he wanted to have a good tool, a good bread bag, food from the canteen. The other was to serve social and psychological needs. To own and dispose of things makes a man feel like a human being, with choices and decisions of his own—no matter how limited they may be. To have things in his pockets which were his own represented the last remnant of privacy, at least as far as his fellow prisoners were concerned. He dressed and undressed, washed, used the toilet or the latrine, ate, worked, and slept in the company of other people. He couldn't make a move without a dozen fellow prisoners watching him. But none of them could search his pockets, except his senior, who ordinarily wouldn't do so without serious reason. What he had in his pockets was absolutely his—until some SS man got the bright idea of taking it away from him.

The more personalized and necessary a stolen article was, and the longer it had been in the possession of the owner, the more severely was the thief punished. And of course, as frequently happened outside the fence too, the more powerful the man was from whom the article was stolen, the worse the thief fared.

This was a hungry society where to steal bread meant to threaten the physical existence of its members. I recall cases when in times of great need guards were stationed in the dayroom to watch the bread overnight. And I recall cases where the senior and/or a few other men lay in wait for a thief night after night. When they caught him, he was laid across a table and given the same "twenty-five" as the SS was accustomed to administering.

Stealing money was punished equally severely. On the one hand, money was almost the only thing of value a prisoner possessed; on the other, it usually had to be stolen directly out of his pocket during the night. It was similar to stealing things out of a man's locker. Since nobody could lock his "locker," there had to be some guarantee that a man would find the things he had put there when he returned from work. The watch that men kept on each other, the amount of honesty and decency they preserved within themselves, and the severe treatment of thieves when caught—all these things constituted such a guarantee. Often a thief was handed over to the administration for punishment, sometimes after having been beaten up in his own barrack.

Length of possession, it seems to me, played a considerable role, not only because it lent greater sentimental value to objects, but also because it represented continuity and a man's ability to have possessions and make decisions. To snatch a man's shoe brush while he was using it was not considered a very serious crime, though a brawl might ensue and the snatcher might be forced to return it. But I saw a barrack senior, who otherwise never touched a subordinate, beat a 70–year-old man because he had stolen a shoe brush that the senior had used for five years, ever since he had come to Dachau. It was the only object he had owned during that period.

Theft among comrades (*Kameradschaftsdiebstahl*) destroyed a man's social status. He was ostracized by those who knew about it. If he was transferred to another barrack or working group his new comrades might be warned that "he had stolen in his own barrack before."

To steal from the rich was less dangerous than to steal from the poor—unless the rich man happened to be powerful too. And the man who stole expensive canteen goods would be treated more leniently than the man who stole bread.

In the overcrowded barracks in Buchenwald, men lost caps, towels, and mugs all the time. Since everyone was responsible for his own articles, this led to a sort of mutual snatching, the same kind as is sometimes in evidence in schools and boys' camps. If, for example, a man had lost his towel in the witches' cauldron of the washroom, there was no time and no opportunity to get a new one. The only thing he could do was to keep a sharp eye on his neighbor's towel, and snatch it as soon as he saw a chance. The neighbor, as soon as he noticed his loss, would snatch another towel, and then the snatching made the round. Finally everybody had a towel again, with one or two exceptions. These had better not complain that their towel had been stolen, because the one who complained one day and had a towel the next was branded as a snatcher. He was the man who would steal the barber's towel, which was recognizable by the hair on it. A good way to get a towel was to have a cooperative friend who himself had a towel that he wore openly around his neck. Nobody would suspect him of being on the hunt for another one. That increased his chances considerably

When the week was over and everybody had to hand in a towel, it was usually the senior or occasionally the barber who, through connections of his own, was able to supply the one or two towels that were actually missing.

This type of snatching did not detract from a man's status, even though the victim might holler bloody murder if he caught him.

To snatch a man's cap or mug was more serious, because these were considered his personal belongings which he might keep for years. He might mark them, perhaps in a secret spot, so that he could unmask a thief and reclaim his property if he was able to recognize it.

To prevent discovery, a thief might swap a stolen piece with someone from another barrack while he was on the working ground, and come back at night with an absolutely unrecognizable cap or mug. Neither he himself nor others might yet have considered him a serious thief, but his act detracted seriously from his trustworthiness (especially the swapping to prevent discovery)—while snatching a towel did not harm a man's credit in the least.

The society was well aware of the severe consequences that went with the discovery of a serious theft. Strong measures were taken therefore to protect a man against false accusation. Here is an illustrative case: A friend of mine who very seldom received money and who was very popular, had lost his money. Others wanted to get it back for him, and when it could not be found, they concluded that it must have been stolen. Their suspicion fell upon a man who never had any money himself and was seen with some canteen goods. He could not defend himself properly, and, ignoring his protests, the men searched his pockets. They found nothing. But others, hearing that a man had been searched "knew" immediately that he must be a thief.

My friend did not know about all this, regretted his loss, and was very happy when he found the money in the bunk below his, where it had fallen during the night. The senior, hearing that a man had been searched because another had mislaid his money, called my friend, who did not know about the search, and in front of the barrack at roll call, slapped his face violently thirteen times, counting as he struck. "Another time you will wait before you accuse a fellow prisoners of stealing your mislaid money." The senior was otherwise a good man, an old political, who very seldom beat a prisoner.

The case was typical both in its lack of logic and in the swiftness of decision and action. Had the searched man actually stolen the money, he would probably have received considerably worse treatment than my friend did.

The impression that the whole affair left with his fellow prisoners was also typical. Since my friend was highly respected by everybody, nobody held him capable of doing anything bad enough to deserve the punishment he had received. Therefore people listened willingly to the truth—that he had no idea of what had happened. If, however, the man had not been as highly esteemed by others, the story might have remained a stain on his honor, no matter how innocent he was.

Usurers who loaned money at extremely high interest and black marketers who sold at exorbitant prices were sometimes punished by the men of their barracks. They might be beaten by the senior and ordered to give up their goods or claims, or they might receive an anonymous beating known as "the blanket." At night, while the culprit was asleep, or at least in bed, several prisoners would sneak up to him, throw a blanket over him, and beat him under the blanket, so that he could not tell afterwards who did it. The same punishment was occasionally given to informers, when the evidence against them was not too clear. Sometimes the senior himself took part in such a beating, or even organized it, if he wanted an informer punished but did not want the administration to know about it.

Here is another case that seems worth reporting. The men of a whole table got together to discuss what to do with the table canteener, who had embezzled the funds of his table mates. The men formed the elite of their room and thought it might harm their status as the "best table" if they brought the case before the senior. They decided to give the man another chance to pay back the money. What he did was pay back with money from new embezzlements. This happened a second time. Then the group came to a surprising solution: "This man has been a cheat all his life (a few knew about his past). Apparently he can't be happy unless he has a chance every now and then to cheat people out of their money. Why shall we make life hard for him by persecuting him for cheating us out of little sums?" And they left the man in charge of the table canteen, and tried only to keep a closer watch on their money. From time to time somebody would ask the man, half embarrassed, half nasty, when he intended to pay back the embezzled money. He never did. And nobody cared. What finally made the group appoint a new man was not the untrustworthiness of the embezzler, but his inability to provide them with an adequate share of canteen goods.

The camp expressed its approval or disapproval of punishment that was meted out by the administration. It was seldom that the camp approved, and when it did, it was usually not for the reason the punishment had been given.

One day a man was missing. The whole camp had to stand on the roll-call square until he was found two hours later. He was an asocial who had shirked by hiding in a wood pile and had fallen asleep. When he was found by searching prisoners, they beat him almost to death. While we were waiting and nobody was allowed to leave, a man had to comply with nature's need and relieved himself right on the square. Rödl ordered him to the "door." Later he announced that the two men would get "twenty-five" each—the one because he made an attempt to escape, the other because he shit on the square—that swine!

The camp heartily disapproved of the punishment in the latter case, but approved of it in the former. Not because the man had attempted to escape, which he had not, nor because he had shirked, to which nobody would have objected—but because he had been so stupid that he got caught, and because his stupidity had made 10,000 men wait on the roll-call square for two hours.

When a man was punished for "corruption" because he took another's money for making his bed every day, the politicals might have thought that he should not have done so, but that he certainly deserved no heavy punishment for taking money for something that they did for one another voluntarily. The nonpoliticals might have thought that what he did was an absolutely legitimate way of earning a little money. But the administration punished him for violating a rule—to take money was *verboten.*

When the administration broke up the big rackets of the professional criminals and meted out terrible punishments, they did so because the rackets undermined discipline in the camp. The camp approved wholeheartedly of the action, but for a different reason. These were gangsters, and it was bad enough to be in the hands of the Nazi gangsters who ran the camp; they did not want, in addition, to be subject to an intermediary layer of underworld gangsters.

The administration tried very hard to teach the prisoners that a man was a bad prisoner when he violated the rules and when he disturbed the order. Yet here their power found one of its most serious limitations. They could lash a man to the stand and thrash his life out of him. But whether he and his fellow prisoners thought that he deserved it was entirely outside their sphere of influence.

Chapter 16

Property Rights

Practically all property in the camp is acquired in one of the following ways: by official issue, such as uniforms and dishes; by paying for it in the canteen or black market with money that comes either from home or from straight or crooked transactions among the prisoners; by receiving it from someone else for nothing or in payment for services: by stealing camp material that is brought in for camp use or that is used in the production of other articles, such as bread bags; by acquiring "free" camp material and using it to produce some new object, for example, a knife made from a piece of tin, wood, and wire.

A man may claim an article as his which he has obtained in any of these ways, and he may show marks on it or call witnesses to confirm his claim. A man who happens to possess an item at any particular moment may claim it as his own, and arguments may start, at the end of which the object may remain either in the hands of the man to whom it seems to belong rightfully, or in the hands of the stronger man. In the latter case, others will call it unfair. Nobody doubts the possibility that a rightful claim can be established to a mug or a money purse.

However, property rights and prerogatives are claimed and to a certain degree established in cases where there is no recognized method of acquisition. Tools are handed in every night and piled up in a tool shed, or perhaps in the open. In the morning there is no individual issue of tools; the capo bellows, "To the job, on the double," and everybody runs to the tool piles. Tip-cart loaders run for a shovel, gravel diggers for a shovel or a pickaxe or both, wheelbarrow men run for the barrows. This general melee is often used for a last-minute change of job. A man who pushed a wheelbarrow yesterday, may grab a shovel today, and hope that the capo doesn't notice.

Men who can tell a good tool from a bad one try to get good ones—a sharp pickaxe, a shovel with a new blade and a well-bent shaft, a wheelbarrow with a small box, and so forth. And those who can tell a better working place from a worse one will also try to get that—a place in the shade on a summer day; a place behind a pile of material that protects a man from continual observation by the guards; a place so deep in a gravel pit that the SS men seldom get there, or one on a terrace that is not too far below the next, so that it is not so difficult to throw up the gravel; an inside rope on a steam roller.

One way to get a good tool or a good place is to use force. In the general scramble, the strong push the weak around, perhaps take an article that a weaker man has already laid his hands on, or chase a weaker man from a place where he is just about to begin digging. Another way is stealing. A man may lay aside his tool for a moment; another sneaks in from behind and takes it away.

Neither of these methods is frequently used, and when one of them is, nobody believes that any rightful claim has been established to the tool or the place. If a man has succeeded in hiding a good tool overnight instead of handing it in, or if he put it in the tool shed in such a way that he could find it again the next morning, does he now have a rightful claim to the tool? Does previous use of something that belongs to the camp and is not issued to the man individually, make it "his," so that he can claim it from another?

I think it is Voltaire who is often quoted as having said that the greatest criminal the world had ever seen was the first man who fenced in a piece of land and claimed, "This is mine," and that the greatest idiot was the man who believed him. This is exactly the way most prerogatives on tools or working places in large unskilled labor groups are established or re-established every morning.

The man who finds a good tool that he used the previous day claims it immediately as "his." "This is mine, I used it yesterday." He may even make such a claim about a tool he has never seen before. In either case he may call on (true or false) witnesses who will take an oath for him immediately and confirm, "Yes, it is his." A man may mark the tool, scratch his initials on it, for future proof.

It happened once that a man had taken a good shovel which I had successfully hidden for three days. While we were still yelling about it, he turned around, took a nail out of his pocket and began scratching his initials on the handle. I called the attention of witnesses to it, and the man was unmasked. Most of us happened to be good friends, while the "thief" was an intruder. The whole group yelled at him, and he was forced to let it go.

However, proving one's previous use of a tool and deriving from that the right for further use, is not a generally recognized procedure. Some submit to it, some do not. After all, if the man who happens to have the good tool today submits to these rules of mine and thine, he may lose it to the man who used it yesterday. But a bad tool—a shovel with a straight handle or a bent edge—can make a day much harder than it would be otherwise.

So today's possessor may answer the man from yesterday, "So what? There is no such thing as 'mine' and 'thine' in shovels. Your initials are on it? Look what it says here: KLD or KLB.[1] It belongs to the camp and everybody can use it."

There is no argument that can be brought against this. The two men are speaking different languages. The conflict is always decided by force, explicit or implicit. The men may fight for the tool, or others may take a threatening attitude against one of the two, or a capo or officer may appear on the scene, which puts an end to the argument and leaves the tool with the one who happens to hold it tightest at the moment.

In the case of personal issues such as caps and mugs, one article is as good as another. What people want to establish by claiming a thing as "theirs" is not the possibility of using a "good" mug, but rather the possibility of using one at all. In addition they want to establish continuity of possession. A mug, after some time, becomes the prisoner's property almost to the same degree as something he bought. There practically never arises a situation in which he must hand it in, until the day he is released.

In the case of tools, men are not too much interested in the stability of possession, because nobody succeeds in holding a tool longer than a

---

1. Every tool bears the initials of *K*onzentrations *L*ager *D*achau or *K*onzentrations *L*ager *B*uchenwald.

few days. All they want is to have a good tool. Rightful possession based on previous use is just one handy argument, good enough if the other believes it, and dismissed when the shoe is on the other foot. Men switch from "my shovel" to "there is no mine and thine" from one day to the next, adhering to the one argument when they happen to be the fortunate possessors and to the other when they happen to be in need of a good tool. The man who clung to a shovel yesterday because he "had worked with it for ages," may defend a good place in a gravel pit today by saying, "What do you mean 'your place'? We are all in the same boat."

And yet the quest for a certain amount of stability of possession, relieving the individual from the necessity of being always on guard against his neighbor, arises as soon as groups become stabilized to a certain degree. As soon as a group that is small enough for the men to know each other fairly well has worked as a unit for a few days, and the usual little cliques of friends have been established, snatching tools begins to be considered something one "ought not to do." The more stabilized the group, the more such an action appears as "stealing," while in a large and unstable group "snatching" is barely noticed. This is because the personal satisfaction or relief the men draw from the existence of a little group of friends who know each other, usually outweighs the advantage obtained from a few days' possession of a good tool, which, after all, will soon be in someone else's hand anyway.

People from cooperative groups, especially politicals working with other politicals, adhere to the stability of possession even if they don't know each other personally. If a fellow political claims that a thing is "his," and it sounds reasonable, then it is "his." Since most of them adhere to the same set of arguments and concepts, there is considerably less fighting for tools. They all speak the same language, and in it they can establish which of two claimants is "right."

When politicals clash over tools with nonpoliticals, the former are less consistent in their attitude. As long as the whole situation looks like fair play, that is, as long as the others seem to adhere to stability of possession, they themselves do, too. But if the others switch arguments, the politicals usually switch just as quickly and often get the better of their adversaries, because often several others come to their defense, supporting whichever claim or argument they happen to be using at the moment.

The arguments take a different form when whole working groups rather than individuals are involved. Within any column of handbarrow carriers, the situation is the same as within other groups of comparable size. Within a large column, the men who claim that a good handbarrow is theirs—one with feet to rest it on, smooth handles, and a small box— may get away with it, or they may be asked, "Why don't you print your initials on other boxes? There are enough of them around. Want a pencil?" But if a capo decides to snatch all the handbarrows of another column, he simply marches his men there before the possessors appear and takes the boxes with him. If the other capo has no influence, he can do nothing about it; if he is on good terms with the camp senior, he can complain and perhaps get his boxes back.

If a capo wants to safeguard his handbarrows, he may have the tool shop paint his column number on every box. This is done with indelible tar, and the boxes are recognizable at a great distance. Then if another capo snatches some boxes, they can always be claimed back, because the claimant is no longer an individual capo, but the officially established "Carrier Column No. II." The power behind the claim is no longer individual influence and personality, but the whole administration.

The administration, of course, is not interested in having a particular capo keep his carefully selected barrows. But they are interested in keeping order. Different numbers on barrows in the same column disturb the order. Hence the officer in charge of construction sees to it that the situation is remedied. Then even the individual man who tries to snatch a box from another column is threatened with the whole force of the camp.

When the administration punishes a thief, it is again not because they want to protect the prisoners' property, but because stealing is against the rules. The prisoners realize this, and hand thieves over only in very serious cases, when the desire to get rid of the man is stronger than the dislike of appealing to the administration. And in a fight for tools, if a man makes so much noise that the capo's attention is called to it, the others despise the man even if his original claim was just.

Chapter 17

Corruption

The presence of free money, in this society of shortages and of tremendous arbitrary power in the hands of certain prisoners, led to the development of a system of corruption and racketeering that in Buchenwald reached an extent that was well nigh astonishing, even for an old camp hand who had half a year's experience in Dachau.

There were several reasons why corruption was less pervasive in Dachau, in spite of the fact that the individual prisoner there had, on the average, more money. The main reason was that the political prisoners, the only group with great power in its hands, were opposed to corruption on ideological grounds. This restricted corruption automatically to those political capos and seniors who separated themselves from their own group (and there were not many of them) and to nonpoliticals who were primarily capos in unskilled labor areas. Thus corruption in the barracks was a rather uncommon experience, and if the administration wanted to mistreat certain seniors, it had to interpret as "rackets" and "corruption" what ordinarily would be considered the usual "apple for the teacher" that occurs wherever men are set above men.

Corruption on the working grounds was restricted, partly because the politicals fought racketeering capos, partly because of the inescapable publicity given to every single act; the guard around every individual working place and the presence of an officer in charge restricted considerably the arbitrary use of power by the capo in the distribution of jobs.

A black market in canteen or camp food did not develop in Dachau, because everybody who had money could go and buy for himself what the canteen sold. Since the canteen was well supplied, there was practically no smuggling of food from the outside. Nor was there any reason for hoarding food for a rainy day; the canteen practically never closed—never more than for an evening or a few hours on Sunday, perhaps because Koegel just happened to get angry at the prisoners for being noisy in line. In addition there were no days of punitive fast. Throughout my six months stay in Dachau, there was only one morning with no breakfast; that happened when the boiler in the kitchen did not work, and Koegel let us go hungry rather than delay the work by half an hour. The same applied to smoking. Cigarettes and tobacco were available in quantity in the canteen, and smoking was hardly ever forbidden for more than a few hours.

Thus the only large-scale illicit traffic was in articles that were not sold in the canteen but were still necessary. The possession of these things, incidentally, was ordinarily considered legal; only trading in them was forbidden.

Most common among these articles were wooden clogs, certain cleaning materials such as sandpaper and steel wool, and wooden tools for "constructing the bed." The wooden clogs were primarily produced in the punitive company, which during my time built the great building on the roll-call square and therefore had access to lumber and tools. Both the production and smuggling to the rest of the camp were done at terrible risk, and frequently men wound up in the dungeon for it. Those from the regular camp who had taken the merchandise usually were sent to the punitive company, after receiving "twenty-five," because any contact with these unfortunates was punished by making the transgressor one of them.

The wooden tools were ordinarily produced in the furniture shops, but they were not usually traded on a business basis. As a rule the tools did not belong to individual prisoners but to a whole room, and the senior acquired them for his room from political friends in the shop, who let him have them as a personal favor. However, when discovered, production of these tools was heavily punished, because men had produced them during working hours, and because they were illegally smuggled into the camp (the furniture shops were just outside the fence).

Sandpaper usually came from the furniture shops, and was paid for. The men who brought it had to steal it. Sometimes it was smuggled in through the canteen. Steel wool might be smuggled in through the canteen in a relatively open way. The prisoners there would order it for the canteen and then distribute it secretly, and the officer in charge would keep quiet about it because it was needed and apparently no profit was made. Sometimes it was smuggled in from the SS kitchen or other SS places, and in these cases it was almost always stolen.

One type of traffic was heavily punished for no understandable reason—self-made cigarettes. The canteen sold tobacco and cigarette paper and a little machine to roll cigarettes. Cigarettes made this way were slightly cheaper, and the smoker could reduce the cost even more by being stingy and putting a little less tobacco in each cigarette.

These homemade cigarettes were an important trade article, because the man who paid a few pfennigs for them spared himself the trip to the canteen. He could not pay the other man to bring him a package of cigarettes, because that was forbidden. It was forbidden to buy anything for another man, apparently because the administration hoped in this way to prevent people from buying on a large scale for capos and seniors. Of course, small quantities could not be checked in this way at all.

Numerous so-called "corruption stories" had as their basis nothing worse than one man's buying for another to save him a trip, and perhaps getting a few extra pennies for it.

Another type of "corruption" was lending money, which was strictly forbidden, apparently in order to prevent any sort of money-making from usury. The man who hung two and a half hours by the wrists because he did not want to betray a friend, had lent the man fifty pfennigs, because his regular money order had been delayed. (After he had confessed this, Grünewald could not keep from laughing. He had hanged the man by the wrists because he suspected him of participating in a letter-smuggling affair of which the poor man had not even heard.)

A certain amount of racketeering, though not very much, developed in the larger unskilled labor places, particularly where the capo was a devil and the place was so large that the guards couldn't see everything that went on. The capo might take money to put men on a leveling job, for instance, which was easier than carting gravel. A few men were always willing to pay for certain special jobs, for instance in the tool shed, or to carry water when not too much of it was needed, and so forth. In some highly skilled jobs, such as fitting pipes, money might change hands if the capo did not have any. But this was usually not a regular racket; that is, the men did not pay to get or keep their jobs but simply as a gift developing out of the intimacy in which they worked. When discovered, this was punished as corruption.

In addition there were always cases when a man might have found a way to slip a mark to an individual capo who ordinarily was not involved in large-scale rackets, and then might have found a softer job. For example, at the very beginning of my time, I had landed, more or less by accident, in a wonderful soft job, which by certain little tricks I prolonged for about two weeks. I was working on a cemented heat shaft, which was not yet quite covered. I talked my capo into the necessity of removing from it the water that had gathered there. I did this with a small tin shovel, which I had the plumbers make for me under a fake order. Since at that time (April 1938) we had snow or rain every night, there was always enough water in the morning to last for the day, and if there was not, well, I knew where to get a bucketful or two. In this place I had a companion whom I thought had landed there, like myself, by accident. But after working with him for two weeks, I learned that he had paid a small amount to the same capo, under whom I had the job for nothing.

Altogether corruption was of minor importance in Dachau, up to the summer of 1938, when the mass influx of Austrians changed the situation.

The most important reason why racketeering in Buchenwald reached its almost unbelievable extent seems to be that the group with the most power at the time of our arrival, the professional criminals, were already corrupted through and through before they came to camp. Because of their background and their individual experience, they were accustomed to do things for money, to take high risks for money, and to evaluate men, things, and services in terms of money. They did all this more ruthlessly and were less restrained by ideological considerations than most other groups in civilian society. These men, entrusted in the camp with tremendous power, placed at the key points of a potential network of black markets and rackets, had in their hands the almost completely arbitrary distribution of favors and good or bad treatment. They were willing to sell all of it for money or some equivalent, and when they couldn't find customers for their merchandise, they created them by blackmail and mistreatment.

But not only their past predisposed these men to racketeering; their future did too, and so did their present. They had neither a common goal that required them to keep their morals intact, nor individual goals; they had almost no hope of being released. Thus they made the camp life their permanent life and tried to get out of it whatever they could—and the only "pleasant" things that camp life had to offer were those that could be bought for money. Hence their insatiable greed for money and goods.

These men, conditioned for any kind of corruption and racketeering, found in Buchenwald the most favorable circumstances that anybody could invent for the purpose. They found a society that was half starved, continuously hounded by hunger and a shortage of food, steadily threatened by punitive fast days, or by the cutting off of the meager canteen supplies, and continually in the most precarious situation concerning the only material pleasure that the canteen offered—smoking. In addition they found a guard system that tremendously increased the arbitrariness of the capo. Capos of large working groups of 500 and more men were like mighty kings, with power over life and death. Most of the time the capo himself was not watched, there were practically no limits to his freedom in distributing different jobs, and he could sell positions as sub-capo almost at will—limited only by the risk that the man he fired might go and tell the administration. That risk was not too large, because squealing and being caught was almost equal to a death sentence (and sometimes it actually was).

There were two principal types of rackets, most of them organized on a large scale: food rackets and job rackets. The food rackets consisted of black markets, where practically everything that existed in the camp was traded, including food and anything else from the canteen, stolen food from the kitchen, regular camp food, and food smuggled from the outside, either through the canteen or through the SS kitchen or some other way. Most of the canteen food found its way to the black market through the barrack canteeners, who, instead of delivering the goods to their own customers, either bought for or sold to the black market. The black market itself was composed of more or less separated sections. There was one among the Jews, one among the "asocials," and one among the professional criminals. The politicals, who didn't have one of their own, usually bought from the "asocials" or from the Jews. The Jewish section specialized in canteen goods, because they had more money than the others. The asocial section specialized in stolen kitchen goods, because the kitchen workers lived among them, and in regular camp food, especially bread and sausages, because they were the poorest, and all they had to sell was what the camp gave them. The "green" section dealt in valuable canteen food and stuff smuggled from the outside, because they commanded the key points, and because the money was theirs— not so much money sent from the outside, but money obtained by blackmail inside the camp.

The black marketers bought from the canteeners, and then usually sold, not directly to the ultimate consumer, but to one or two intermediate dealers. Thus a piece of canteen goods was often sold three or four times and might, in times of great scarcity, finally have cost several times the original price. Nonperishable goods, such as canned fish, chocolate, or candy, usually disappeared as soon as they appeared on the market; so did a great part of the tobacco. Much of it was hoarded for the days when the canteen was closed or for fast days. When the canteen was closed (sometimes for several weeks at a time, with no announcement as to when it would be reopened), the black marketers usually waited a few days, until everything had disappeared from the hands of the regular customers; then they began to sell at high prices, which rapidly increased as the supply dwindled. On such occasions, cigarettes might have gone up from four pfennigs to fifty or more apiece; a can of fish from eighty pfennigs to three marks; a loaf a bread from twenty pfennigs, which was its trading value when the canteen functioned normally, to as much as 1.50 marks. Not only did the prices rise, but also the differences between prices for different articles almost disappeared; there was no choice of merchandise, so all the money went into whatever item happened to turn up.

Black market operations were carried out on the basis of personal acquaintance, contacts made on the working grounds or in the camp streets. After some experience, people found out which men usually had food in times of scarcity and tried to make close contact with them in order to learn the secret. Then the man who knew might either tell the newcomer to whom to go, or might perform the transaction for him, which relieved him of the necessity of giving away the secret—or he might even buy the goods from his original source and resell them to the new man, thus establishing himself as a dealer.

Black market goods were hoarded in tool sheds, which usually required the cooperation of the capo, or in the barracks, which usually required the cooperation of the senior, because the hiding places had to be protected from the inspection officer. To hide anything in a straw bag was dangerous, because these were frequently inspected.

Job rackets were established in one of two ways—either by direct negotiation between capo and man, perhaps with a sub-capo as an intermediary; or by an agreement between capo and sub-capo, under which the sub-capo collected a regular tribute from his group. Establishing groups and sub-capo positions for this purpose was an intermediate step, so was appointing a sub-capo in order to get his personal contribution.

Often the sub-capo established his own little racket, either by deducting from the general contribution for the capo, or by selling little favors on his own account.

The capo himself seldom openly requested money, but once he had taken some, he simply became known as one who did not repudiate offers. Offering a cigarette or some delicacy from the canteen was usually a good method of starting the approach when the capo was a fairly friendly type. If he was the violent type, approach through a sub-capo was usually the only way. However, it frequently happened that a capo began mistreating a man, persecuted him for some length of time for no visible reason, and then some friend would tell the despairing victim, "Don't you see, he only wants money?"

When my hand was halfway healed and I was returned to work, but could not use my right hand yet, my political friends arranged a place for me in a working group that was generally dreaded in the camp. I protested, but they told me that it was all to the good. And to my surprise it was. There was a sub-capo who was on excellent terms with the capo, and the little group with which I worked had one of the easier jobs, the main advantage of which was that it was fairly out of the way of inspection, and that part of the crew always had to work in a cellar. We arranged a nearly perfect warning system, and the cellar shift worked very little. Of course the shifts rotated.

One day the capo suddenly appeared, made a lot of fuss about our being lazy bums, and took us away to some heavy tip-cart loading work. Our sub-capo was absent at the moment. On returning and finding that he had lost his command, he ran all over the mountain until he found us, and then found the capo. Suddenly he reappeared, shouting and scolding us for having run away from our jobs, and that he would show us what it meant to jump a job. He made us drop our shovels, abandon the carts, arrange in formation, and, yelling, he drove us off. When we were back at our old place, he beamed and told us joyously that for this time great grievance had been spared us—he had fixed everything. And it was very cheap. The capo had run out of smoking material, so first he wanted some cigarettes right away, and then twenty-five pfennigs per man, which was about three marks, or four packages of cigarettes. The whole incident was repeated about three weeks later. In between the sub-capo asked only occasionally for small contributions, in an irregular fashion.

I was one of a group of four Austrians who for a large part of our time in camp, particularly in Buchenwald, tried to keep together. Two of us were politicals, two nonpoliticals. One day one of our nonpolitical friends came with good news. He had made a good contact and all four of us should report the next day with a new working group. At that time we happened to be on very hard work, carrying heavy oak logs, but the work had its advantages: while carrying the logs, we were safe from persecution, for nobody could speed up a dozen men who were balancing an oak log on their shoulders. We could take rest periods and carried no load on the return trip. We had practically no supervision because the capo was occupied at the place where the logs were needed. And he was a political man who did not touch us. As a matter of fact, I had established contact with him when we had worked on tip carts under capo Berg, the killer. We had had several days of hell, including some bleeding wounds on my head from stones thrown by Berg. And this capo had freed all four of us. Hence I protested against leaving him. When our friend insisted, I arranged with the capo for some "leave of absence"; he promised to take us back, if the new arrangement should not turn out to our liking.

The new capo was an asocial, which was in itself suspicious; asocial capos were rare. His deputy was a professional criminal. We were a group of about twelve. He had us select heavy long sticks, and then a strange journey through the forest started. After about half an hour's pleasant walk we came to a big pile of tree trunks, practically all of them fir, with a few oaks buried underneath. And now we set to work with our sticks, and, using them as levers, eased out the oaks from underneath. It took us about two hours. Then we walked in the sun for another hour or so, and pulled out some more oaks from a pile of firs. The oaks we simply left where they lay.

We enjoyed that very much, but on the second day I began to get suspicious. On the third day our friend let the cat out of the bag. This job cost a mark per man each week, and the capo wondered why we hadn't come across yet with the dough. For the moment there was nothing to do but to pay, and to enjoy the good rest we got. But I, not trusting this business, wanted to go back. It was too pleasant to last for any length of time. Soon I found out that the man was no capo at all, hardly a sub-capo. His capo had given him a few men to pick out a few oaks, and the man had made a business of it by collecting other workers and their contributions. On the fourth day we almost got caught. Suddenly an SS officer appeared, just as we were "tickling" an oak out of a pile of firs. He was puzzled by the strange assignment, which seemed quite unfamiliar to him, and called for the capo. He stared at him for quite a while, then asked him, "What crooked deal is going on here?" "We are getting the oaks ready to be picked up by the punitive company and carried to the sawmill." "Hmm … Give me that stick of yours." With the stick he hit the capo over the head—not too much, just enough to rip the skin a little. "Listen, son, if you are doing something crooked here, I'll be sure to get you! And then you'll get more. Have I made myself clear?" "Yes, Herr Barrack leader." The officer disappeared. The "capo" was rather quiet, had us line up and marched us off the other way to another pile.

To me the incident was warning enough, and I talked the other three into returning to our old job. As it happened, we got out by the skin of our teeth. The group was caught the next day and got their "twenty-five." The "capo" and his deputy wound up in the punitive company.

Both stories are fairly typical, except for the fact that apparently the real capo of the man was not involved in the log affair. Ordinarily the sub-capo would have delivered about sixty pfennigs per man to the capo each week, while he himself would have kept some forty pfennigs.

One of the largest jobs rackets I know of occurred in Dachau after the arrival of the Austrians. Capo Zock, the pimp, was in charge of leveling the barrack yard in the SS camp. He had about 200 men digging and transporting gravel, which was heavy work, and all the harder because Zock was a sadist who was on the run all day, beating and harrying his charges. In addition he had forty men leveling the finished parts, which was easy work, and 160 men pulling two steamrollers on ropes. In April we had been pulling the steamroller with forty men, and that was hard work. Now, since there was not enough work to keep everybody busy, there were two steamrollers in use, and eighty men pulled on each. That made the work easy, compared with digging and wheelbarrowing. Since none of the four hundred jobs required skill, the workers, for the most part Austrian nonpolitical Jews, were assigned to him by the barrack, two barracks every day.

Zock made a German Jew, Shyftan, his deputy. Shyftan wore a red badge, like Zock, but he was not a political man either. With his Jewish star he could inconspicuously mingle in the barracks at night and organize the racket. He made the barracks pay not to be selected by Zock, and of those who were selected he made some pay for not being assigned to shovel and wheelbarrow. Since Shyftan could not direct this huge organization alone (it covered about eight barracks), he appointed sub-cashiers for the barracks and sub-sub-cashiers for the rooms. Of course tribute was not exacted for everybody; a certain amount was requested "per barrack," and it was the barrack cashier's business to get it where he could.

And there were always enough personal relations, and personal payments, because the fact that a barrack was working on the steamrollers did not necessarily prevent Shyftan or Zock from shifting a particular man to the wheelbarrows.

A different type of job racket developed, primarily in Buchenwald, in connection with the invalid jobs. Places in the stone knockers' hut were sold for one mark a week, and places close to the little fire for two marks a week—the latter being a serious inroad on a maximum allowance of seven marks. Places in the stocking-mending room were sold, in spite of the fact that a certificate from the infirmary was needed for the place— the certificate, genuine or falsified, was sold with it. Prices amounted to two or three marks a week, depending upon the customer's capacity to pay. Of course, not everybody could get into one of these shops; the worker had to have some evident ailment or handicap, because once the officer got suspicious and investigated, the game was usually lost. Officers checked up regularly on men's certificates and ailments.

Places were sold in the invalids' stone carrier column, and at other places where invalids worked. But it is important to remember that almost everybody who bought himself into such a place was, by his age, illness, or weakness, so conspicuously incapacitated, that even a scrutinizing officer would automatically concede that he belonged in the column anyway.

The only place that started as an invalid column but finally became a haven for perfectly healthy individuals who had money enough to buy a place, was the famous column "4711"—4711 was a well-known German brand of eau de cologne. The men in this column were equipped with tin cans with a capacity of about a gallon (old jam jars), with which they emptied the latrines and carried the contents as fertilizer to the flower beds and lawns along the neutral zone. Every officer avoided the horrible stench of this column, which was so bad that one could still smell it in the midst of the forest ten minutes or more after the column had passed. There were about twenty-five men in the column. Their fellow prisoners refused to sit with them at the same table; after much protest they were put together in one barrack. It was a common joke in the camp that quite a number of these men were highly educated men, university professors and so forth, who saved their lives and health in this way. I was told by members of this column that conversation during "work" was on a amazingly high level. When typhoid fever came to the camp and the latrines were thought to be infected, some of these men tried everything to buy their way out again. Only a few succeeded. Several died.

The racket in invalids' certificates also extended to certificates that gave the holder permission to go to the infirmary during work time—particularly to certificates that allowed the holder to line up during work time in front of the dentist's office. The infirmary racket was a relatively impersonal one, primarily based on forged or stolen certificates. The attendants in the infirmary, being politicals, were practically never involved in selling them, but occasionally handed them out for nothing to their political friends. The dentist racket was closely tied up with the person of the dentist or his attendant. Since he had to keep a written record of his treatments, every certificate could be checked immediately. The dentist, who was, of course, also a prisoner, made a lot of money by using inferior materials for repairs, instead of the valuable ones for which he charged. The better materials either were not bought, or disappeared for illegal treatment, which brought extra income.

The Buchenwald counterpart of the Dachau wooden clogs (that is, articles which were illegally produced and traded, but legally possessed) were the bread bags. Practically every one of the ten thousand prisoners had one. It was carried openly, slung over the shoulder; every officer saw the 10,000 men in the morning marching out with their bags. The official Buchenwald song mentioned it. And yet, all 10,000 bags were made from stolen burlap, canvas, or linen; all of them were produced on sewing machines that were accessible only during working hours (in the clothing repair shops, etc.). And of course, all of them were sold, at from one to three or four marks apiece, in a camp where trading was forbidden. Most of the bags were produced and sold by the asocials, many of whom had access to the material. In ordinary times, when only few newcomers were added to the camp, the trade was conducted on a personal basis. A man who needed a bag would start asking where to get one, until he came across somebody who knew.

But when large numbers of new prisoners arrived, for instance, when 2,300 men came from Dachau within two days, the trade immediately became a big racket, with mass production and artificially high prices.

There were also "local" rackets, restricted to barracks and rooms, and involving individual seniors. For example, in many rooms in the morning, before the people left for roll call, one man inspected all the beds, and called the men back if something was wrong. In many barracks this became a racket; the "inspector" messed up the beds until the men paid either to be let alone or to have him make the beds. Professional criminals who were seniors either meted out mistreatment in regulated quantities to blackmail prisoners who were known to have money, or harassed the whole room continuously, until the men organized the racket among themselves to placate him with gifts. Afterwards he could say that they hadn't been asked for money; it was a gesture of friendship.

In barracks where carrying the food, sweeping the room after dinner, and cleaning the toilets and hall were not done on a pre-arranged schedule, but by men whom the senior selected every day, these tasks were often made a source of income. Men paid for not having to do these tasks, or they paid others for taking their place.

In certain cases prisoners paid each other for services. Men who had difficulty making their bed or keeping their shoes clean and so forth, might pay a small regular sum to have somebody else do it. Unless exorbitant prices were asked, however, the prisoners did not consider these payments a corruption racket, although they were forbidden and persecuted as such by the administration.

In addition to the widespread food and job rackets, there were always a great number of smaller rackets, often based on the ingenuity of individual men who discovered something that could be sold. Since it was forbidden to drink the supposedly contaminated water, there were always men who would find some sort of a container and some way of reaching a faucet during working time, and then sell the water. Others might in some way procure a key to the washroom, which was ordinarily locked after the washing period was over, and sell water that way. A man might happen to have a sizeable quantity of cigarettes, find out that others don't, and sell them at a small profit, without being in any way mixed up with the black market. Repair equipment, such as rags, needles, and thread, were sold when unavailable in the canteen and clothing department.

The most impressive types of rackets did not affect the average prisoner, nor the average receiver of money, but only the owners of big money—a select number of professional criminals, capos, seniors, a few asocials, and a few politicals. One type was smuggling from the outside; the other was the transfer of money. The importation of tea, coffee, on rare occasions liquor, but more often fruit, fat, chocolate, and smoking material, especially better brands, was accomplished either through the SS kitchen and SS canteen, in which case SS men were invariably involved, or through the civilians who brought the goods for canteen and kitchen. Since the latter did not have access to the prisoners' camp, ordinarily not even to places where prisoners worked, contact was extremely difficult to establish and maintain without SS men being involved. The risks that went with this kind of traffic, particularly for SS men and civilians, were so tremendous that the prices asked went way beyond what an ordinary "rich" man in the camp (one who regularly received the maximum of 30 marks a month) could possibly pay. Thus the goods were kept within the small circle of those who made big money from the various rackets. The rest of the camp knew about this only by hearsay, but details were quickly broadcast every time the administration uncovered a case and a civilian or an SS man landed in the camp for it.

Since nobody was allowed to receive or possess more than ten marks at a time, the owners of the big money had no legal way to transform this money into goods. Transfer of big sums of money was performed through the smuggling routes, in part through the canteen. The owners of big money ordered through several barrack canteeners simultaneously, or simply got in touch with them as soon as the goods came in and had first choice.

The transfer of money in order to hoard it outside was effected so seldom that it cannot be considered typical of the camp, in spite of the fact that it was often spoken of. Money was usually sent out either through the SS or through the clerk's room. A certain amount of racket developed when the "November Jews" came in. With them came a great deal of money in bills. The professional criminals robbed them of it, but it could not be used legally for payments at the canteen, since only coins were legal tender. SS men, both inside and outside the canteen, were persuaded to get the bills exchanged, in return for which they got a heavy percentage that increased with the size of the bills.

Chapter 18

Conflict

Up to the summer of 1938, the prisoners' camp in Dachau gave the outward impression of a society without any major internal conflicts. True, there were antagonisms between groups, based on their different social, political, and economic backgrounds, and all the prejudices brought along from their former world; true, these differences led to discrimination in the distribution of jobs and favors. But the politicals dominated the field to such a degree that they were able to prevent these antagonisms from turning into open conflict.

After the "Austrian Invasion," the politicals lost in numerical importance. They still dominated the camp, but their attempt to organize the Austrians in accordance with their own concepts of solidarity and fighting spirit soon broke down. It was a major achievement of the politicals that neither anti-Semitism nor rivalry between Austrians and Germans led to large-scale fighting or persecution between the groups involved.

In Buchenwald, at the time of our arrival, the situation was different. Neither of the two groups that were in open conflict was strong enough to dominate the camp alone. The administration used this to play various groups against one another, now persecuting the "greens" for corruption, now giving power to them so they might checkmate the "reds." All antagonisms between groups were more clearly visible, in the form of bitter fights, persecution, mistreatment, and treachery; but solidarity within the groups was also more evident.

Political versus Nonpolitical Prisoners

Political and nonpolitical prisoners, lived together in the same camp for months and years, were beaten and mistreated by the same SS men, yet lived in completely different worlds. What to one was a meaningless and insufferable inferno, beyond which there was nothing but, at best, the hope of individual survival, was to the other a battlefield, beyond which there lay a final victory, if not for him individually, at least for his group. Crowded into a tight corner by a temporarily powerful enemy, he fought on, and nobody but he himself could call off the battle. Hard labor, mistreatment, torture were seen as planned moves on the part of his enemy to break his fighting spirit; to cry or beg or make confessions meant to admit defeat. So he gritted his teeth and suffered silently. He made it a point of honor not to show his feelings, not to break down, to outdo whatever challenge was thrown at him. His conviction that he was indefatigable, that he would outlast his enemies, was one of the strongest sources of his continued resistance.

If the enemy tried to finish him off by having him shovel gravel, he would outlast the gravel period. If he was made to work in ice-cold water knee-deep and deeper, he would outlast the water. If the enemy tried to make him give up by proving that he could not live up to the requirement of discipline, he would keep his barrack so clean that not even the most malicious inspector could find a speck of dust. If he then got punished anyway for "having made a pigsty of his barrack," he knew that this was just a foul blow, which of course always had to be expected from this type of enemy. And if they hung him on the "tree" or threatened to kill him unless he betrayed his friends, then he would silently hang on the "tree," and if need be give his life, and die as a victor. Only if he broke down, would he admit defeat.

As an individual, the political man was as little inclined to slave for his tormentors as anybody else. But his past life, devoted to faithful fulfillment of his duty, had perhaps conditioned him more than others to feel uneasy when loafing, particularly if individual loafing might involve the risk of punishment for a whole group. But if loafing could be arranged as an organized action, he would do it with pleasure, even at great risk. A political "moor express," after shirking a whole afternoon, would take more pride in having cheated the camp than pleasure in the rest period gained by this action.

I could imagine a competition, say, in shoveling gravel, between well-nourished SS men and underfed political prisoners, and I am convinced that the prisoners would have won. This notion, perhaps a little far-fetched, is closer to reality that it might seem at first glance. Occasionally it happened that a weak man was picked at random by the officer in charge, to replace for an afternoon a man on a moor express. This man was immediately conspicuous because of his less efficient work. Now it might happen that an officer, seeing the whole crew working well and the one man lagging behind, might try to make him hurry. He would yell at the man, push him around, and perhaps in his anger grasp the man's shovel to show him, in full fury, how to load gravel onto a wagon.

The other three men, who would have started piling up the gravel, each from his corner of the wagon, would immediately take this as a competitive challenge. It was not meant this way, it was only an incautious act on the part of the officer. But there he would be, on the spot. Now he shovels ahead like a fiend. And invariably the prisoners shovel ahead like two fiends, their piles rise faster and higher. Those who are not shoveling try to encourage with their eyes and with nods those who are at it. As soon as the officer realizes what is going on, he tries to extricate himself from the embarrassing situation. He throws the shovel back into the weak man's hands, perhaps beats him up, barks at the rest of the crew, and leaves the scene.

But the crew, on the way back to the camp, would discuss the incident in all its details and treat it as a minor victory: "Eh, we showed that guy this time, didn't we?" "He certainly won't try again to lick us shoveling."

Jehovah's Witnesses had a similar attitude toward work and the whole camp. They were working for the Lord and therefore must not be defeated. They couldn't let down the Lord. A martyr must not give up. To this was added a certain fatalistic element in their philosophy: If the Lord wants us to work, we have got to work. If he wants us to work in a concentration camp, then we have to do good work in a concentration camp. Why the Lord should want them to build good barracks for the SS, was not subject to discussion. Undoubtedly He knew what He eventually would need these barracks for.

The general attitude of the politicals and the Jehovah's Witnesses was reinforced by the fact that they belonged to their groups not only ideologically, but also quite physically. They stood around a man and watched him, and if he gave in they despised him, considering him almost a traitor: "Look at him, he can't even cope with a lousy SS man." The social pressure of the group became extremely strong when the composition of a group was fairly stable, such as in a barrack or on a moor express.

When men were together for years, a loss in social status was a hard blow, and one difficult to recover from.

In the beginning the politicals suffered a great deal from this attitude. Their sense for order and organization made them comply with any regulation; thus they could easily be brought to despair when the administration set the standards higher or multiplied the number of rules. But in the long run they profited from it; the administration, caught up in its own principles, turned against the disorderly barracks and left the political ones more or less alone.

However, this was only a secondary achievement. The main goal was to keep alive the fighting spirit of the group for future action. For years they fought with their backs against the wall. They lost dozens and hundreds of their comrades on this battlefield. They mourned their dead and swore revenge, but for those who survived, every single day was a triumph.

All this seemed to the nonpolitical man, inside or outside the camp, a strange, romantic attitude. But men in a concentration camp were not too prone to romanticism, and to the politicals themselves their own attitude seemed the most natural thing in the world for a group that still had political goals left outside the barbed wire. They talked about death in the most casual way, as they did about the weather. Only after strong friendships had been established would they talk about their own feelings.

When we arrived as newcomers in the camp, they told us from the very beginning, "You can't win by giving in. You must take it on the chin. You'll get used to it." They themselves had worked under harder conditions and longer hours than we did in later years. They had gone through outrages of sadism about which we, already accustomed to mistreatment by our own experiences, could only hear with a shudder. They had endured in silence. They had held together, proving that they could be and remain Socialists, Communists, and Jehovah's Witnesses, under any sort of test.

When comparing himself to the nonpolitical prisoner, the political felt vastly superior. He knew that he had at least tried to do something to stem the rising Nazi tide, although he might be sorry that he did too little or not the right thing, while the nonpolitical had done nothing or perhaps had hindered him in his fight. And he despised the man who had no principles, no ideals to fight for, who was not ashamed to show the SS men his feelings, the weakling who whined and broke down under mistreatment. He had only contempt for the lazy shirker, who got caught because, with his basic tendency to shirk, he took risks that should not have been taken. He considered him a stupid and unimaginative creature, hardly worth bothering with, and certainly not worthy of any place in a well-cooperating crew.

The nonpolitical prisoners considered the politicals an assembly of men who, for the most part, were utterly respectable, but slightly mad in their ambition. They knew that most of these men had the courage of their convictions, and that they behaved in a most comrade-like and helpful way, not only among themselves, but also to the nonpoliticals, in spite of their contempt for them because of their lack of principle. There were fewer crooks and gangsters among the politicals than in any other group, except for the Jehovah's Witnesses. But, at the same time, the nonpoliticals hated the politicals for their very ambition. They despised and called "submissive" the political man who worked calmly and undisturbed, and thus attracted attention to the fussy and shirking man beside him.

The nonpolitical prisoner could not be defeated, because for him there was no battle going on. In a sense, he saw the situation more realistically than did his political brother: Here is a strong SS man with a revolver on his hip and a stick in his hand, and here am I, underfed, without enough sleep, untrained in the work I am doing, and harried and tortured. Small wonder I don't do the work. Let *him* try under these conditions and see whether he can do any better. There is no sense in being enduring and indefatigable. If the SS man is around and kicks you with his boots, you work harder, not in order to show that you are the better man, but to spare yourself a kick in the pants. One kick less is one kick less. And if the man goes away, just take it easy. Too bad that they are around most of the time.

When the nonpoliticals were mistreated, they screamed. It is perfectly natural for a man to scream when you twist his arm around behind him. And when you strap him to a stand and whip him, what else do you expect but that he will scream at the top of his lungs? Every dog howls when you beat him like that; every animal squeaks when you trample upon it. There is no point of shame involved. It is no challenge to beat a defenseless man. Give *me* a revolver and a whip, and strap *him* to a stand; you'd be surprised how I would make him scream.

What may perhaps make him keep his mouth shut is the knowledge that many SS men keep beating as long as you scream. One slap in the face less is one slap in the face less. See above. But not being upheld by any ingrained principle, too often his past will betray him, the past in which a weeping child is an object for pity, a weeping man an object of utter compassion.

Since the behavior of the political prisoners was determined to a high degree by their ideology, there is little value in asking whether in the camp it led to more or less suffering. Having accepted the camp as one of the risks involved, they would probably not have changed the behavior that derived from their ideology in return for a slight difference in treatment. A slap in the face less, if paid for by a loss of self-respect, was more than just a slap in the face less. On the other hand, the behavior of the nonpoliticals, since it was not based on ideology but, as they claimed, on common sense, is open to judgment on the basis of its results.

The amount of suffering the two groups endured cannot be compared easily, because the groups differed in several respects which have bearing on the issue. I do not know the actual statistics, but on the basis of hundreds of personal acquaintances, it seems safe to say that the politicals on the average were younger, had a higher proportion of laborers and workers among them, and were so much better trained in teamwork that they would probably have fared somewhat better even if they had given up their ideology.

Yet the difference in suffering is so much in favor of the politicals, that it cannot simply be explained by a difference in age and physical training. It is true that the politicals spent more of their leisure time cleaning up their barracks, but it is equally true that the men of their barracks were practically never punished for disorder. On the working grounds they were beaten less, and it hardly ever happened that a political old-timer was reported for punishment, although the young guards of course didn't know who was an old-timer and who wasn't.

It seems possible to make the following general statement: At any single moment, the nonpolitical man who shirked could claim a gain, while the political man who worked on suffered a superfluous loss of energy. But in the long run, the nonpolitical ran the higher risk. Out of a thousand nonpolitical prisoners, a considerably larger number would have gone through a whipping, been hung on the "tree," or had their limbs broken by mistreatment on the working grounds, than the number per thousand of political prisoners during the same period of time. In addition, a considerably larger proportion of nonpoliticals would have gone through all sorts of group punishments, such as punitive drill, constructing beds, or standing at the "door." And finally the politicals had the lowest rate of sickness and death, comparable only to an equally low rate among Jehovah's Witnesses. The apparently close connection between moral and physical powers of resistance was much discussed in the camp.

Actually the connection was not as simple as it appeared in people's minds. Apparently there were two factors involved. One was the strength the individual man gained from his conviction. A man whose whole mind was directed toward his future task, would perhaps overcome the exhaustion of a punitive drill or of individual mistreatment longer than a man who fought only for the moment. In a decisive situation, when it was a question of enduring one more half-hour, he might have gritted his teeth and decided, "All right, this one more half-hour I will try it. If I want to be there when we turn the tables on them, I have to survive now." The other, at this decisive moment, might have given up and said, "What the hell is the difference whether they kill me today or tomorrow."

The other factor was the fact that the politicals generally worked under better conditions because of administrative regulations (for example, in the furniture shops in Dachau, or as seniors and barracks details) and also because they had the best network of relations. Both were fairly direct consequences of their ideological behavior. They got the positions as seniors because they were better able to organize the camp, and they dominated the camp unofficially because of their superior organization among themselves.

With the help of this better organization, they were better able to take care of their people than any other group by securing better jobs for them, by having them transferred away from dangerous capos, and by having them treated in the infirmary. For example, when the men from Dachau discovered what a murderous killer Capo Berg was, the politicals among them were soon transferred to other places, and those whom Berg killed or injured were primarily nonpolitical people.

In addition there was the solidarity the politicals developed among themselves in areas other than those of work and immediate danger. They were not the richest group in the camp, but they took the best care of their poorer members. In a situation where the majority of deaths was caused less by mistreatment or the sickness which preceded it, than by the general weakness of the body due to overwork and undernourishment over a long period, the small support that the group provided for its destitutes became an important factor.

There was one more point in which the politicals were superior. There were practically no suicides among them. The few that did occur were either cases of men who were involved in an investigation in the course of which they expected to be tortured or killed, or cases where a political was taken to the dungeon and nobody ever found out how much truth there was to the claim that he had committed suicide. Suicide as a voluntary giving up of the battle by a man who simply does not want to live any longer was almost unknown among them. The rare exceptions occurred when men killed themselves on their "camp anniversary," after having decided long in advance—I am going to stand this so many years. If then there is no reasonable chance of a turn for the better, I will quit.

On the whole the politicals fared better in the camp, and it seems that this fact was either directly or indirectly related to their political convictions. They themselves felt justified in sticking to their accustomed way of life and their principles of cooperation, and in regarding the camp as a battlefield. It also seems that most of the things that were true for the politicals were true for the Jehovah's Witnesses, which would indicate a conflict between ideological and non-ideological prisoners. But since the "Jehovah's" in Dachau were kept in the punitive company and in Buchenwald were not very active, and since they were numerically not very important in either camp, the main antagonism appears to have existed between political and nonpolitical prisoners and took the form of attempts by the politicals to try to enforce their ways of thinking upon the rest of the camp. At the same time, for political reasons, they tried to prevent this same antagonism for turning into an open fight.

Anti-Semitism

Ever since its beginnings, Nazism depicted the Jews as the source of all evil. This was not a very new theory in a country which had practiced persecution and discrimination against Jews for centuries. What was new was the emphasis on racial rather than religious discrimination, and the violence with which they went about putting their ideas into practice.

The Nazis' anti-Jewish propaganda was never very successful among politically trained workers, who had always cooperated with Jews in their political and cultural organizations. In the concentration camps, their relations with the Jews continued in their old forms; they made close friendships with Jewish leftist politicals and a few selected others, and left the rest alone, just as they did with non-Jews.

Hitler's propaganda was more fruitful among the middle and upper classes, who had always harbored a vague, never clearly defined anti-Semitism based on social prejudice rather than on racial or religious differences—a prejudice which had poisoned the political and social life in Germany for generations. The conservative parties had always nourished either an open or a creeping anti-Semitism, even those which admitted Jews as members or as financial supporters.

These people, when brought to a concentration camp, did not lose their prejudices simply because they happened to be imprisoned and beaten along with Jews. But they did not develop any violent hatred for them either. There was nothing to be gained by it, and there was nothing inside the camp to blame the Jews for. They established personal relationships just as they had done outside. Those Jews whom they liked, they accepted as human beings, admitting that there are good people everywhere, regardless of parentage. Those whom they disliked, they rejected for being Jews, "because all Jews are dishonest and bad." The only difference was that in the close daily contact of the camp it was more difficult to overlook the fact that Jews are like other people, and to explain every acceptable one as an exception to the rule.

This vague anti-Semitism became more active when an individual derived some social or economic advantage from avowing it publicly. After Hitler had deprived the Jews of their legal rights and property, any nobody could raise himself a few notches on the social ladder by emphasizing his clean Aryan descent, which automatically placed him above all Jews. And if he was vociferous enough and joined an appropriate organization, he could even share in the spoils which accrued from their expropriation.

In concentration camp the same principle applied. The asocials and some of the professional criminals, treated by the politicals as second-rate beings, raised themselves on the social scale by looking down with contempt upon several thousand Jews beneath them. In Dachau this had no serious consequences, since the politicals prevented any serious strife between the various groups of prisoners. In Buchenwald the conflict was more open, because one of these groups had considerable power in its hands. Professing anti-Semitism if one's capo happened to be against the Jews possibly meant sharing in the favors he had at his disposal.

However, it appears that much of the so-called anti-Semitism of many capos and seniors was more a rationalization of an existing state of things than a deeply felt racial or social prejudice. Rackets in which capos attempted to get Jewish money were occasionally carried out with anti-Semitic threats, and so was mistreatment and violence when capos were in charge of large Jewish groups. Berg, for example, was not so much an anti-Semite as a primitive brute who beat anyone who fell into his clutches. He did so with the most colorful curses, which, when he happened to turn on Jews, were spiced with anti-Semitic oaths. Sterzer, known as the worst anti-Semitic murderer among the capos in Dachau, turned out under closer scrutiny to be an abnormal sadist, who ordinarily happened to have Jews under his rod and therefore developed an anti-Semitic vocabulary. He really persecuted the Jews, perhaps even believed at times himself that he was an anti-Semite. But when he happened to get non-Jews under his command he beat them just the same, only he did not call them "dirty Jewish swine, dirty," but just "dirty swine, dirty."

But there were of course real anti-Semites among them, such as Azzoni, who had been an SS man. He really preferred to mistreat the Jews under his command and left the others more or less alone. Zock usually turned more against the Jews than against the non-Jews, but the fact that he organized his largest rackets with the help of a Jew seems to indicate that his was an opportunistic type of prejudice.

Generally, Jews were cautious in the presence of non-Jews whom they didn't know very well, without being actually afraid of them. When they worked together for some time, the racial barriers usually broke down, and a friendly atmosphere developed, which in individual cases led to close friendship. The men helped each other, shirked together, shared their food, made little deals, warned one another, and only when they had a fight did they occasionally spice their squabble with anti-Semitic epithets. When the quarrel was over, a bitter taste might be left for some time, and it might take several days before trust was restored among the men. People with anti-Semitic prejudices simply abstained from close contact with Jews, usually without anything more than an occasional disparaging remark.

The various categories among the Jews behaved similarly to their non-Jewish counterparts. The politicals exhibited the usual cooperation and leadership, and the nonpoliticals had the usual difficulties in adjustment, perhaps somewhat aggravated because the proportion of professionals and business men was larger. Jewish asocials had a considerably higher standing than non-Jews in the same category, because of their different background. The large majority of them were middle-class people, who would probably not have been in concentration camp had it not been for their being Jews. Jewish professional criminals were considered smarter, since among them the proportion of violators of property laws was larger, and that of killers and slayers smaller.

The "Austrian Invasion"

The first two transports of 150 Austrians each, arriving in Dachau in April and May 1938, were distributed among the old barracks, Jews to Jews, non-Jews to non-Jews, and were soon absorbed by the camp. The real "Austrian Invasion" began with a transport of 600 Jews from Vienna on May 27, followed by another 600 on June 3, and several more mass transports within the following three weeks. All told about 3,300 Austrians, 2,000 of them Jews, were added to 2,500 Germans of whom only 300 were Jews.

All numerical relations changed. The politicals, up to that time by far the largest group, suddenly became a small minority and had to make a tremendous effort to keep their dominating position. The Jews, previously a very small group, now comprised about half of the camp, forming a large body with a social life of its own. And the majority of the camp as a whole became Austrian.

The three groups overlapped considerably, since the majority of the newcomers, about 1,800 of them, were at the same time Austrians, Jews, and nonpoliticals. Thrown together in barracks of their own, they exhibited the difficulties of the nonpoliticals on a vast scale. The camp as a whole, not realizing that their lack of organization and their disorder was caused primarily by their lack of training in cooperative behavior, ascribed it either to their being Austrians, or their being Jews, or both. And not realizing that the SS had picked as many rich Jews as possible, they looked at the money of these men and the corruption that went with it not as a middle-class but as a Jewish phenomenon. It took all the organizational ability of the politicals to disentangle this hodgepodge of ideology and prejudice and facts, and to reduce the resulting antagonisms to a point where they would no longer be a threat to this politically relatively frictionless society.

* * *

The Austrians were by no means the homogenous mass which they first appeared to be to the Germans. Yet differences among the various subgroups were not conspicuous for various reasons. The majority of their politicals, both Jews and non-Jews, lived in German barracks, where they became an integrated part of the existing community and thus were no longer considered especially Austrian. The same was true for large numbers of the remaining Austrian non-Jews. Several hundred others were either professional criminals, who played no role in Dachau anyway, or gypsies, who were hardly considered Austrians. The only outstanding Austrian group, which could be noticed everywhere, were the 2,000 nonpolitical Jews.

About 1,500 of them wore the red badge of Gestapo prisoners, as a result of which the political Jews, both Germans and Austrians, who wore the same color sign, would no longer be distinguished from them. And those Austrian Jews who wore the green and brown badges (professional criminals and criminal police prisoners) were really, in social background and behavior, much closer to the nonpoliticals with the red badge than to the other Austrians or Germans with the green and brown color signs. This was due to the way they had been selected rather than the fact that they were Jews, but the camp could not very well be expected to make such fine distinctions.

Of the 1,300 Austrian non-Jews, about 200 were Socialists and Communists, both old party and trade union men and underground fighters against the Dollfuss regime. Another 200 to 300 were conservative party leaders, high officials of the Dollfuss regime, police officers, or prominent members of conservative parties. In addition there were some 200 to 300 men with the red badge who were known for their anti-Nazi attitudes without having been prominent in political life, most of them business men, government and city employees, and so forth. Most of these people had been on the Nazi blacklists long in advance and were arrested soon after the Nazis came to power in Austria.

The 250 professional criminals were rounded up either in penitentiaries or from civil life, practically all of them with serious crimes and long years of incarceration behind them. When talking to these men, it was never quite clear why the Nazis had arrested them so soon after Austria was annexed—why these and not others, and why not more of them. They did not seem to be distinguished from any other criminals who were either left behind in the prisons or let alone in their civilian life.

Three hundred gypsies were rounded up in the part of Austria that had formerly been Hungarian, the Burgenland. Apparently they made up the whole adult male population of one tribe, led by their chieftain, an old man of more than 90 years, almost blind, who used to be led around by two sons who were well over 70. In the beginning they had difficulties wearing shoes, and during leisure time preferred to walk barefoot. Their barracks were opposite those of the Viennese Jews, and they used to go there and beg for bread or other food. Not much of course was to be had. When they got nothing, they became angry and repeatedly denounced the Jews to the commander as being "lazy," which did not help to improve relations. The commander did not pay any attention to these complaints.

Among the Austrian Jews only a small proportion were arrested in the same way as the non-Jews, that is, on the basis of political or other blacklists or on the basis of previous convictions. The bulk were arrested during the pogroms in Vienna known as the "Gestapo action of May 24, 1938." From this derived the camp expression "Action Jews," by which both administration and fellow prisoners designated them.

Without any previous warning or announcement, the police, SA, and SS began suddenly, on May 24, to arrest Jews in the streets of Vienna. Nobody knew why or for what purpose. The Nazis simply walked along the streets, entered public places, warehouses, restaurants, parks, and so forth, asking people if they were Jewish. If they admitted it, the Nazis took them. Others went through the Jewish districts and arrested shopkeepers, small tradesmen, and the like, or looked at the signs of professional men and arrested those with Jewish names. Lawyers, doctors, dentists, merchants, etc., were the main victims. Added to these were handpicked business and professional men, journalists, and so forth, and a great number of men who had been denounced by their neighbors.

The way in which these arrests were carried out influenced considerably the social composition of the group that finally was brought to Dachau. First, there were practically no industrial workers among them, because most of the arrests took place during daytime, when the workers were in the factories. Also, because men were selected by their names on business and professional signs, there was an exceedingly large proportion of these two categories. In addition, this method of arrest brought in only a very small proportion of politicals. Therefore the whole group was composed predominantly of those elements which had the least training in cooperative behavior, the most individualistic backgrounds, and the very smallest basis for adjustment to the crowded life of a concentration camp. Nor did the stay in the police prisons in Vienna prepare them, because most of them did not stay there for longer than a week or two. The first 600 came to Dachau three days after they had walked for the last time unmolested through the streets of the city.

In the camp they were crowded together in unfinished barracks, 100 to 150 in rooms designed for fifty, with no beds, no tables, no closets, no chairs, only a few straw bags, about one for every three men.

About 130 new capos and seniors had to be appointed within a couple of weeks to supervise these thousands of people. Practically everybody who had been in the camp for a very long time, or had ever had a similar function, got an appointment. (Thus the politicals could not exercise their usual influence upon the selection.)

Most of the appointees, in particular almost all the seniors, were political old-timers. The great majority were former workers, accustomed all their life to living with people who were trained in cooperation—in organizations, in workshops, and finally in concentration camp. Now suddenly they were faced with this crowd of uncooperative people, who were slow in organizing anything, untrained in hard labor, but accustomed to talking back when anyone bossed them around. Those of the seniors who for political or personal reasons abhorred beating a fellow prisoner, simply could not manage the discipline, and those who did beat their charges, soon became outcasts among their own friends. Some of them did not care, and after so many years of being underdogs, enjoyed their new position as bosses, beating their subordinates whenever there was a chance. But beating or no beating, the barracks did not become orderly.

The administration enjoyed this confusion. "Aren't the Jews an uncivilized pack, justifiably put in concentration camp! Just look at the mess in their barracks!" And they strapped the "messy" Jews on the stand and hanged them on the poles and thus proceeded with dispatch to teach them German orderliness.

The Jewish politicals from the "old" barracks took the initiative. Systematically, they searched from room to room for political people, and introduced them to their new seniors, who in most cases were their political brothers-in-creed. The seniors, glad to find a few people to whom they could speak in their own language, supported these men, and soon little political cliques ruled a number of these nonpolitical barracks and established a minimally routine organization. Through their close contact with the "old" barracks, the 2,000 men were to some extent linked up with the existing society of the camp, and the domination of the politicals was restored to a certain degree.

In the non-Jewish Austrian barracks, order was sooner established, in part because there were more political men among them, in part because there were fewer barracks and it was easier to exercise a certain amount of control from the German barracks. This was especially true because so many of the Austrians lived in German barracks anyway.

The efforts of the "old" barracks were less successful in barracks where the new seniors were not politicals or where, in spite of their being politicals, they had set up regimes of terror and mistreatment. There the dominating cliques originated in a different way. A few fawning creatures would flatter their way into the tyrant's heart, with or without money support, become his favorites, and boss the room. Or the whole barrack would become utterly corrupted within a short time. The newcomers, mentally afraid of the reign of terror that awaited them every night, and seeing that in other barracks life went on smoothly, tried to gain the favor of their seniors by bribes of all sorts. They filled their lockers with canteen goods and offered part of their coveted money to placate the almighty lords and kings. Some of the lords mellowed under the treatment, and only occasionally did their wrath flare up in the old fury. Others, realizing their opportunity, slackened the terror a little and used the marginal terror as an everlasting threat, which proved a wonderful "Open Sesame" to the Jews' cash. Some created a regular racket with weekly payments.

The administration enjoyed it as they enjoyed the whole mess. "The Jews *are* a corrupt pack, they *have* corrupted our Aryan society! Look how they corrupt our Aryan seniors!" And they hanged the Jews on the poles to save civilization from being corrupted. Occasionally they put one of the seniors in the punitive company, and sent with him a few of the Jews whom he had robbed. But that did not suffice to extinguish the spirit of money.

The political prisoners fought desperately against the corruption. Their reputation as a group was at stake. They talked to the seniors, and if that did not help, they ostracized them. In some cases this did not work, because the new kings, drunk with their power, thought they could easily forego membership in their own society. The politicals as a whole did not think so. They began to aid the Jews, political or not, and they plotted to bring about the fall of the self-styled kings. In quite a few cases they succeeded.

In the non-Jewish barracks, corruption played a much lesser role, partly because the politicals had the situation better in hand, partly because there was less money. The Jews, having such a large proportion of well-to-do people among them, received on the average considerably more than the others. Also there was the general prejudice that it is easy to make a Jew use his money for bribery, which caused seniors in Jewish barracks to try harder to get at it.

That was exactly what the administration wanted to happen—that the rest of the camp would turn against the Jews as being rich and corrupt.

However, it did not happen to any great extent. The only ones to turn against the Jews were either the corruptionists themselves, or those non-political capos who had been anti-Semites before and who had beaten and blackmailed German Jews before they even knew what an Austrian looked like. The only difference was that now they were able to carry on large-scale rackets, such as the one that Zock organized.

The politicals were not taken in. The overwhelming majority of them had not been anti-Semites before, and they did not become such now. They picked their political friends carefully and selected others from the great mass, as they had done with the Germans before. They despised the rest as crooks and lousy trash, but it did not seem relevant to them that this trash happened to be Jewish, because so were their accepted friends.

* * *

It proved more difficult to overcome the other major antagonism that followed in the wake of the "Austrian Invasion"—the national cleavage between Austrians and Prussians. Based on differences in history and cultural traditions, social and economic structures, and Prussian nationalism on one side and the more cosmopolitan outlook of the Austrians on the other, this division found its expression in an open animosity that rendered it difficult for large numbers of these people to get along.

It seems hopeless to attempt to portray these differences with stereotyped thumbnail sketches of "The Austrian" and "The Prussian." Each group within itself was as heterogeneous as any other nation, and whatever generalizations they used to justify their mutual animosity were based more on prejudices than on facts. Yet there were some differences visible in the behavior of the prisoners, which might well be traced back to differences in their education.

Prussian schools and traditions fostered zeal, ambition, and Spartan virtues, a rigidity in behavior which forbade the display of feelings and emotions. To fulfill one's duty and be proud of it, without wasting time asking for the reasons, was a chief virtue. These were taught not as common human values, but rather as "German" or even "Prussian" virtues. "Prussian consciousness of duty" (*Preussisches Pflichtbewusstsein*) was taught to children while they were still in grammar school. That it was "Germany's mission and destiny" to make the world a place worth living in was a stock phrase in German schools long before Hitler was born.

The Austrian tradition on the other hand fostered sentimentality, *"Gemütlichkeit,"* compassion, and sympathy for all that lives, with little concern about what national label it bore. To save face and suffer silently played a less important role in education. They did their duty as well as any Prussian, yet they didn't consider this quality specifically Austrian—rather they considered it the obligation of every honest man.

The Austrians were as proud as the Prussians of their national tradition, but the points which they emphasized were less aggressive. They were not proud of being good soldiers, of producing superior armaments, and winning wars; they were not even proud that their great philosophers and scientists had forced the world to think in ways they themselves discovered. They had always thought that they were good enough to defend themselves if necessary, and they knew that they had great thinkers from whom the world had learned much. In addition, the popular mind dwelt with affection on the fact that they have given the world the Viennese waltz and other music and dances, and these were things that could not be spread by force. In comparison with the rough Prussians, they considered themselves good-natured, and the fact that they were treated as such by others encouraged them to continue to teach friendliness as a virtue.

The "Prussian spirit" had been despised in Austria for centuries. When the Germans took Austria in 1938, the majority of the Austrian people felt that they had suffered not so much a defeat at the hands of fascism—of which they just had gone through a certain home-made, though weaker, brand during the past four years—but a defeat at the hands of the Prussian spirit. Only the leftists in Austria saw it primarily as a fascist victory; the conversations among the nonpolitical parts of the population saw it primarily as an attempt of the Prussian arch-enemy to extinguish Austrian mentality and culture.

That Nazism had swept the whole German nation, from the Rhine to the Memel, that some of its most important strongholds were in Bavaria, that a few of Hitler's leading politicians were by no means Prussians, and that he himself was born in Austria—none of this entered into the argument. The conquerors were "Prussians."

When the Austrian prisoners came to Dachau, they found something that looked utterly Prussian to them; the SS, though completely Bavarian, represented to them the utmost bestiality of the Prussian spirit. The old prisoners, who tried to outdo the administration in hard work and meticulous order, were nothing but "goddam Prussians." Their ambition was a freak of nature. How could a man work hard in a concentration camp for his own self-respect? What satisfaction could you get out of slaving for gangsters? This was unintelligible. Well, there's no understanding these creatures. They are and remain Prussians, even if you knock the daylights out of them.

It escaped their attention or at least their argument, that the majority of the politicals, whose ambition was so conspicuous, were not Prussian at all, but Bavarian—workers from Nuremberg and Augsburg and Munich, whose ways of life and even whose accents were more closely related to those of the Austrians than to those of the Germans. I even remember an ambitious deputy from the village next to Hitler's birthplace.[1]

That this apparently meaningless ambition was a struggle for political self-assertion, they could not possibly realize. Nor did they fully grasp the extent to which the nonpolitical Germans, many of whom were Prussians at that, were forced into line by the dominating politicals.

However, among the German Jews, with whom the Viennese Jews came into closer contact, the Prussians were in the majority. That made their zeal appear even more Prussian than that of the non-Jew. And it may well have been that their Prussian education wielded a certain influence, but as long as there were only Bavarians and Prussians, and both developed the same behavior on the basis of the same political ideology, the difference was fairly insignificant.

But now the Austrians called them Prussians, "lousy, goddam Prussians," who had servility to their overlords so deeply rooted in their bones that they couldn't get away from it even in a concentration camp— so stupid in fulfilling their duty that they could not stop it, even if the duty was nothing but the dictates of their arch-enemies.

And the Prussians retorted, "The Austrian is an intermediate step between the monkey and the Bavarian."[2] That was of course not meant as an insult to their Bavarian political friends but to the SS men, who were such an illiterate and uncultured breed as only Bavarian backwoods farmers could be. Scornfully, they made fun of the Austrian *Gemütlichkeit* and *Schlamperei,* their proverbial easygoing ways and sloppiness. They teased them for their amiable language, which overflowed with diminutives; they aped their *Bittschön* and *Dankschön* and *'tschuldigen schön*— "if you please" and "thank you ever so much" and "pardon me." Later,

---

1. Hitler's birthplace, Braunau am Inn, is near the Austro-Bavarian border.
2. Bismarck is often quoted as the originator of the phrase, "The Bavarian is an intermediate step between monkey and man."

in Buchenwald, what an Austrian reportedly had asked a capo became a camp slogan: *"Bittschön Herr Kapo, a leicht's Tragerl."* (Please, Herr Kapo, give me a light little handbarrow.) The melodiousness, the sentimentality, the grotesqueness of this sentence cannot be translated. This complete misunderstanding of the whole situation, the naive idea of placating one of those beasts by calling him "Herr Kapo," the diminutive *"Tragerl"* for the instrument of torture, the handbarrow, drew laughter and scorn from the Germans, to whom a *"Trage"* is a useful, if hated, instrument of serious labor.

The Germans felt that all their prejudices against the sloppy Austrians were justified. It did not occur to them that most of the Austrians simply could not do the work, even if they wanted to, because there were so many old men among them, and so many who had never handled a tool heavier than a pan or a scalpel or a pair of scissors. And it did not occur to them that these people, the great majority of them lacking any fighting ideology, simply could not see any reason for working hard, even if they had been able to do so.

The administration was faced with the same problem from another angle. They tried very hard to make the Austrians the same type of prisoners as the Germans were—orderly and disciplined and hard working.

The Austrians could not be remodeled in this fashion. They were fully convinced that order and discipline are good only in order to achieve a goal. If there is no goal worth working for, just take it easy. They could not be taught the sense of order for its own sake, which was so well-developed among the Germans, whether they happened to be SS men or prisoners. It proved impossible to teach masses of Austrians to march like well-fed and drilled soldiers. Half a mile away one could tell an Austrian from a German marching column. The fact that many Austrians who had formerly been soldiers were used to different military commands helped to increase the difficulties.

And they could not be taught the basic law of the concentration camp—always be on the move. They simply were not always on the move. There was not sufficient supervision for so many thousands of men, and in addition to that the Austrians developed a mastery in shirking that aroused both the contempt and envy of their German fellow prisoners.

I remember how a fellow Austrian, one morning, taught me one of the basic laws of shirking. We were working in a ditch when suddenly he invited me for a stroll through the camp. I thought he was crazy, but he kept urging me to come along. Finally I climbed out of the ditch to join him. He looked me up and down, critically and severely, shook his head and said in a fatherly voice, "Where is your shovel?" "My shovel?" "Man, are you dumb. Do you really think you can go strolling without a shovel?" He was right. Nobody questioned us as long as we had our shovels on our shoulders—probably we were about some important job.

The most important thing, however, was not their inventive genius for shirking, but their passivity toward the camp as a whole. Hundreds and hundreds of them, working together in a gravel pit for instance, shoveled around in their slow and uninterested way, skeptically scratching the surface, obviously convinced of the absolute meaninglessness of their actions. Others, again by the hundred, dragged their way along with wheelbarrows, slowly, cautiously, even if the box was empty. And if one did run he was most certainly asked by another, "What's your hurry? There won't be a train to Vienna for another year." Or, "Are you afraid you won't have carried enough gravel before you kick the bucket?" Or, "Don't you think you can die without this damned gravel being moved over a few yards?" Or, "Gee, is that man busy! Must be his own gravel!" A man who would tell another, "Don't throw bricks that way, you'll break them," would be asked," Are they yours? No? Then why do you worry?"

The SS guards and their officers had busy days. They chased around like hunted beasts and tried to keep up with the situation. They beat and cursed and kicked people and trampled them to death. They hit them with sticks and threw stones at them. They shouted their throats hoarse and ran out of breath. The prisoners got scared to death when the fury broke loose, but as soon as the officer went around the next corner, they simply stopped working.

The capos began to despair. They wrote reports upon reports, and the Austrians were given the whip by the dozen and hung on the poles and screamed. But on returning to work they were as lazy as before, as soon as the shock was over.

They realized that there was no use working fast, the guards wouldn't stop beating you anyway. They beat you because they liked to beat you, all you could do was avoid attracting attention. If some prisoners worked fast, those who worked slowly would be conspicuous. If all three thousand worked slowly, several hundred in each place, then it was no longer conspicuous to work slowly. Mistreatment wouldn't decrease for that reason, but it wouldn't increase too much either, because the SS man wouldn't beat you more than he enjoyed, and he would not beat you less, no matter what you did. Your work had nothing to do with it.

And they also realized: If they want to kill all of us, we can't prevent them from doing so. But anything else they can't do to all of us at the same time, we are too many. They can't whip more than a dozen every day and they can't hang more than a dozen on the poles, otherwise their schedule gets out of gear. And an officer can only beat so many people every morning or he will get tired before noon.

It was similar in the barracks. They welcomed the help of the old political prisoners in organizing their routine, as long as such routine related to the barest necessities of life. But beyond this minimum they rejected it. It was quite clear to them that they would never be able to achieve the smooth functioning of the political barracks. Any attempt to do so would leave them completely at the mercy of the hundreds of non-cooperating people among themselves, and of any SS man who took offense at the slightest sign of disorder. So they did not try it in the first place. And they told each other—if they want us to do punitive drill, they will do so whether our barracks look like doll houses or not. There is nothing we can do about it.

Lacking the ability to organize themselves, they discovered the tremendous power of disorganization. Many of them understood it quite consciously, and the great mass felt it without verbalizing it: This concentration camp, which tortured them with discipline in the minutest details, could be fought only with one weapon—absolutely passive disorder. They demonstrated to the astonished camp what had never been seen before and never imagined by men who had lived all their lives with organization and cooperation—that unorganized large-scale disorder could be as powerful and as active a force as the best organization and cooperation.

They were no heroes in suffering. They screamed and yelled when beaten, and begged, "Please don't, please don't." But they were heroes in sticking to their ideology, and that made them invulnerable. However, lacking as a group any of the high ideals, and being stuck to their self-image of as *"Gemütliche Österreicher"* made them highly vulnerable. They were whipped and beaten and blood ran in streams.

But they were the real victors in Dachau in the summer of 1938. The SS men might work themselves to the bone, and the capos might bounce around like rubber balls, be everywhere at the same time, harry, hurry, beg, beseech, curse, beat, report, insult, and injure. They were absolutely helpless against this mass passivity. You can kill a jelly-fish, but you can't lick him.

And slowly, slowly but irresistibly, the work tempo slackened. When we compared the hell we had gone through in April during the destruction of the old dungeon with what was going on in the gravel pits and barracks yards in July, we couldn't believe our eyes. Within a few weeks the famous "Dachauer Tempo" had died away, faded out, disappeared under the mass passivity of 3,000 Austrians. Dachau was licked in Dachau.

Theirs was not a political victory nor had it been a political fight. They had not been engaged in the long-term struggle against fascism, only in the struggle against the working and living conditions of the concrete camp in which they happened to be. They had no ideological concepts except perhaps not to become slaves of the German brand, with the law of subservience written into their every thought. Where the political prisoners accepted death willingly, as long as it was death in action, they only wanted to survive. They did not want to die as heroes. All they wanted was to live a few more years, perhaps with their wives and children. Hundreds of them were exactly what was known as the "Viennese cafe Jews," and a sarcastic allusion to this became a camp slogan: "A Jew belongs in a cafe, not in a concentration camp."

No other goal had led them but the natural drive for self-preservation. It was a triumph not of the human spirit but of human existence as such.

When finally there was not enough work to do and some of the prisoners were left in the barracks every day, they added this incidental fact to the joy of their victory. They developed a cockiness they had not possessed before. And when later they were confronted with the horrible conditions in Buchenwald, their first reaction was, "We finished off Dachau, we will finish off Buchenwald." And they set to work and they did it. For some technical reasons, roll call was delayed the day after our arrival. That was taken as a good omen: " We have hardly arrived and the camp is already out of gear." Again men lost limbs and life, were beaten and punished, but this mass of nonpolitical Austrians changed the spirit of Buchenwald as they had changed the spirit of Dachau.

It took a long time before the cleavage between Austrians and Germans was overcome, at least to the point where it consisted of nothing more than slightly benevolent contempt on both sides. The Austrians began to understand in part the political concept of their German brothers, they respected them for their honesty and courage. As to their stupid ambition, they shrugged their shoulders: "Prussians, what else can you expect of them."

And the German political prisoners, after having seen before their amazed eyes this incredible picture of a victory won by poor wretches who screamed on the stand and whined on the poles, began to understand that this was battle and action as well as their own. They were still contemptuous of the dull and unintelligent creatures who had won it, but their contempt became good-natured and friendly, a sort of fatherly condescension. Never would they let themselves sink so low as to adopt this passivity as their own method, but they respected it as a method of the weak. And when a German political prisoner teased one of them— "Hi, brother Austrian, want a *leicht's Tragerl?*"—this was a battle cry as good as any circulating among fighters on the same side of a barricade.

Political Prisoners versus Professional Criminals

At the time of our arrival in Buchenwald, the struggle between the "reds" and the "greens" was already in full swing. The "greens" were greatly outnumbered by the "reds," but they still held the most important official appointments. Places changed hands as the result of all sorts of intrigue, pressure, treachery, betrayal, and corruption. The "greens" used every opportunity to play a hated "red" into Rödl's hands, and the "reds" did not fail to retaliate in kind.

Here is one example of how it was done. The leading man among the politicals was a former Communist member of the Reichstag, Karl Bartel. He was senior of a Jewish barrack, and had in his barrack detail a few "greens" who had been appointed by Rödl. One morning these men were enjoying themselves, munching smuggled food without Bartel's knowing it. Camp senior Hubert Richter, himself a "green," saw them, went for Rödl, showed him the men eating through a window, then asked for the removal of Bartel as a barrack senior. Rödl instead, apparently in order not to upset the balance of power, gave Bartel "twenty-five" for not having reported the case.

Of the more important positions, the professional criminals held all three places as camp seniors (though two of them wore a red badge). They also held positions as barracks and room seniors and barracks details in their own barracks, as well as in most of the asocial and in some of the Jewish barracks, and as capos for most of the unskilled, many of the semi-skilled, and a few of the skilled labor groups.

The political prisoners held about half the places as seniors and barracks details, most of them in either political or Jewish barracks. They were capos for practically all the skilled but almost none of the unskilled labor, and they shared with the "greens" the positions as capos in the semi-skilled groups.

Places in the various offices, such as the registry, mail office, bureau of construction, and clerk's room, were about equally divided. So were the various special jobs, such as plumbers, mechanics in the bath, electricians, etc. The infirmary was almost exclusively in the hands of the "reds," and so was the clothing department. Places in the repair shops were divided, the "reds" having at their disposal legal ways to bring people there through the infirmary, the "greens" controlling the illegal methods of forged certificates and bribery.

The "reds" had most of the working places in the special workshops, such as the carpenter shop, sawmill, pigsty, and riding school; in addition they held the great majority of all skilled jobs. The "greens," in close association with the asocials, dominated the smuggling routes inside and into the camp, as well as the black market in canteen goods. The camp canteener, chief of all barracks canteeners was a "green."

The whole scene in Buchenwald changed rapidly after the November pogroms. Eleven thousand newly arrested Jews were crowded into five temporary barracks, erected on the roll-call square and fenced off from the rest of the camp by barbed wire. They lived under the most horrible conditions that could be imagined: 2,200 in one barrack, the whole furniture of which consisted of five tiers of shelves, running along the walls. The distance between shelves was about three feet, which hardly left room enough to sit up. To get in, the men had to crawl in on their bellies, head first. Those in the uppermost tiers used rough ladders loosely nailed together. There they lay, huddled against each other, 440 men in each tier, trying to keep warm in a barrack that had no floor, except for the clay on which it stood, and no windows except for a few holes sawed out of the walls. A small stove in the center gave no warmth.

There were no hygienic facilities. One latrine, hastily dug out behind the barracks, served 11,000 men. Six faucets which gave water for a few minutes each day were the only means of keeping clean. No drinking water. (The rest of us could at least get hold of some illegally.) Almost no food. That most of them stayed alive can only be ascribed to the amazing ability of the human body to survive on less food than even the Nazis were willing to supply. And the "November Jews" had no medical care except for what was smuggled to them. Treatment in the infirmary was barred to Jews after the pogroms.

When they were delivered to the camp by the thousands, there was not time enough to register their names. Men died by the dozen without their names being known; living and dead got mixed up in a horrible confusion. Men died in their shelves, to be noticed only when the stench aroused their neighbors' indignation. Wives received bodies or ashes allegedly belonging to men who had already returned or who were still in the camp—well, who the hell can keep track of them, they die so fast you can't even count them. Others could not be released because they did not exist at all as far as the camp in which they suffered and died was concerned; there were no records that they had been arrested.

We in our crowded barracks, clad in rags, underfed, and overworked, were envied by those poor devils as if we were kings. Gratefully they thanked us for everything that could possibly be smuggled to them; a glass of water, a bite of bread might save a life. So might a piece of toilet tissue that served as a bandage.

The administration had had no time to take away their money and other belongings. These they stuffed away in their civilian clothes—no uniforms were available for them—for future scrutiny. But here the professional criminals proved equal even to the Nazis. They descended upon the Jews like vultures, beginning to devour them while they were still alive. Before Rödl even knew what was going on, they had already robbed them of a fantastic amount of their money.

The controllers and camp seniors had free admission to the camp behind the fence, and they were supposed to see that nobody else entered. They let slip through those "greens" with whom they organized the racket. They began to smuggle food and medical supplies in addition to the smuggling that went on with help of the politicals who established their own channels. The politicals and hundreds of nonpoliticals, both Jews and non-Jews, including even some of the "greens," gave their help for free to save the threatened lives of the Jews. But most of the "greens" sold their goods for amounts for which the word "price" is a misnomer. Many of the unfortunate Jews were made to pay 10, 50, 100 and even 1,000 mark bills for a drink of water, a bar of chocolate, a bandage, an aspirin, a roll of toilet paper. Money had lost its value. What counted was the number of bills. Do you want to give me one hundred marks for a piece of candy and perhaps an apple? You'd better, because Rödl will take it from you for nothing.

There was so much money that suddenly corruption passed beyond the barbed wire. SS men got involved, receiving big bribes for changing the paper money, which could not be used in the canteen because only coins up to five marks were legal tender in the camp.[3]

---

3. It is impossible to say how much they got, but conservative estimates of people with some insight into the story run around 150,000 marks. This means that 150,000 marks rolled around in the camp of 10,000 prisoners, completely beyond the control of the administration, and most of it must have been in or run through the hands of not more than 500 people.

The most fantastic things happened, things that could never be explained in ordinary terms. For example, anyone who left his barrack after "lights out" was shot to death without warning. But there were nights when the Herren capos, the real gangsters among them, sat out in tool sheds in the forest, playing cards and winning and losing hundreds and thousands of marks a night. Alcohol was smuggled into the camp. Some SS men in the kitchen were involved along with the milkman who delivered to the SS kitchen. He wound up as a prisoner among us. Koch's famous after-New Year's celebration with mass whipping occurred in that connection.

Rödl fought a terrific battle for this money. He did not want the "greens" to have it, because it destroyed discipline and morale in the camp. And he wanted to have it for himself. This money had not gone through any records, it was just as good as if he had found it in the street.

One night he gave us a little speech. "There is Jewish money in this camp. Jewish money stinks. This stink must be rooted out from the camp. I am not going to rest, until I have torn out of your dirty claws the last penny of Jewish money, even though it may take weeks." The "greens" apparently figured that Jewish money would not stink less in Rödl's dirty claws and it might just as well remain in theirs for that matter. And there it remained.

For weeks and weeks investigations proceeded, and discipline went to pieces in the camp. Rödl made a desperate attempt to re-establish it by introducing new punishments. The attempt to outlaw prisoners was made during that time, and Hubert Richter invented the black dungeon. People were locked up there for any sort of racket that was discovered. But the big money was not found.

One night during roll call, Rödl suddenly ordered, "Every man cross his arms over his chest." A company of SS men came in, searching every one of the 10,000 men for money. As the search proceeded, the first culprits were reported—those with more than the permitted ten marks in their pockets, men with 11.25, 10.50, 12 marks. Angrily Rödl told them over the loudspeaker not to bother with small transgressions. Then they found a few men with 20 marks or so, but it turned out that they were table canteeners who simply had not settled yet yesterday's accounts with their clients. Rödl chased them back. He was after the "real" money. But when the search was over, not a single man had been found with an amount worth mentioning. It was a mystery who had tipped off the "greens." The SS men who made the search did not know about it until they were on the square. It seemed an almost unavoidable conclusion that some of the higher officers must have been involved.

Finally Koch unraveled the mystery. Two men whom he caught drunk were whipped into confession. From there he traced the affair through the camp to the barrack of the "greens." Once he had got that far, the going was easier; the "greens" betrayed each other by the dozen. The whole barrack was involved. The controllers were unmasked as the leading crooks and gangsters. They had drunk and smuggled and stolen and robbed and blackmailed; they had committed and perfected and covered up every crime on the books.

When the investigators got hold of the camp canteen man, SS men became involved, because through his hands the greatest amounts of paper money had left the camp. One morning he was missing at roll call. At the familiar order—"Barrack details to the forest, search for the bird"—the barrack detail of the "greens" went straight to one of the tool sheds. Lo and behold, there the corpse was hanging, in a hut that was no higher than he was tall. Both Rödl and the camp took it for granted that the "greens" had hanged him to prevent further confessions. Rödl even asked for a commission from the court in Weimar to investigate the murder. But nothing ever came of it.

Finally, Hubert Richter got involved. He turned out to be the chief gangster of them all. This was no surprise to the camp, but it was to Rödl. He had placed great confidence in this man, who had been so effective in mistreating and killing other prisoners, particularly Jews, and who had hanged Peter Forster and his companion on the gallows. The second hangman, Osterloh, barrack senior of the "greens," was also in the money racket.

Without Richter's knowing it, the administration got wind of where his "cabinet" was and searched it. "Cabinets" were in themselves nothing unusual; every now and then one was discovered. They were cavities in the huge brick piles, cleverly constructed and hidden, where the Herren capos occasionally went for a puff on a cigarette or for a nap. But Richter's cabinet was something extraordinary: He had a bathtub in it! After having soiled his hands killing other prisoners, his highness had taken baths! In this cabinet 2,000 marks were found.

Then the administration threw Richter into the black dungeon. From time to time they took him out and tortured him. One evening during roll call he got the most horrible "twenty-five" a man ever got. He roared like an ox when they hit him. He shook off the SS men who beat him, sprang up with the heavy wood stand strapped to his chest and staggered across the square, shouting, "Shoot me, shoot me!" But they brought him down again and continued the beating. When it was over, Johnny with his boyish voice lisped, "That was only the first installment, Richter."

And finally Richter broke down. One of the most pitiful sights I have ever seen was when he led the commanders down through the camp to barrack 45. Koch, Rödl, Johnny, all the higher officers were in the procession. Richter could hardly walk by himself. But the SS officer from the dungeon whipped him along the street. His face was ashen, and his eyes were sunken like those of a death's skull. He looked utterly shabby and pitiful, this powerful king and murderer.

In barrack 45, he showed the high overlords the hiding places. A window panel, an old shoe, a table leg, a straw bag, a glass of jam, and similar places. Thousands of marks were found there. Yet it was only a fraction of what they were after.

One morning Richter was found dead in the black dungeon, his own invention. It was such a dramatic act of justice, that it would look cheap in a movie. But the camp enjoyed it as if it were the most wonderful fairy tale.

Richter's death however did not solve the problem. There still was money and corruption.

The political prisoners saw that their time was ripe. They had been careful not to get involved in the robbery and crimes. They stressed their own clean hands—and this time they covered up those among themselves whose hands were not so clean. It was important to stand out as honest against the professional criminals.

As one after another of the mighty "greens" was felled by the investigations, the "reds" took over position after position. Here a capo, there a barrack leader, several room seniors. The "greens" did not dare to get their men in.

Then on January 30, 1939, the big change occurred. It was more radical than anyone had expected. Each and every "green" dignitary, room, barrack, camp senior, controller, and all other privileged men were unseated and sent to work in the quarry. In their places, politicals were appointed. Karl Bartel was made first camp senior.

The idea apparently was that the politicals would be less corruptible, and that, if led by a man to whom they were willing to listen, they would stamp out the corruption in the camp. This speculation proved right. Within a surprisingly short time, Bartel brought corruption down to its "normal" level, below which no influence whatsoever could bring it in view of the prevalent living conditions. But in addition he achieved something which Rödl had not bargained for—he stopped the worst terror of the capos. Beating and mistreatment decreased considerably. He himself never touched a man. Yet his word was obeyed by everyone, and he had much more power than Richter had ever been able to achieve.

But with this change followed another, more unexpected and more radical. In order that the new setup might not be corrupted again by Jewish money, Rödl removed from the Jewish barracks all non-Jewish officials and appointed Jews as seniors, barbers, clerks, and canteeners. And within each major working group a Jewish capo was appointed who was responsible for the Jews, and who was subordinate to the non-Jewish capo of the same group.

Since all this had taken place on the anniversary of Hitler's rise to power, it was immediately dubbed the "day of the Jews' rise to power." This nickname perhaps expressed best in a single phrase the full force of the change. Whole groups that had been masters and underdogs changed roles. The unofficial society of the prisoners withstood the shakeup better. After all, large numbers of the prisoners had always considered the politicals as their true leaders and the rule of the "greens" an artificially bolstered regime of subhuman creatures.

About 140 Jewish capos and seniors were appointed. There was no time to search for capable ones, and there was no time to search for special bloodhounds. Everyone who had ever held a similar position in concentration camp or in civilian life was appointed. Many of the new appointees were nonpoliticals; there were even some old Jewish professional criminals. But the politicals immediately assumed the leadership. Their leader went from barrack to barrack the same night, called out the new dignitaries, and told them, "We are not going to tolerate any corruption among the Jewish capos and seniors. We will not shrink from finishing off or handing over to Koch every one of you who proves to be a crook." And an amazing thing happened: Not a single one dared to answer, "Who are you to issue orders?" I happened to be visiting the barrack where this leader himself had become the senior, when he rose and made a similar speech to the new capos who had been appointed from his barrack. Without naming a single one of them, he frightened them all. Shyftan, the chief corruptionist from Dachau, shifted uneasily about on his chair. He had become capo of a large group. But the speech proved effective. Shyftan could not be prevented from taking money, but he was prevented from making a big racket of it.

The new Jewish appointees were less violent than the old capos and seniors. Some did not want to beat their fellow Jews; others were afraid of future revenge, as nobody expected the new order to last very long.

Rumors circulated every now and then that by the following week the whole thing would be reversed. But when I left the camp four months later, the Jews were still in charge.

As they began to feel more secure in their positions, those who were crooks and gangsters began to follow their own impulses, and beat and blackmailed their subordinates. But the rule of the politicals among them and over the whole camp kept terror and corruption within relatively narrow bounds.

The professional criminals fought to regain their power. A few of them, like Berg, the killer, had been left in power or were reinstalled because they were not easy to replace as slave drivers. Control had to be maintained by "greens" or former SS men or similar people, because the politicals simply would not file reports. A few of the former capos and controllers saw their chance; they made confessions by which they sought to involve leading "reds." They brought about the fall of one of the new deputy camp seniors and one or two capos.

One morning the former control was reinstated. A shudder ran through the camp. We knew what could be expected from them now. That morning I was working in an invalid stone carrier column. Slowly we dragged along through the forest, hardly bothered by anybody, since our bandages were visible at a great distance. Suddenly Rudi, former chief of the control, appeared. He made us stop, form ranks, and begin a punitive drill. After a few minutes of "up-down" and "crawl on your belly," he made a little speech to us. " For this time I will let it go at that. But let it serve you as a notice and warning. From now on *we* have the power again. We'll knock hell out of you. We will show you who is the master in this camp." It was the most impressive statement of consciousness of the power and "we"-feeling of a group that I had ever heard in the camp.

But the episode was soon over. After a few days the old control was withdrawn again, new men were appointed, and Rudi, along with others, was returned to the dungeon. Rudi himself was involved in a homosexual affair, which the politicals transmitted to the administration, in order to finish him. When he left the dungeon soon afterwards as a corpse, the power of the "greens" was definitely broken.

Chapter 19

Why Don't They Hit Back?

People who listen to reports about the concentration camps ask again and again, "If someone mistreated me like that, I would strike back. I would rather die than not hit back. Why didn't they hit back in concentration camp? Weren't they men?" They didn't hit back. Still they were men.

The prisoner is expected to hit back in anger, revenge, self defense, defense of his honor, and for a number of other reasons. There is a simple explanation why the vast majority didn't hit back. The camps were under martial law. The slightest sign of resistance was immediately answered by a bullet through the head. As in so many other situations, the majority of men preferred to live, no matter what they had to suffer. The outsider who asks, "Why don't they hit back?" usually realizes that. What he really means is, "Aren't there any exceptions? Aren't there at least some real men, who don't count the odds and who strike back even in the face of certain death?" There were real men like that in concentration camps. But they didn't strike back.

Hundreds of the second-termers, after having gone through the hell of a concentration camp once, returned to their underground movements, knowing that if they got caught, they would be brought back to camp and to circumstances in which a bullet through the head would seem like a welcome relief. They certainly were "real men" by any standards. But in concentration camp they didn't strike back.

Others, leftists and liberals, sometimes conservatives, fought on against the Nazi regime, under the constant threat of winding up in a concentration camp or of getting their heads chopped off. But in the camp they didn't strike back.

There were others—similar to most of the people who ask, "Why don't they hit back?"—who had never dealt with politics. They had been courageous all their lives, had gone through serious danger, professional and otherwise, without counting the odds. They had developed very rigid concepts of honor, and if anybody in the outside world would have dared to slap their faces, they would have struck back immediately and with a vengeance. But in concentration camp they didn't.

Nor did the professional criminals, many of whom had brutal and impulsive dispositions, men who had killed and mutilated in anger and excitement. Again, for the majority it was the martial law, the threat of the bullet, that prevented them from striking back. But the question remains, "Weren't there any exceptions?"

I do not know of any exceptions. I was in two of the largest camps for fourteen months. I have met dozens of people who passed through practically all the German concentration camps.

Still, there may be some cases of which I do not know. But it seems that not much would be proven if, among the hundreds of thousands of prisoners who passed through the camps during all these years, finally one or another could be found who was shot because he hit back. The general statement would still hold: In concentration camp they didn't hit back.

There are cases known of people who hit back at the SS men when they were arrested or during their first hearings at SS or police headquarters. I knew a man in Dachau who hit back at the SS men in the famous headquarters in Berlin, Columbia Haus. He was almost torn to pieces. Ernst Winkler, in his book *Four Years of Nazi Torture*,[1] tells about his own similar experience when he struck back during his first hearing. But these things happened before the people were brought to concentration camp.

From what knowledge I have from people who were still in concentration camps when the war broke out, and from reports in the American press after the liberation of the prisoners in the various camps, it seems that even after the beginning of the war, there were practically no cases of prisoners hitting back in concentration camps. Not even from the worst annihilation camps, where people were gassed and burned by the thousands and ten thousands, were there reports indicating that the victims resisted their impending death or their general mistreatment.

---

1. Ernst Winkler, *Four Years of Nazi Torture* (New York, 1942), pp. 50ff.

Detailed newspaper reports of the mistreatment undergone by American and British prisoners of war in German concentration camps—especially in Buchenwald—never mention any resistance on the part of the beaten prisoners. It seems that these men, when put into concentration camps, accepted the situation in a way similar to the German civilians, and I am inclined to believe that they did so for the same reasons set forth in this chapter.

The reasons camp prisoners refrained from hitting back are not quite the same as those for which a man in the outside world would accept a beating. It was neither simple cowardice nor resignation and indifference, and of course it had nothing whatsoever to do with the prisoner's stolidly accepting what he considered a well-deserved punishment.

One possible way to arrive at an explanation for this behavior is to follow the prisoner step by step on his way from "civilian" society to camp society, and watch him go through the metamorphosis from "man" to "camp prisoner."

Individual Prisoners Enter the Camp

Individual prisoners usually come from penitentiaries, prisons, or courts. Ordinarily they are not delivered directly to the camp but, for administrative reasons, have to pass through several prisons, until after several days, sometimes two weeks, they arrive at the city near the camp. On this transport they are guarded by regular police or prison personnel, whose only concern is to deliver their charges safely to the next station. There is practically no pushing or beating on the transport.

From the city—in our case, Munich or Weimar—a prison van is dispatched to the camp once or twice a week, usually with six or eight, seldom with more than ten prisoners from all over the country.

Up to the moment when they leave the van, the prisoners are in the hands of civilian authorities, even though legally they already are prisoners of the Gestapo. Now they are handed over to the SS guards of the concentration camp. This is the moment when they lose their status as human beings and become something different—"prisoners under protective custody" (*Schutzhaftgefangene*) or "camp prisoners."

Without any transition, they are faced with a completely new world. In the greatest hurry they are chased through an administrative procedure, which, in spite of all the beating, works as smoothly as if it were the most natural thing in the world.

Guards swarm around the prisoners, striking, hitting, beating, and shouting that they will teach them how to behave; cursing, swearing, kicking them with their boots, and occasionally threatening them with a bullet from an openly carried gun. It is like being thrown into a witch's cauldron. Nobody understands what is going on, why he is beaten or yelled at, what he has done wrong or how. All he sees is that everybody gets beaten no matter what they do, and that the same is the case for other prisoners who apparently have been there for a longer time.

During all this time, it never happens that an individual prisoner faces an individual guard. Instead, the small group of prisoners simultaneously face a sort of many-faced and organized mechanism, that pushes, shouts, beats, and hits. Not for a single moment does it occur to the prisoner to strike back. He is completely occupied with getting through the procedure, and he is overwhelmed by the smoothness with which it turns. If he needs an additional explanation, he can always get it from the SS man's gun, but ordinarily he grasps the rules of this mechanism by himself.

After evening roll call, the newcomers are led to their barracks, where they make contact with the old prisoners. During the night they recover to some degree, and in the morning it all looks like a bad dream. The newcomer feels himself a man again, though in a strange world. Perhaps he feels ashamed for having been beaten and had his face slapped. His desire to keep his status as a man, and if need be to defend it, has not yet been entirely broken.

But it has to be broken. Otherwise the administration could not keep thousands of prisoners together under conditions which, in ordinary prisons, would lead to riot and mutiny every day. The newcomer has to understand that he cannot escape, nor resist, nor attack, nor have any chance to feel himself a man. He has to learn this lesson: Five hundred prisoners at work, guarded by twenty riflemen, are not 500 men opposing twenty men, with the twenty rifles as the deciding factor. They are 500 numbers who carry out orders, while the rifle men happen to be around to watch that nobody is lazy or perhaps crazy enough to run off.

They are taught this lesson.

Every morning when the camp marches out to work, the order is given: "Newcomers and retransferred step forward."[2] They are either sent to Capo Sterzer in the gravel pit, who will surely knock every thought of

---

2. "Retransferred" means camp prisoners who have been away for some time, for example, for a court hearing.

resistance out of them, or they are dealt with by a few officers, usually one for every two or three men.

These officers mistreat the newcomers systematically for several days. Each of the poor devils will break down many times during the ordeal. He will faint over his wheelbarrow, topple over under the burden of heavy stones, collapse while being hit over the head with a club. But he will not be allowed to stay down. The officer's boot will bring him to life again, and if that does not do the trick, a jar of water, poured over his head, surely will. Sometimes it won't.

The worst comes when the man says, "I can't go on." Then the officer really crashes down on him, and teaches him the lesson for which he has gone through this whole thing. "'You cannot' means 'you don't want to.' But you must!" He will be trampled upon again and again, he will be beaten and driven, and when he breaks down he will be chased up again, and always he will be told, "Remember, 'you cannot' means 'you don't want to.' But you must."

There was a dreadful scene once when an officer kept shouting this lesson at a man. The man simply did not get up. The officer taught him more and more, with curses and kicks, with water and boots. But the man did not grasp the lesson. He was dead.

After a few days with the officers or with Sterzer, the new men are assumed to have learned their lesson. They are now expected to behave as depersonalized numbers with no more thought of resistance left in them. They are now attached to regular working groups, like the old prisoners. The initiation is over.

Large Groups Enter the Camp

When the prisoners began to arrive by the hundred and by the thousand, this method of careful individual mistreatment to break the personality and resistance of the newcomers could no longer be applied. Something new had to be found, which would achieve the same effect in one decisive blow, with no waste of time.

A method was found, and the blow was dealt.

Large transports of prisoners were usually brought directly to the concentration camp by train, guarded by one or two companies of SS men who were sent from the camp for the purpose. These SS men knew how to deal with prospective camp prisoners. They knew that they had to teach them their lesson in one single night on the train. They did it.

* * *

The 150 prisoners with whom I went to Dachau on April 1, 1938, were the first Austrians sent to German concentration camps.[3] After that thousands made the same trip. All of us saw and experienced scenes of horror, hell at its deepest, where the last idea of humanity died away with the cries of tortured prisoners and the curses and abuses of their tormentors. Yet we all agree on this: There was nothing like the night on the train from Vienna to Dachau.

In the police prison we had been under the supervision of Austrian police. Although a great number of policemen had already been Nazis before the Anschluss, we were not mistreated, except when some prisoners were taken to hearings before the German Gestapo and SS. But these were rare exceptions. Most of us were sent to concentration camp without any hearing at all.

One evening some of us were taken out of our cells and collected in other cells. Next evening we were ordered out, led through the vast building, over staircases and corridors to a back exit. There we were loaded into prison vans.

I was the last man in the line. In front of me marched Dr. Bick, Director General of the Austrian National Library, a tall man of about sixty-five, who walked through the lane of staring and sneering policemen with an admirable calm and dignity. Just before we left the building, a young policeman caught sight of him and said, "Look at him! Looks like the head of a department." And he spat right into his face. Dr. Bick did not turn an eyelash.

We entered the vans, and as soon as I was inside, we rolled off. There we sat in the darkness, crowded, sweating, and hardly daring to speak. We tried to guess where we were going. Through the little window we could watch the van crossing the "Ring," then turning up Mariahilfer Strasse. This is one of Vienna's main thoroughfares, leading up to the Western Railroad Station. Suddenly we realized we were on our way to Dachau. All talk ceased. We were on our way to hell.

At a back entrance of the station, the car stopped. The door was thrown open, somebody yelled at us to get the hell out of the van. Half-blind after the darkness in the car, we jumped out and were immediately chased through narrow gauntlets of SS men. They shouted and cursed at us, kicked

---

3. A few days earlier the two Hohenberg princes and one Hapsburg archduke had been sent there.

us with their boots, hit us with the butts of their rifles, tripped us, trampled upon us, kicked us up again, and made us run for the railroad cars.

And we ran for dear life. None of us had time to think about hitting back. All we could do was to try to avoid their rifle butts. With all the hell they raised, they might have scared the life out of a hero. Panting for breath and trembling with excitement or fear, we climbed the stairs up to the cars. In the corridor there were more SS men, more yelling and beating. Each one of us ran into the first compartment with an empty seat. In came the next man, and the next, and the next, til all eight seats were taken.

After the last man, an SS man stepped into the entrance, in full battle dress, with steel helmet, rifle, side arms. He gave orders: Sit up straight! Open your eyes! Shut your mouths! Put your hands on your knees! Do this! Do that! Don't move or you will be shot! Don't look out of the window or you will be shot! Don't open your mouth or you will be shot! Don't do this! Don't do that! You will be shot! You will be shot! Do this! Do that! You will be shot! Don't do this! You will be shot!

And each one of us obediently did what was ordered.

This was the moment when the man in us changed into an automaton that carried out orders.

I remember telling myself, "If they intended killing all of us, why should they put us on a train?" I ventured a look at my neighbors. Most of them were old men. I told myself that I was in better physical shape than the others, and therefore probably had the best chance of getting through this night.

We heard the order passed through, "Don't let them fall asleep." We were ordered to stare into the eyes of the man opposite us. All night long I stared into Dr. Bick's eyes. When I seemed to be falling asleep. He gently shoved his foot against mine, and I did him the same service.

The torture went on all night long. Exercises, drill, invectives, slaps in the face, beatings with rifles, kicks with boots, interspersed with curious questions about our professions. One of the young hooligans slapped Dr. Bick's face and then asked him what he had been before. Dr. Bick answered in a firm and fearless voice, "Intellectual laborer (*Geistiger Schwerarbeiter*). I have worked sixteen and eighteen hours a day." Only those who know the Nazis' contempt for intellectuals can appreciate the grim humor with which the old man made a fool of the Nazi boy with a rifle in his hand.

In another car Herr Schmitz, fascist mayor of the City of Vienna, had to bear the brunt. A secretary of state, warned by Schmitz's fate, answered that he was a lawyer. He got away a bit cheaper.

One incident seems characteristic to me. A man in my compartment was asked, "What are you?" "First Public Prosecutor of the State." Immediately he received a blow. "You are an asshole." "What are you?" "Public prosecutor." He received another blow. "What are you?" Now he said it. "An asshole."

Step by step one could follow the change in the man's mind from looking upon himself as the First Public Prosecutor of the State and in this capacity defying his enemy, into a poor wretch, trying to keep alive during this hell of a night. He kept alive. He certainly would not have, if he had insisted upon his being the First Public Prosecutor.

Every two hours the guards were relieved. Many of them were drunk. As far as I know, bringing prisoners to the camp was the only occasion when guards were allowed to be drunk on duty. It was part of the system.

Sometimes for brief intervals nothing special happened. We simply stared into the eyes of the man opposite. Then it would happen again that some passing SS man would ask the guard on duty why we were "at ease," and whether he thought that we were on our way to a sanatorium. And he would start a little celebration of his own.

It seemed as though the night would never end. Beating, shouting, staring, beating, drill, shouting, staring.

We had left Vienna at about seven o'clock at night and arrived in Dachau about six o'clock in the morning. We were loaded into SS trucks and ordered to bend our heads down on our knees. If anyone looked up he would get shot.

In the camp we were unloaded amidst great yelling and beating. Since we were the first Austrians and there were many well-known people among us, Commander Loritz himself came and made a speech. He explained to us that there was corporal punishment in the camp, that we had better behave damned well, there was no fooling about the lash. He read our names from a list and introduced us to his beloved comrades. Those with resounding titles, like the Mayor of Vienna, the Secretary of Finance, the Head of the Police Department, the Consul General, were greeted with a cheer and had to run a little gauntlet.

Then we were lined up and not allowed to move. Snow had fallen overnight. There we stood freezing, at rigid attention. After that horrible night, one single man was enough to keep us in order.

The sun came up, rose higher and higher, and began to burn our bare heads. Old men fainted. We were not allowed to help them up. They were trampled back to life.

Finally the administrative procedure began. Amid yelling and beating we were rushed through the regular routine, then lined up on the roll-call square. All day long SS men swarmed around us, teasing us, beating us. After roll call at night we were led to our barracks, and we got our first food in thirty-six hours. Then we fell asleep on the straw bags that covered the floor of the otherwise empty barrack. We were dead tired and slept the deep, deep sleep of an overworked horse that simply can't go on any longer.

The next morning we were formed into a special working group with an unusually large number of officers and capos.[4] For weeks we were accorded the camp's "special treatment," until finally the terror ebbed, the old men and invalids were sent to easier jobs, and the rest were attached to ordinary working groups. From then on we were subject "only" to the "ordinary" terror of this hell. We were swallowed by the great mass of the older prisoners, we adjusted ourselves to their way of life, the initiation was over.

I want to add lest there be any doubt: I have not tried to describe every detail of the horror of the night on the train. I have left out everything that might possibly be construed as a manifestation of a guard's own ingenuity. There occurred outrages of sadism which I also consider part of the system, but which others might ascribe to individual action. I have only described what was beyond doubt part of a well-planned system to break the spirits of the new prisoners.

Later on the administration learned that they could save themselves a lot of the breaking-in procedure in the beginning by stepping up the terror of the train. The 150 men who arrived on May 24 had to keep their hands clasped behind their heads and stare into the electric light all night long. They were more severely mistreated than we had been. But their initiation inside the camp was easier. It is difficult to say which was preferable. But it is important to indicate that it was part of the system.

The larger the transports became, the more terrific became the terror. When the Viennese Jews were brought in groups of 500 and 600, they were so mistreated and tortured that men went mad and jumped through the closed windows. These men were shot "on attempt to escape." One transport arrived with eight dead. When another transport arrived, one man went mad during the disembarkation and ran in the wrong direction. He was shot to death immediately. Other SS men, hearing the shots,

---

4. See the chapter "A Day in a Concentration Camp" on the destruction of the old dungeon.

got nervous and also began to shoot. Within a few minutes five prisoners lay dead, others wounded. Incidentally an SS man was wounded by a bullet.

When large groups arrived, there were not enough tools to keep them busy. But to let the men go idle until the new tools arrived might have given them time enough to recuperate from the shock on the train. So a relay system was organized; men made a long trip with a heavily loaded wheelbarrow, emptied it, turned it over to a new man, and lined up for their next turn. Officers were placed all along the way who made them run and beat them. So the period at the waiting station became only a short interruption between two long stretches of agony.

Finally there were not enough wheelbarrows even for such a system. The next batch of 600 men were made to carry heavy blocks of cement on their shoulders for a distance of about half a mile. The stones were not needed, but the men had to be kept busy. Officers along the way made the men with their stones move faster, and those on the return trip they made run. No water or rest was allowed them. Under the blazing sun many of them suffered sunstrokes. Broke down. Were kicked to their feet. Broke down again. Kicked up again. Some went mad under the torture. All of a sudden such a man would throw away his stone and run in wild circles around the roll-call square. The circles became smaller and smaller until finally the man collapsed in the center. Death had put an end to the run. Others were carried in wheelbarrows to the infirmary and suffocated before they arrived. To increase the terror, a few people were shot "on attempt to escape," and the record showed eighteen dead within thirty-six hours.

But the purpose was fulfilled. Any spark of resistance that might possibly have survived in these 600 men after the night on the train was thoroughly stamped out within a few days.

* * *

The same "breaking-in" procedure was applied in a different way to the 300 Austrian Gypsies. Both prisoners and the administration seemed to expect that these "sons of the steppe," famous for being indomitable, for knifing and for fighting the police, would behave differently. They might hit back, primarily because they did not understand that this situation was basically different from any other situation they had faced in "civilian" society. Nobody thought them capable of work and discipline.

All talk about the "free sons of the steppe" proved just so much romanticism. They reacted exactly as we others did. They got the shock of their lives during the night on the train, even more so than the rest of us, because they understood less what it was all about. They forgot completely about their famous indomitability.

The administration let loose at them more than at the others, just in case. On the first day they shot several "on attempt to escape," and that successfully terrorized the rest. Then Commander Koegel proceeded to teach them "regular work" and "civilization." Together with barrack leader Wagner, he inspected their working grounds, picked out a few of them for being lazy, and Wagner administered the "twenty-five" on the spot. After this had been repeated for several days, the gypsies were assumed to have grasped their lesson. And as a matter of fact they had—there was practically no more trouble with them at all.

That all this was part of a carefully planned system, and not haphazard mistreatment, was confirmed to us very clearly on the way from Dachau to Buchenwald. Again we spent a whole night on the train, guarded by Dachau SS. Yet for most of us the trip was relatively quiet, only in a few cars was there some excitement and beating. Apparently we were considered "old prisoners" who knew the ropes and did not require any special attention.

But in Weimar we were taken over by Buchenwald SS, who thought that they had to break us in to our new environment. They were very proud of the hell they kept going up there and kept yelling at us that the "good times of Dachau" were over now. Before we were loaded into the SS trucks, we were lined up in a street tunnel, and there they fell upon us with all the extreme cruelty accorded to newcomers.

Later on we learned that the attack in the tunnel was a regular thing for newcomers to Buchenwald, when they came in numbers too large to be loaded directly into the trucks. This attack reached its height when, a few weeks after our arrival, the 11,000 Jews were brought in during the pogroms. Many of them came by truck and car from different parts of Germany and had not yet gone through even the regular night on the train. Thus the whole initial blow had to be concentrated into the short time in the tunnel. Blood flowed in streams, limbs were broken, skulls were smashed; they entered the camp with the most horrible injuries. But the purpose was fulfilled again; with one decisive blow the very idea of resistance was knocked out of these unfortunates for good.

Why They Don't Hit Back

As I said before, the vast majority of the prisoners don't hit back because they fear the bullet. What we are trying to answer is the question, why aren't there any exceptions? Or at least no more exceptions than perhaps one or two among hundreds of thousands of prisoners?

One reason why people are expected to hit back is that they might go insane and attack, bullet or no bullet. It is quite possible that that could happen. However, not many men go insane under mistreatment, and of those who do, not many fall into a violent sort of insanity. The chance that a man might happen to go insane in a violent way, and that an SS man would happen to be around, and that the madness of the man would direct itself against him, seems to be rather small. And besides, the question, why don't they hit back, is hardly directed at these cases.

Yet it is often asked in a similar sense. "If they beat me, I would get so mad, I would forget what I was doing, I would not think of being shot, I simply would strike back blindly and without a thought. Sure I would."

You would not. Nobody does. It seems inconceivable that the people who ask the question are of such exceptional stature, that what applies to hundreds of thousands of men, among them some who have proven themselves courageous above and beyond the call of duty, should not apply to the man who asks the question, and who feels so vastly superior to those who didn't strike back. It seems more plausible to assume that the man who asks the question would not have struck back either, just as the others didn't, and for the same reasons, whatever they may be.

The implication of the question is usually not that of self-defense, except perhaps in an unconscious way, because most people will admit that if a man has sense enough to defend himself consciously, he also has sense enough not to do it, if that might cost him the very life which he wants to defend.

The implication is usually, that a man is expected to be ashamed of being beaten; he is expected to strike back in defense of his honor and dignity as a man. "I would get so mad, I would not care what I did," implies getting angry at the humiliation and shame of having one's face slapped.

To understand why the prisoners did not strike back, we must first ask, why does the man in civilian society hit back? Which of the reasons that make him hit back do not hold up in the camp? At what point on his way from one society to the other does the man realize that the rules which govern his behavior have been changed?

"Honor" is a social concept, and so is the necessity of defending it. It cannot, like the necessity for self-preservation, arise within one individual alone, but must be seen against the social situation of which it is a part.

To strike back when attacked is one of the basic references in our society. Only a small minority will, in the concrete case of a slap in the face, follow the Christian rule and turn the other cheek.

He who does not strike back is considered a coward, both by other people and by himself. Because the frame of reference of his society has become an integral part of his personality, there is practically no alternative left to him, except when the odds are so obviously unfavorable that he is excused for not striking back. But that is seldom the case. The man who strikes back against heavy odds is admired as a hero. If he has to suffer for it, he is praised as a martyr for his honor. The increased acclaim is in part a compensation for his suffering.

The man who does not strike back loses status in his community. Recognition by the community in which we are living is one of our basic needs. Many a suicide has been committed as a way out of a community in which a man felt he could no longer carry on after having lost status for not striking back when he was beaten.

When a country is occupied and a man is insulted by a member of the enemy's army, he usually has a choice of action. If he hits back and gets the better of the enemy, he is admired as a hero. If he receives more mistreatment, is perhaps arrested and executed, he will be regarded as a martyr who died for his country. He knows that his death will be a signal for his friends, and he expects them to avenge him.

The man who does not hit back will usually not be considered a coward, but a victim of the brutality of the enemy. His insult will be glorified as martyrdom. He will not lose in social status.

The man in concentration camp who gets slapped or whipped on a stand, has no choice but to take it, unless he wants to commit suicide. But here is the main difference from civilian life: Nobody expects him to strike back. If he really does strike back and is immediately shot to death, nobody will glorify him as a hero or martyr. The only comment he can expect from his fellow prisoners is, "Damned fool." They may elaborate a little: "Who is he that he thinks himself too good for what we have to endure every day? The hell with him!"

What affects the man's status is the way he takes the beating. If he cries and weeps, he is considered a weakling. If he begs for quarter (which is never given anyway), he is held in contempt. I should add that men who beg and cry under the lash or on the "tree" get additional blows or have to hang longer. Because the guards have the same basic idea, that it is dishonorable for a man to cry under torture. They show a little respect (though not much) for the man who takes it the right way.

On the part of the guards, this is only the Teutonic image of the redskin at the stake, as they learned from reading Karl May.[5] But on the part of the prisoners, beyond the redskin image, it is self-preservation, pure and simple. They are faced with this conflict: On the one hand, the ordinary way of gaining and retaining status, namely to hit back, is practically blocked by its absolutely suicidal consequences. If a whole society does not want to commit suicide in response to acts that are not a supreme insult, but daily routine, it has to adjust its concepts of honor and social status to this routine.

This adjustment is made by not letting an insult affect a man's status. No social pressure is put upon him to hit back. On the other hand, terrific social pressure is put on him to take it the right way, to remain silent and stolid, both before, during, and after the beating.

The beating itself becomes a completely impersonal matter, like the weather, or an accident. When the sun burns hot, or when rain and hail fall upon him, the prisoner does not like it. But it does not affect his status. When a worker is injured by a machine, that is his occupational hazard. Nobody holds him in contempt for it—possibly his fellow workers might cast doubt on his craftsmanship. To get slapped and beaten is one of the occupational hazards of the man who happens to have the profession of "camp prisoner." To say of a man, "He got 'twenty-five' yesterday," is simply a factual report, with no value judgment involved. To say of him, "Don't know what's the matter with that guy. Every now and then he gets his 'twenty-five,'" is a derogatory remark, implying that the man through his carelessness gets caught and beaten more often than is considered his proper share.

From a man-to-man affair, the beating changes into a group-to-group affair. Here are defenseless prisoners. There are guards with rifles and machine guns. Well, there is nothing the individual can do about it.

To the prisoner, the SS guard or officer who slaps him is not so much a man who humiliates him through an insult as a sort of low animal, unpleasant and dangerous. To be bitten by a snake or a mad dog brings many unpleasant consequences. One may even die of it. But it certainly does not arouse the contempt of one's fellow men.

---

5. Karl May was the author of numerous American Indian stories which were widely read by German youth.

Several parallels come to mind, where people do "get mad" and hit back in situations where they should not. Children sometimes hit back at their parents, pupils at their teachers, sometimes prisoners in ordinary prisons at their jailers, and civilians in the streets at an arresting policeman. All of these situations have two characteristics in common—hitting back is not identical with suicide, and for both parties the concept of honor and defending one's honor is an accepted thing. The individual involved may be punished for violating the law, for hitting back in a situation where it is specifically forbidden to do so, but those who punish him still consider him somebody who ordinarily is encouraged to strike back when attacked.

The citizen who is beaten by a policeman finds himself in a conflict. There is the basic rule that tells him, strike back, but there is also the exception—never at a policeman. Against him you can only go and lodge a complaint. Sometimes people do get so angry that they hit the policeman. Then they are sentenced in court, not because the policeman was right, but because the policeman, representing the power of the state, must be protected. The individual policeman may then be sentenced for having beaten a citizen. Occasionally a defendant may plead, "I had to defend my honor. I got so mad I did not know what I was doing. I am sure your Honor would have done the same in my place." Sometimes this kind of defense proves successful.

Our civilian society can afford an occasional exception from the rule that the policeman is sacrosanct. The concentration camp cannot afford a single exception regarding its SS men—the very existence of the camp would be threatened immediately.

The man who hits a policeman is judged by his fellow citizens according to his motives. People who are given long prison terms for having hit back at a policemen in political fights, never lose and usually gain social status.

"Getting mad" in situations in which one should not, is recognized by the community as an understandable form of behavior, though perhaps punishable. The noble outcast, who robs the rich and gives to the poor, is accepted and glorified by folklore, though he is hanged if caught, and though that also is considered just. If he puts up a terrific last fight against the police, that only adds to his glory. Even the movie gangster who fights for his life receives a lot of admiration for it, although the eventual triumph of justice is almost necessary to absolve society of approving his defense.

The prisoner in an ordinary prison is, of course, forbidden to strike back at the guard. But the guard is forbidden to beat the prisoner in the first place, except in self-defense. The relations between prisoners and guards are covered by written laws, which are guaranteed by the law. In these rules the prisoner is treated as a man, a member of human society, who happens to be in prison, and some of whose rights happen to be curtailed or postponed for the time of his stay there. Both he and the guard, and in the case of a trial, the judge, know that after his term in prison is up, he will return to his community.

Thus the frame of reference of civilian society, of which the guard is a member when off-duty, and to which the prisoner will return, influence greatly their relations to each other. They may be enemies, but they are, in their relations, a man who happens to be a prisoner and a man who happens to be a guard. And between them the idea is still prevalent that a slap in the face is an insult, and that hitting back is the proper reaction, though it may be punished by a week in a dark cell. The fellow prisoners consider the one who struck back a real man, who does not let "those guards" fool with him. And the fact that he was heavily punished for it, perhaps after an unofficial heavy beating by the guards, does not detract from his status.

The prisoner in a concentration camp is there not for a definite crime for which he serves a definite sentence, but for his attitude toward the Nazi state, or because he belongs to a category of people whom the Nazi state wants to get rid of. By being a Jew, a Jehovah's Witness, a Communist, he has forfeited his membership in this Nazi society. He is ejected and outlawed.

There is no time limit set on the period for which he is outlawed. During the first few years, when the pattern of relations between prisoners and guards was established, there were so few releases that release was spoken of as a miracle. But even when, in the fall of 1938, they began to release masses of Jews on condition that they leave the country, and when in 1939 they released 1,100 non-Jews from Buchenwald alone on Hitler's birthday, release did not become the logical end of imprisonment; it remained something like an accident or a gift from heaven.

Thus the relations between guards and prisoners are considerably less influenced by the concepts of the outside world than is the case in a regular prison. Both know that the civilian rights of the prisoner are not suspended but abolished. To his guards the prisoner is no longer a man whose personality has any meaning. He no longer has an "honor" that has to be respected. And to the prisoner the guard becomes part of a machine, or a dangerous beast whose every move he watches and studies carefully, in order to get hurt as little as possible, but to whom any concepts of honor simply do not apply.

And so, while the civilian strikes back in order to defend his honor—that is, his social status among his fellow men—the camp prisoner for the same reason takes his beating stolidly—to retain the recognition of his fellow prisoners. The civilian reasons, "If anyone dared to slap me like that, I would surely hit him over the head," (which actually means, "I live in a society where striking back is necessary to retain my status, and I certainly want to retain it.") The prisoner reasons about the man on the stand, "Your turn today, mine perhaps tomorrow. But I'm sure I wouldn't cry out," (which actually means, "If that is the way it is done in this society, then I surely will do it. I wouldn't want to lose my status among the only people for whose judgment I have to care, perhaps for the rest of my life.")

The difference between the two societies, that outside and that inside the camp, seems at this point one of rules of behavior rather than basic concepts.

In a situation where there is no goal worth sacrificing your life for, and where there is no one to accept the sacrifice if you make it, sacrificing your life becomes worthless and meaningless. "Sacrifice" is as much a social concept as "honor," and where the society does not recognize an act as a supreme sacrifice, the act might, as far as readiness to sacrifice goes, just as well remain undone. And for this reason, in concentration camp, sacrificing one's life for the sake of hitting back is not done.

One question that outsiders often ask is, "But if they know that so many of them are going to die in the camp anyway, if so many of them have given up the hope of ever getting released, why don't they simply jump at one of these SS men, perhaps snatch his gun from him, shoot one of two of the gangsters, and bring their own life to more rapid and dignified and perhaps useful end?" This question is aimed particularly at the political prisoners of every party denomination.

The answer is that if they saw the slightest reason for doing so, they would probably do it. Enough of them would be willing to give their lives, if it would serve their cause. But there is not the slightest bit of sense to it. The outside world to whom it might be a symbol of the unbroken spirit of its fighters, would never learn of it, because nothing would happen spectacular enough to be told. The man would be shot to death while still in the unspectacular act of lifting his arm. His fellow prisoners would not get much satisfaction out of it, because all they could do to carry on his revolt would be to lift an arm again—and be shot too, for this unspectacular move, before landing the blow. It would not impress the SS either, because for them shooting defenseless prisoners is not a rare sensation anyway. They would not take the prisoner's life as a supreme sacrifice—they would shoot him in the same matter-of-fact way in which they slap his face. His fellow prisoners, utterly convinced that he had not the slightest chance of success, would also not see any supreme sacrifice in it. They would condemn it as an absolutely foolish undertaking.

In addition to all this for the political prisoner, there is the political isolation of the camps. No regular contacts are established with the underground movement. The prisoners learn about the still-existing movement through the newly arrested, and the movement in turn learns about its incarcerated members through the few who are released. No messages go to and from, no encouragement, and no promise of help. The political prisoners in the camps, though informed that their movements still exist, know that these movements are too weak to support them in the case of any attempted uprising.

If per chance once in a hundred thousand cases a man should seriously attack an SS man, because, due to some accidental circumstances, he thought that this time he might be able to land at least one blow, the administration would most certainly take the necessary precautions so that such a situation could not arise any more. We have a good illustration in the case where two men escaped from Buchenwald and killed an SS man in the process. The day after, in all the concentration camps, new orders were given about the guarding of prisoners. The guards from then on carried their rifles not over their shoulders but under their arms, ready to shoot, and with bayonets attached. The greatest care was taken that one guard would never be alone with one prisoner, not even on some special mission such as getting a special tool from a distant tool shed. The distance within which a prisoner could approach a guard without being shot immediately was increased from three to six yards, with the exception of the chain of sentinels, where the guards stand so close to each other that the neighbors to the left and right can always shoot the prisoner while he is trying to approach a guard.

The question remains: When and how does a prisoner realize that the old laws do not hold any longer, that this society has different rules, and that here he is not expected to strike back? Why are there no exceptions at least among the newcomers, at least on the very first day, before they have talked to anybody? In my opinion this is due to the shock they experience the moment they are taken over by the SS.

Up to the moment when they leave the prison van, the prisoners have had no occasion in which to make use of their old rule, when beaten, strike back. They have been in the hands of civilian authorities, civilian police perhaps, or prison personnel, who ordinarily did not beat them at all. The change from one society to the other follows with practically no transition.

Emerging from the dark prison van, they are suddenly faced with this machine that hits, that beats, yells, shouts, and tramples, for no understandable reason, and all in such a hurry that the prisoners have no chance to stop for a single moment or to think about what to do next. They are drawn into the witch's cauldron as though it were a whirlpool so disproportionately stronger than themselves that they can do nothing but try to lie still and wait to see whether it will let them loose again. A man sees others being beaten like himself and doing nothing about it. When he makes his first contact with old inmates, he is told that it is that bad only in the beginning, that after a few days it will let up somewhat, and he will be beaten less than might appear at first glance. As to the shame of being beaten—the old inmate will just laugh at it or dismiss it. Don't take it to heart, don't take it too seriously, it doesn't count. This is not like where you come from. Here it is different. It doesn't matter to us.

Once he has gone through this initiation, he has already learned from his own experience that you can survive having your face slapped and not striking back. And he has learned that he did not have to perish with shame, because nobody took any notice of it. Having learned in addition about the suicidal nature of any attempt to strike back, he gives up this notion for the time of his stay in camp.

I got my first realization that a slap in the camp is not the same as a slap outside of it in a strange way on the train from Vienna to Dachau. Some time during the night, a young boy of about 17 or 18 took over our compartment. For a while he kept silent and did nothing. Then he inquired quietly about our professions. One man answered, "I am an Austrian general." The boy saluted militarily and said, "Yes, general, I know what that means, general." The last man was a "major in the Austrian army during the World War." The boy saluted again, "Yes, major," and began a quiet conversation with the man. After a short while he said, "Anyone who wants to sleep, do it." We stared at each other in amazement. A miracle. A human being among the devils. He continued to talk to the major in a low voice. I sat next to the major and overhead the conversation. The boy asked the major about his experiences during the Great War. Suddenly he said, "One thing I want to tell you, major. If anybody should beat you, perhaps even slap your face, don't think of it in the same way as if you were free and a major. Here it is different. Just ignore it."

The whole interlude lasted only for a few minutes. One of us really slept for a minute. He was the president of the Vienna Commercial University, a man of almost 70. Another guard, chancing by, saw the sleeping man and asked the boy whether he was crazy to allow us to sleep. He brought in another SS man showing him the spectacle of a man who could sleep during that night. They started beating us. Somehow the boy disappeared during the scene.

Having gone through my share of being slapped and beaten both on the train and during the first weeks of special terror, I still wondered whether it would be any different if I should meet an SS man face to face and be beaten by him. The situation soon came up. On a fine spring day I was working with another man in a side street of the camp. We were in an out-of-the-way spot and so began chatting. Suddenly an officer appeared. He shouted at us, but soon went away again. Smiling, I said to my companion, "That was luck, wasn't it?" At that moment the officer turned around again: "What are you laughing at? Are you joking about me by any chance?" How could I dare to? I denied it. He came closer. We stood face to face at a distance of a few inches. "You are a damned liar!"—and crash, a blow landed on my face.

Of course there was no choice between hitting back and not hitting back. The only choice I had was whether to take it standing upright or to drop. If you drop, there is always the chance that nothing more may follow than an additional kick with the boot. If you take it on the chin, the guard may feel the resistance and keep on beating until there is no choice left but to go down.

The incident happened to take place in front of my barrack, where I had been moved only a few days before. The barrack senior and my room senior were looking out of the window, curious to see how the new inmate would behave. In addition there was the man with whom I was working, whom I knew from Vienna.

I decided to take it on the chin. I stood straight and stared into the officer's eyes. They are cowards. They can't bear your staring into their eyes. Stare an SS man in the eyes, and he will behave like a dog when you stare into its eyes. The dog will bite you or howl at you or pull his tail in and get off. The SS man will either kick and beat you, just to get rid of your eyes, or he will howl at you, "Don't you dare look at me! Don't you dare look at me!" ("*Schau mich ja nicht an!*") This one hit once more. I did not move but kept staring into his eyes. A third slap I took in the same manner. Then the dog pulled in his tail and went off.

This one incident I remember better than any beatings I got before or after, because I was so completely aware of my surroundings—in fact I felt more like the observer of a psychological experiment than a victim in the hands of tormentors. Not for a single moment did I think of the shame of having my face slapped. I only watched myself, curious to see whether I was able to take it and to show the devil that he could not hurt me.

When, on the trip from Dachau to Buchenwald, we were loaded into the SS trucks in Weimar, I looked out of the car to see what sort of people the policemen in the streets were. One of them saw me looking at him and immediately shouted, "Don't you dare look at me!" Here it was again. I turned my head back into the car. An SS man who had seen me looking out of the car, which was forbidden, began to howl at me. That reminded me of my theory about the dogs. I stared into his eyes. The theory proved right. This particular one bit. To get rid of my eyes, he gave me a heavy blow over the head with his rifle. Then I kept my head down as ordered.

In Buchenwald once, when my hand was still bandaged, I was at work carrying water from a garage, together with two old men, both about 70. They always wanted to take time off inside the garage. I kept warning them of Officer Becker and Capo Azzoni.

The two old men kept insisting, "Becker can't be everywhere." Finally I consented to a little rest. We had hardly put down our pails when suddenly the door was flung wide open—Becker and Azzoni entered. Becker gave a mock-surprised "Ahhh?!?" and grinned like a boy who is out for a prank. He held a stick in his hand. He had the first of the two old men step forward. "Bend." The man bent forward. Becker walked slowly up behind him, lifted the stick with a wide swing, and let go. The old man lost balance and toppled a few steps forward. When he was back in position, he got another blow. He moaned slightly. All told he got five blows, and that was very cheap. The next man got five blows in the same manner.

While Becker was busy with the old man, I was only angry at the boy for beating these people each of whom could have been his grandfather. But now, when it was my turn, I felt deeply ashamed—not at the fact of being beaten, though I must confess that the elaborateness of the procedure made me gulp a little—but at the fact of being caught in such a childish manner. It was beneath my dignity as a political prisoner to get a thrashing for such a stupid thing as getting caught in a dark garage that had only one exit.

But here I was, and the best I could do was to take it in a good way. I grinned at Becker, bent, and stood firm as blow after blow fell. Becker, being a relatively decent man within his own standards, made a difference between the two old men and the young one. I received considerably more and harder blows. But it was soon over, and Becker and Azzoni left the scene.

My imagination and feeling of shame had not deceived me. When I told Walter the story, he called me a little boy whose momma can't let him take a walk by himself in a concentration camp without having him run into trouble. Jackie added some funny remarks, and then we stopped talking about it. But none of them saw anything shameful in the beating itself. That was an accident. What they teased me for was my stupidity in getting caught.

A good illustration that a beating does not affect the status of people was an incident in Buchenwald, when all thirty-seven barrack seniors "went over the stand." Discipline had slipped in the camp, relations between seniors and their charges had become very close. To pep up their lax spirits a bit, Rödl first gave them a speech, threatening them with repeated thrashings of "twenty-five" if they did not file reports. Then he had every single one of them receive ten heavy blows, promising that the missing fifteen would soon follow if they did not tighten up camp discipline at once.

Each barrack senior was strapped to the stand. The blows echoed over the square. Not one of the men made a sound. And a feeling of admiration ran through the 10,000 men—Aren't they grand, our seniors! Of course when some Satan of a senior had his turn, the men of his barrack would smile—Why not, he has given us so much of the same.

The commander hardly achieved what he had wanted. Where the relations between senior and barrack had been bad, they grew worse. But where they had been good before, they grew better now. On coming home from the stand, the senior was treated with the greatest respect; his friends cheered him up and brought the good old home remedies, fat and warm water, and tried their best to get him into shape again.

Another effect was that the esprit de corps of the seniors was strengthened. They were reminded of our common enmity for the administration and felt themselves more a part of the community than they had before. As to the shame of being beaten—nobody thought of it as shameful.

Fear and social habit simultaneously tend to form a strong barrier against any conscious attempt at hitting back, either in self-defense or to defend one's honor and social status.

The administration may not have been aware of the social implications, and possibly attributed it to fear only. In accordance with this, they arranged the terrifying initiation on the train and during the first period after arrival. Their maxim seemed to be: If you want to prevent any riots, you have to break the prisoners' personalities, knock the spark of resistance out of them at the very moment they enter the camp. If you are able to crush them with one decisive blow at the beginning, they will never recover again.

This pattern was carefully carried out for years in concentration camps all over Germany. It was planned and carried out in such detail, and was so identical from camp to camp, that there cannot be the slightest suspicion that these were incidental sadistic outrages of individual camp commanders.

Statement on the Validity of the Observations That Form the Basis of the Dissertation

This dissertation is based almost exclusively upon the author's recollections. Additional material was provided by discussions with about ten former fellow prisoners. All of them are living in the United States, all of them saw all or part of the book while it was in the process of being written, all of them have added valuable criticism. However, there was not much of it. We almost never disagreed. When we disagreed on facts, it was concerning trifles, such as whether we had to remove our shoes more or less often in Buchenwald, and whether the wolf we had to pay for cost us 7,000 or 12,000 marks.

When we disagreed on interpretations, we usually reached agreement or compromise very soon. Some of my friends blamed me for painting the Austrians in too friendly colors; others thought my picture of the Prussians too friendly. But again, others blamed me for treating the Prussians too badly, and others thought I might have been more considerate of the Viennese Jews. All this apparently is the kind of criticism every author has to expect when he is dealing with complicated social phenomena, especially where no numerical proofs are possible, for instance, regarding statements such as, "Most of the asocials had a very low educational level," or "The political prisoners were the most incorruptible group in the camp." These statements can be criticized by anybody who comes along and says, "I knew a former banker who wore a black badge, but he had two doctor's degrees," (I knew him too), or by someone else who says, "I had a room senior who was a Communist and had been in camp for four years, but what a crook he was! The racket he organized was one of the worst in the camp." That is right. I, too, have known such men.

But the important difference between this kind of criticism and the dissertation as it is written is that I almost never speak about individuals, or if I do, it is only to illustrate a statement about a group. The same people who remember the banker with two degrees and the Communist with his racket, are considerably slower in remembering an SS man who did not beat the prisoners, or a professional criminal who, during the November pogroms, brought half of his sausages to a Jewish barrack without charging a penny. When describing whole groups, I mention these cases as well.

However, here is one of the great difficulties of the whole dissertation. Given the circumstances in which the author found himself, in a society of 10,000 or 20,000 people, not as a scientific observer but as a suffering participant, none of the customary tools of social research were at his disposal. No notes, no interviews, no questionnaires, no documents, no figures, no correlations. The question which I am frequently asked by academic people—"Could you take notes?"—is identical to asking—"Didn't you want to commit suicide by being beaten to death?" Aside from the impossibility of taking notes, it would have been still more impossible to smuggle them out of the camp. A man who was released went through a routine administrative procedure, in the course of which he removed his clothes at a given moment and, absolutely naked, passed a wooden bar, where an SS officer watched him. He then crossed a large room and got his civilian clothes. From that moment on he had no further contact with other prisoners who remained in the camp. There was no possibility of smuggling "notes." All that occasionally got smuggled were small objects, such as a purse or a pipe, which a man could carry in his hand while distracting the officer's attention. If the officer noticed it, the man could always quite innocently ask to be allowed to keep it as a souvenir. What the prisoner did not have in his head, he couldn't take with him.

It seems to me that two different types of questions may be raised as to the validity of observations and interpretations under such circumstances. One type deals with the facts as such. It is the simple question, how far does the man tell the truth, and how far does he lie, consciously or unconsciously? The other type deals with interpretations: How far has the man been able to organize his observations? To what degree can the picture of the society in the camp be correct?

The question of the truth or untruth of facts can be settled relatively easily. Books have been written by other people who have been in concentration camps. I am going to cite in the following pages only books by people who were in Dachau and Buchenwald, the two camps where I was. Bruno Heilig (*Man Crucified,* London, 1941) was with me on the train from Vienna to Dachau, and we were together in both camps for thirteen months. He was released one month before I was. He was one of Austria's foremost liberal journalists. I had many interesting discussions with him in the camp. Peter Wallner (*By Order of the Gestapo,* London, 1941) writes under a pen-name, and I therefore do not know whether or not I am personally acquainted with him. He came to Dachau during the first days of June, 1938—that is, with one of the big mass transports of Viennese Jews. He left Buchenwald about the same time as Heilig did, in April 1939. Wallner says of himself that he was formerly a business man. His identity and trustworthiness is vouched for by Lord Davies, who wrote a foreword to his book.

Georg M. Karst (*The Beasts of the Earth,* New York, 1942) came to Dachau in October or November 1938, and left it in March or April 1939. He writes under a pen-name, but says that he was a high official in the Schuschnigg government and a former employee of the *Reichspost,* the official party newspaper of the Dollfuss and Schuschnigg party. His identity and trustworthiness are certified in an introduction by George N. Shuster, president of Hunter College, New York.

The facts in these three books agree with mine in so many hundreds and thousands of details that an attempt to refer to them in footnotes bogged down in the superfluity of material. It seemed to me not only a hopeless, but also a fruitless task to cut up other people's books into footnotes. It would take more time to read the incoherent footnotes than to read the whole books. Particularly Wallner's book, the best I have read so far about the concentration camps, would need to be dissected into at least 1,000 footnotes. This would not only be a tremendous task, but would also destroy the general effect of both his book and mine.

I therefore take the liberty of considering the question about the factual truth of my book as settled. I know there may always be the question, "But

perhaps the first man invented the whole story, and all the others copied it."
Yes, this question can be raised, and nothing can be said to refute it. Because each of the thousands of witnesses who are now in America may be a liar. In the early eighteenth century, a man earned a doctor's degree in Milan by proving that Toricelli's vacuum was merely imaginary; the truth, he said, was that Toricelli's quicksilver was pulled upwards by invisible threads which were fastened on a cloud. Torricelli did not need to worry about it, because he was long since dead, and his followers could say nothing against it. No proof is possible against invisible threads. If there is a claim that all people who report what they have gone through are members of an invisible network of scoundrels and liars, let there be such a network. It is beyond our power to send doubting men to Dachau to convince themselves. They might be beaten there and then say that we arranged it for them in agreement with the SS in order to have our lies substantiated. As far as I know, Torricelli's vacuum is today accepted as a fact, and the doctor's dissertation from Milan is quoted as a *curiosum.*

The question about the truth of facts becomes more involved when we inquire not about the obvious facts of mistreatment, the layout of the camps, or the administrative organization, but about the undercover organization of the prisoners, the social structure of the camps. The honesty and truth of an author being granted, it is still an open question whether, in his position as a suffering participant, he had a chance to see enough of the camp to come to a comprehensive understanding of the situation. Particularly as far as the distribution of power, the struggle for power, and the struggle between ideological concepts are concerned.

In this connection, I have to talk about my own role in the camp. Nobody ever tells the prisoner why he is brought to the camp, but many of us had definite theories about the system of arrests and the reasons why certain people were arrested. The 2,000 Viennese Jews were apparently arrested in order to terrorize the other 200,000, so that they would emigrate. I was arrested as a name on a blacklist the Nazis had prepared long before they took Austria. It appears they considered me one of the young intellectuals who were fairly well known in Vienna, and who could be expected to become points of crystallization for future resistance. They knew that I had been fairly active in anti-Nazi propaganda ever since 1930, and in addition they seem to have known what Schuschnigg's police knew about me—namely, that I worked underground against our homemade fascism, as well as against the foreign brand. They did not know any details, because Schuschnigg's police did not either, although they tried very hard to catch me red-handed by making numerous searches of my home between 1934 and 1938. This weaker brand of fascism persecuted me as much as it was able, considering that they did not have any evidence against me. Thus the Nazis had at least all the material that Schuschnigg's police had gathered against me. The Nazis, being politically much stronger than the Schuschnigg government, did not need to have evidence in their hands. Suspicion was enough to send a man to concentration camp.

When I arrived at Dachau with the first transport of handpicked political cases, I was one of the first men to be accepted by the German political prisoners. I am not a Jew but a Protestant; I spent ten years in a Protestant children's home, and never had any contact with a Jewish community. However, some of my grandparents were less Protestant, and I was given a Jewish star. That, incidentally, brought me into a position where I could discover how it felt to be persecuted as a Jew, without having anything in common with this group but a yellow badge. Up to the time of Schuschnigg and Hitler, the race problem never played any role in my life. I lived in a milieu of mixed marriages between Jews and non-Jews; a great number of my relatives were scientists, professors at the university of Vienna, artists, and so forth.

From the very first day I played a dominant role among the new Austrian prisoners. I was the unofficial leader of the sixty-three Jews in our transport; that is, I organized them into a cooperating group, since our non-Jewish senior, a German Communist who had spent four years in Dachau, was completely unable to cope with the situation. When we were distributed among the old barracks, I still kept this dominant role to some degree. With three others, I was one of the first Austrians to be selected by our German political friends as a worker on a moor express. Later, when most of the old German prisoners on the moor expresses were removed, I was one of the first Austrians to become an unofficial leader on a moor express. When I describe how we tried to bring our political friends to the wagons and to get rid of everybody who did not live up to our standards of cooperation and comradeship, then I describe not only what others did, but also my own activities.

From the very first day, I had insight into the power structure and the struggle for power, both in Dachau and in Buchenwald, because most of the time I played an active part in this struggle. In the rooms where I lived, both in Dachau and in Buchenwald, I was the leader of the political clique that dominated the room.

In addition, I had the benefit of being in very good physical shape up to the time when my hand was frostbitten. I am physically stronger than intellectuals usually are, and I had experienced very hard years before I came to Dachau. Therefore I could resist the physical strain of the situation fairly well. As a result, I could also resist better psychologically, since I could always find some comfort by telling myself, "I will outlast it longer than anyone else—as long as there are a few of us alive, I will be among them, unless an accident strikes me." (A bullet, of course, is an accident.) Political position and good physical condition made it possible for me to get through the camp fairly well, compared with the burden of mistreatment that the average prisoner had to endure. This made it possible for me to study with more calm what was going on around me. I developed a certain self-possession, even in very exciting situations, and used to keep a sharp eye on general developments. After all, I had the idea of writing a book from the first day, when I saw that there were things happening that had never been reported, in spite of all the books that had been written, and I was eager to get as much information as possible about the power structure in the camp, in order to have the book as complete as possible.

I speak a strong Viennese dialect, stronger than is common among intellectuals, and that made it possible for me to associate a great deal with people whom intellectuals seldom have a chance to know well, because they almost speak different languages. I encouraged people to speak about their backgrounds and their activities inside and outside the camp. I did it systematically and consciously. If I could have taken notes, it might almost be called "interviewing." I made it one of my brain games to watch people a short time, and then to tell them what their background had been. I could almost tell it from the way they handled their tools, from the way they walked, and from the way they talked about the weather.

Throughout this book I have avoided stressing my own role, because I did not want it to be a report of my personal suffering and experience. I have left out my own part where it could safely be left out without destroying the value of the story. I have described the moor expresses without saying that I was one of the leaders, because what I have described was absolutely typical for all moor expresses. I was as much part of a certain pattern as any of the other leaders. And in other stories, where I described beating and mistreatment, it seemed to me unnecessary to tell when the stick bit me and when somebody else—we were all under the same stick. I might have told how I got wounds on my head and my blood ran over my shoulders when an SS man threw a stone at me–but it would have deprived the story of its property of being part of a pattern.

I considered it my task not to show what I went through, but what is typical of the treatment in the camp. For the same reason, I avoided as far as possible mentioning names of people whom I could safely have mentioned. I have, by and large, mentioned only the names of persons who played a unique role, such as Karl Bertel and Hubert Richter, the camp seniors in Buchenwald, or the four outstanding killers among the capos, Sterzer, Bock, Berg, and Azzoni (each of whom, except for Azzoni, is also carefully described by the other authors).

As for my ability to observe complicated social phenomena in a way that enables me to put them into the framework of a sociological concept, I can add the following information. When I came to Dachau, I had already studied law for six years at the University of Vienna. (I took my doctor's degree at Christmas, 1937.) Studying law involved a great number of subjects which, at Columbia University, are taught under the discipline of political science, such as public law, philosophy of law, general sociology, labor relations, and so forth (and also elementary statistics). Beyond this minimum as prescribed in the curriculum, I took a large number of classes and seminars in economic and sociological subjects, since I had been interested in these fields for a long time. Among my teachers in sociology, I may mention two strong antipodes: Othmar Spann, who taught "universalism," and Max Adler, who taught "socialism." Among my teachers in economics, I may again mention two antipodes: Othmar Spann with his universalism, and Hans Mayer, the representative of the "Austrian school" of marginal utility. I studied social politics, involving a great deal of labor relations, economics planning, etc., under Degenfeld-Schonburg.

Aside from my scientific training, I had a many-sided training in dealing with groups and observing groups in different social milieus. At the same time that I was studying law at the university, I went to the commercial academy, where I met nonpolitical, middle-class people. Also for two years I attended evening classes in electrical technique and machine construction, where I was the only university student among a hundred workers, most of them unemployed. They were for the most part radical political people. During the same period, I learned acetylene welding in classes with factory workers who were sent by their companies, and in classes with engineers as the only students. In all these classes I was always the only university student.

Most of my political activities took place among workers and lower-middle-class people, in scout groups, youth groups, student groups, and party life. I was a member of the Social Democratic Party. For five years, from 1926 to 1931, I was a leader of scout groups. Most of the groups I established myself by going to schoolyards or parks and playgrounds and gathering children there. After I had organized my third group in this way and had observed how such a group comes into shape within an astonishingly short time, it began to dawn upon me that there were patterns in the way groups are formed. I was about 17 then, and had not yet scientific training enough to generalize from my observations. But I registered them in my mind.

During the years in scout and youth groups, I was frequently in summer camps, most of the time as one of the leaders, and I again had an opportunity to watch how groups were formed and how whole systems of power grew up. We used to have in those camps youths from different districts of Vienna. The various groups were distinguished to a high degree by their background—and they formed the unofficial power structure in the camp accordingly. The groups from the intellectual districts tried to put themselves up as leaders, but the workers' children would not let them because they had already taken over their fathers' class consciousness and class pride, which played a considerably stronger role in Austria after the war than, for instance, in the United States.

After the scout period, I was a member of political youth groups and adult groups, and had a chance to watch the formation of cliques and groups and their struggles for power and leadership. As I grew older, I found more and more that the background of people played a decisive role in the way they formed groups. Even within one political group, intellectuals formed cliques against non-intellectuals, and so forth. It always seemed to me that personal relations and personal roles had but little influence on people's choices. They joined up with the cliques that corresponded most closely to their backgrounds.

Between 1931 and 1937, that is, during my studies at the university, I spent altogether almost a year hitchhiking on European highways. I traveled on my own feet and in other people's cars about 15,000 miles, all the way from Stockholm to Sicily, through most of the countries of central Europe. I used to travel alone for two or three months at a time during my summer vacation. I met hundreds of people who populated the highways at that time—tramps, vagrants, unemployed workers, journeymen, students on vacation, adventurers, runaways, broken beings, powerful gangsters, young boys curious to see what the world looked like, and grey-haired old men who had forgotten it long ago. Again I studied their backgrounds. I made it a game, exactly as I did later in Dachau, to watch people a short time and then to guess from what country they came and what their professions might be. I was not always right, of course, but I was right surprisingly often, and when I looked for the reasons, I found that apparently the background of people determines their behavior to such a high degree that it is fairly easy to deduce their background from their behavior. During my third journey, in 1933, when I hitchhiked from Vienna to Sicily and back, I began writing a "sociology of the highways." The purpose of this somewhat pretentious title was to express that I had learned at the university how to systematize what I could see with my eyes on the highways. This paper never reached the stage of publication. In 1938 I began working on it again, using as my notes hundreds of pages of letters that I had written to friends during those travels, letters which were kept in diary form. But Hitler interrupted this, as he did my other activities. The manuscript is lost in Vienna.

I had a fairly good chance to watch group formation in the underground movement between 1934 and 1938, where I could see in particular how, under these somewhat peculiar circumstances, a type of leadership developed which was completely different from that in a democratic movement. But I did not have to change the concept which I had developed fairly strongly by that time, that it is their background which makes people join in cliques, even within groups with the same ideology.

I also gathered some experience in the observation of human relations as secretary at the Vienna trade court, a position I held up to the day I was imprisoned.

Even if the ability to interpret social phenomena should be granted, it is always possible that people may have different concepts and different ideas when dealing with the same situation. That is unavoidable. I have indicated a few differences above. Some people wanted me to treat the Austrians better and the Prussians worse, and others wanted me to treat the Prussians better and the Austrians worse, and each of them brought numerous examples to stress his point. I even have a friend who seriously objects to my treating the prisoners in groups according to their background, and who is always willing to demonstrate with numerous examples that every word I say can be interpreted differently or can be proven wrong. He claims that the politicals were gangsters and the "greens" were gangsters too, and the most he is willing to admit is that the "greens" were even worse gangsters than the "reds." The same man claims that the distinction I make between the politicals and the nonpoliticals is nonsense, and that the only important distinction is that between the Austrians and the Prussians. When I remind him (he was a fellow prisoner) that almost all non-Jewish politicals in Dachau were Bavarians, he says, "Yes, but they were all Prussianized." This seems to me about as logical as the Nazi argument, when you tell them that there are very bad crooks among the "Aryans." They say, "Yes, but these are 'white Jews,' who have excluded themselves from the Aryan community." Our argument against the Nazis in this case would be, that apparently the distinction between Jews and Aryans is not very useful in describing the phenomenon of cheating in our society. In the same sense, I would answer here that if a whole group can be classified as "Prussianized" without a single Prussian among them, we might as well look for a more useful subdivision which better describes the fact that there are prisoners who are ambitious and others who are not. The division into politicals and nonpoliticals covers, in my mind, about 70 or 80 percent of all cases, and the division into Prussians and Austrians covers perhaps only 40 percent or less. These figures are given as examples. I do not, of course, know what is true numerically.

Afterword

Christian Fleck, Albert Müller, and Nico Stehr

This text, published here for the first time in its entirety, is Paul Martin Neurath's doctoral dissertation, which he successfully defended in June 1943 at Columbia University in New York. In this Afterword, we would like to introduce the author, elucidate the circumstances of the dissertation's unusual genesis, place the work in the context of the literature on concentration camps, and finally outline Neurath's further life, which led him again and again back to his native city of Vienna.

Paul Martin Neurath was born on September 12, 1911. His father was Otto Neurath, then twenty-nine years old. His mother Anna Schapire died at the age of thirty-four, two months after the birth of her son. As a result, Paul grew up in a children's home, which he was not to leave until the age of ten. His stepmother, whom his father married in 1912, had gone blind, and according to prevailing opinion, was in no position to take on raising the little child. For many years, Paul believed his father's second wife, Olga Hahn, to be his natural mother.

The Neuraths belonged to the assimilated Jewish Viennese middle class. Paul's grandfather Wilhelm taught economics as a professor at the

Hochschule für Bodenkultur (College of Agricultural Sciences). Wilhelm's eldest son Otto, after successfully completing his studies at the Friedrich Wilhelm University in Berlin in 1906 and fulfilling his obligatory military service, took up teaching at the *Wiener Handelsakademie* (Vienna High School for Commerce), a secondary school. Paul's mother Anna Schapire, faced with restrictions that prevented women from studying at Austrian universities at the time, had studied at the University of Zurich. She entered public life as a translator, suffragist, and poet, not hesitating to engage in polemic exchanges with the academic mandarins of the time. At the age of twenty-four, she had challenged Werner Sombart, who objected to university education for women on the grounds that "a woman between her twentieth and fortieth year must be ready, willing, and able to take up the burden of pregnancy at twelve-month intervals." Hahn explained to the esteemed professor that the eleven pregnancies he thus calculated were pure fiction.[1] Although she had already gone blind, Olga Hahn graduated in mathematics from the University of Vienna and published several scholarly papers on logic together with Otto Neurath. The latter made his name both as a teacher and as an author of studies on national economy, and surrounded himself with a group of scientists and philosophers who later became known as the first Viennese Circle.[2] Otto Neurath played a role on a wide variety of stages. During the First World War he qualified for a lectureship (*Privatdozent*) in Heidelberg, published articles on war economics, and was summoned to Bavaria during the period of the *Räterepublik* as an expert on socializing industry. After the suppression of the short-lived experiment in direct democracy, the latter activity earned him imprisonment, conviction, deportation, and the loss of his Heidelberg lectureship. Max Weber appeared in court as a witness for the defense, and Otto Bauer, then foreign minister in the first government of the young Austrian Republic, intervened in writing on Neurath's behalf. During the 1920s Otto Neurath managed the *Gesellschafts- und Wirtschaftsmuseum* (social and economic museum) he had founded in Vienna, in which framework pictorial statistics also came to be developed.[3] In addition, he was the tireless organizer of the logical empiricists' philosophical circle. His attempts to gain a position at a university failed re-

1. Schapire 1902.
2. Haller 1985; Haller 1993.
3. Stadler 1982; Hartmann and Bauer 2002.

peatedly. He was also politically active in the Austrian Social Democratic Worker's Party.[4]

It was in the milieu of "Red Vienna" that Paul Neurath, too, experienced his political socialization—first as a participant in the so-called "summer colonies"[5] as a member of the Red Falcons, and later as a member of Social Democratic front organizations. At no point, however, did he ever take a leading role. On his father's urgent advice, after his high school graduation from Vienna's Humanistic Gymnasium No. 5, he decided to study law.[6] In the winter semester of 1931/32, Neurath began his studies at the University of Vienna. He completed the required studies in eight semesters, as anticipated, and registered for the last time in the summer semester of 1935. Like others in the small group of left-wing students, in addition to the normal legal curriculum he also registered for lectures in sociology, psychology, economics, and history. Even in his first semester, he signed up for both "Political Problems of Marxism" under the Austro-Marxist Max Adler and four hours per week of "Psychology" with Karl Bühler. In the second semester, he took "History of Socialism since 1889" taught by Adler, and in the third and fourth semesters he completed "Sociological Seminars," also with Adler. The Austro-Marxist position, already marginalized at the University of Vienna, had indeed been completely suppressed by 1933. Many left-wing students now attended the lectures of the Austro-Liberals. In his fifth semester, Neurath attended lectures in economics by Hans Mayer, and in his seventh semester a seminar led by Richard Strigl and Oskar Morgenstern. Neurath's future career as a specialist in statistics was foreshadowed by his attendance in Wilhelm Winkler's "General Comparative and Austrian Statistics." Classes in art history and economic history demonstrate the student's broad interests, as does his attendance in "History of the United States" and a course on "Russian for Beginners."[7]

In 1935 Neurath received the *Absolutorium,* a graduation without academic degree. As he himself later described it, he saw little chance of a career in jurisprudence and was working hard to acquire additional credentials. Under the prevailing conditions of Austrofascism, this strategy was unquestionably justified. In 1937, however, after he had spent

---

4. Cartwright et al. 1996.

5. Scheu 1985.

6. Neurath 1987.

7. These data were assembled from the certificates of registration that the "nationals," preserved in the archives of the University of Vienna.

about two years "struggling" in various activities, he nonetheless applied for a doctorate in law and sat the three required oral examinations. The theorist of the authoritarian state, Othmar Spann, was unimpressed by Neurath, to whom he gave an "unsatisfactory." The majority of the professors, however, voted for a positive outcome to the examination in political science.[8]

The list of additional qualifications that Paul Neurath acquired during this period is astonishing. Besides completing the high school equivalency course at the Vienna Business Academy, which gave him a basic education in business, he also graduated from a two-year foreman's course in electrical engineering and mechanical engineering at the Arsenal Technical College. During the summer holidays, Neurath spent many weeks as an itinerant. Setting out on the traditional wanderings of the journeyman was a common strategy for unemployed young men in the 1930s who wanted to escape forced inactivity. His travels led Neurath through Germany, Switzerland, and northern Italy. In his letters Neurath repeatedly mentioned that he would have liked to work these experiences into a sociological book. In the last week of February 1938, he began a year-long practicum at the Vienna *Gewerbegericht* (Commerical Court), which was required to complete his law training. After only three weeks, the invasion by German troops and the surrender of government power to the Nazis ended his work as a trainee. Two days after the *Anschluss* the Gestapo was at his door, looking for an alleged propagandist—"Neuman's the name, or some such." Neurath was able to escape arrest only with difficulty. "They say he's a doctor," a helpful neighbor woman told the Gestapo.[9]

In the next few days, he attempted to cross illegally into Czechoslovakia. He was arrested only a few miles short of the border. After several days in solitary confinement outside Vienna, he was transferred to the Rossauerlände police prison in Vienna. On April 1, 1938, he arrived with the first transport of 150 Austrians at the Dachau concentration camp, where he received the prisoner number 13,868. The city magistrate of Vienna terminated Neurath's residency in his Vienna apartment in the Penzingerstrasse on July 1, 1939.

In this so-called *Prominententransport* were to be found leading representatives of the authoritarian state, and those Social Democrats who

---

8. University of Vienna Archives, Jur. Fak. (Faculty of Law), Rigorosenprotokoll (oral examination report) 1937.

9. Neurath 1987, p. 515. Also see "Prelude," above.

had not managed to escape the clutches of the Gestapo. To this number were added nonpolitical but wealthy Jews, whose relatives were to be blackmailed into ransoming them. The fact that Paul Neurath was included in this transport is somewhat surprising. He was by no means prominent, which leads to the conjecture that both his arrest and his early transfer to a concentration camp resulted either from his having been mistaken for his father, or from a desire to take him into custody as a kind of hostage in his father's place. (Otto Neurath had been living in exile in the Hague since 1934.) From the moment of arrival in Dachau, to be sure, it hardly mattered anyway why someone had been sent there.

Concentration camp Dachau, in the vicinity of Munich, had been established in early 1933. In April 1933, SS units replaced the Munich police as guards. At the end of March there were 151 prisoners, and the number grew continually. By the end of July 1933 there were 2,038 prisoners. The SS-imposed camp system in Dachau rapidly set the example for other early camps, and has been designated "the Dachau model" in the literature.[10] The camp was considerably enlarged and expanded in 1937 and 1938 by means of the prisoners' labor. Altogether, more than 200,000 people were incarcerated in Dachau.[11] In the course of a temporary evacuation of the Dachau camp (probably in preparation for the planned seizure of 10,000 Jews during the *Kristallnacht* pogrom six weeks later) and the associated transfer of its Jewish prisoners to Buchenwald, Paul Neurath arrived in Buchenwald on September 24, 1938, together with 1,082 other Dachau prisoners. His first prisoner number was 9506, the second 2086; category—political Jew.

The Buchenwald concentration camp, which at first bore the name "K. L. Ettersberg," had been opened near Weimar in July 1937 with 149 prisoners. During that month, protests from Weimar led to the camp being rechristened. The city's Nazi cultural authority took exception to the original name on the grounds that "Ettersberg had connections to the life of Goethe."[12] The first prisoner transports began arriving in mid-July. Between mid-1937 and 1945 about 240,000 people were admitted. Of these, some 34,000 are entered in the camp's death register. Thousands more of the Buchenwald prisoners died in other concentration camps and during evacuation marches. The camp was meant to hold between 6,000 and 8,000 prisoners on average. On November 10, 1944,

10. Orth 1999, pp. 26–33; Tuchel 1994.
11. Marcuse 2001.
12. Drobisch and Wieland 1993, p. 269.

there were 59,267 inmates, including those in the peripheral camps; on April 10, 1945, 80,900 prisoners were counted.[13]

The history of the Buchenwald camp can be subdivided into two periods. Paul Neurath's memoirs relate to one part of the first phase of Buchenwald's development from 1937 to 1942. From 1942 on, the function of the camps was expanded. Now the prisoners' economic usefulness as forced labor for war-related industry became significant, for example in the production of "V-weapons" (the V1 and V2 rockets) in the infamous Mittelbau-Dora camp, and the establishment of a multitude of further peripheral camps. Moreover, both the composition and the number of the prisoners changed.[14]

Neurath belonged to the group of political Jewish prisoners in the camp who were finding life particularly difficult at the time of the transfer. This was not because they had been labeled political Jews, however, but because of the huge number of new arrivals. If anything played a role in Neurath's survival, it was the fact that he was still young, not yet 27, in good physical condition, and having few material needs—thanks to having been on the road and a manual laborer. Moreover, Neurath was "lucky," for he was released from Buchenwald on May 27, 1939—before the outbreak of war—probably because he was in possession of an exit visa. His girlfriend Lucie had done all she could in Vienna to effect his release.

After only a few days in Vienna, Neurath set out in mid-June 1939 for Sweden. In the next two years, he completed a one-year retraining period as a metalworker in Stockholm, and then worked operating a boring and turning mill in a shipyard in Göteborg. His emigration to the United States was the result of chance and a sudden change in the manner in which the Americans determined their national immigration quotas. After the German Reich attacked Denmark and Norway, the American immigration authorities transferred the now useless immigration contingent from those countries to Sweden, and Neurath was suddenly given the green light for entry to the United States. Aboard the Swedish merchant ship, Neurath was in good company. Among his few fellow passengers were the philosopher Ernst Cassirer and the linguist Roman Jakobson. The ship docked on June 3, 1941, in New York Harbor. Half a year later, following the Japanese attack on Pearl Harbor, the United States entered the Second World War.

---

13. Schwarz 1990.
14. See the comprehensive documentation in Stein 1998.

In New York, Paul Neurath turned to his father's cousin, Waldemar Kaempffert, who, as science editor for the *New York Times,* was in a position to help the newcomer find his bearings. Kaempffert was extremely pleased to find that the young man, with whom he had not been personally acquainted, asked him not for money, but rather for advice, which he gave willingly. Neurath revealed to his uncle that he now wanted "to study sociology at last,"[15] upon which Kaempffert put together a list of names of professors whom Neurath should approach. On this list Neurath found the name of Paul Lazarsfeld, whom he knew from the old days in Vienna. A few days later Neurath began work as a "sketcher" with statistical counts and calculations in Lazarsfeld's Office of Radio Research, where his proficiency with a slide rule, which he had gained in Sweden, proved to be very useful. This work certainly did not make him wealthy, but he was able to make a living from it, as he wrote in a detailed letter to a friend in Sweden, Rudolf Pass, a few months after his arrival.[16]

In addition to his job at the Office of Radio Research, Paul Neurath inquired into the chances of earning a diploma from Columbia University. His Vienna law studies were accepted as equivalent to an M.A.; thus it would be possible to earn his degree within only two years. Beginning in the summer term of 1941, Neurath rapidly completed the mandatory courses in the graduate program.

Given an opportunity "to be able to show proof that I'm good for something," he seized it with both hands. In October 1942 he recounted his successes in a quite exuberant tone: "So now I've been in this blessed country for sixteen months. Sixteen months ago I didn't even know what statistics was, and now I've already spent a month as the assistant of my old statistics instructor at Columbia University. . . . [I] have a University Fellowship . . . those are the highest fellowships that they give out, they're considered to be great distinctions. Every department has only one of them, and so I've got the one in the Sociology Department."[17]

According to Neurath's own statement, during his stay in the Dachau and Buchenwald concentration camps, he had already contemplated

15. Neurath 1987, p. 521; Neurath 1982.
16. Neurath to Rudolf Pass, Oct. 22, 1941, Paul Neurath papers, Department of Sociology, University of Vienna. Neurath's German-language letters exhibit peculiarities of style and syntax that well illustrate his process of acculturation. It is not usually possible to convey these qualities in translation, though his English-language letters, some of which are quoted here without alteration, show some similar peculiarities.
17. Neurath to Pass, Oct. 30, 1942.

working his observations and experiences into a book after his release. "I had the concept of this book in my head when I was still in camp. I always knew that it had to be written, because I know what people usually write about. In most of the books, we get transmitted only the high spots, like when they hanged a man on Dec. 21, 1938, on a gallows, and twenty thousand prisoners looked at it at attention."[18]

In New York, Neurath was now offered the opportunity to earn a further doctorate with this project. In October 1942, he informed Rudolf Pass that he "already [had] two hundred typed pages" of the dissertation finished. "It is a sociological study of my experiences in the camps.... I'm writing as, what they describe here with the technical term, 'participant observer.'"[19] This last remark is likely only partly correct, because before his arrival in the United States, Neurath had surely not been acquainted with this method of social scientific data-gathering. Moreover, he would hardly have been in a position to act as a participant observer in the concentration camp. For want of a better designation, however, it was probably acceptable for Neurath, or one of his teachers, to furnish his approach with this label. However, the participant-observer method enjoyed less respect among Columbia's sociologists than it did in other sociology departments in the United States.

In Chicago, which was considered the home of the open, qualitative approach, a recent immigrant with a thesis based almost exclusively on his own experiences would probably have met with a much friendlier reception and more stimulating reactions. For example, William F. Whyte did not submit his *Street Corner Society,*[20] which was quite comparable in its methodology to Neurath's dissertation project, as a dissertation at the university where it was written and financially supported—namely Harvard University—but rather transferred pro forma to Chicago, where he was able to obtain his diploma without difficulties. The band of young sociologists who had written dissertations under Robert Park's supervision, often making use of their own life histories, had by this time already produced several journeyman studies. These had met with such a strong response that the Social Science Research Council felt obligated to initiate a methodological debate over this type of social research.[21] In 1937, this umbrella group of professional organizations in the social

18. Neurath to Robert MacIver, Mar. 29, 1942.
19. Neurath to Pass, Oct. 30, 1942.
20. Whyte 1943.
21. Cf. Dollard 1935.

sciences authorized Herbert Blumer to produce a critical assessment of the classic example of the use of personal documents—William I. Thomas and Florian Znaniecki's monumental investigation, *The Polish Peasant in Poland and America,* first published in 1918. Blumer, who was later to become famous as the patron saint of symbolic interactionism,[22] was extremely critical of Thomas and Znaniecki's methodology in his report, but he did not go so far as to reject outright the use of personal documents such as letters, diaries, or personally composed life stories. Blumer's central objection was based on the view, which had then only recently become respectable, of a "scientific" social science modeled on the natural sciences. This view prioritized causal explanation and the ability to produce prognoses. This high hurdle could be surmounted neither by *The Polish Peasant* nor by the many Chicago dissertations that had been written under Park's direction and published by Chicago University Press in a series of their own. Nels Anderson had based his 1923 study, *The Hobo: The Sociology of the Homeless Man,*[23] on his own experiences as an itinerant laborer, and Clifford R. Shaw had graduated with a thesis that consisted largely of reproductions of a pickpocket's autobiographical notes.[24] These and other Chicago dissertations met with a critical reception in further methodological studies initiated by the Social Science Research Council on the use of personal documents in the social sciences.[25] Neurath's claim that he at least did not have to read any books for his dissertation, is thus only a half-truth. In fact, there already existed a series of texts about life in German concentration camps. These publications, whose authors included such social scientists as Karl August Wittfogel,[26] were written in the style of eyewitness reports and not as attempts at social scientific analysis. Moreover, there were methodological essays on the problems connected with eyewitness reports, autobiographies, and personal documents in general, which played such a prominent role in the contemporary debate in the American social sciences that many interpreters came to the view that the criticism leveled by Blumer and others at what was later to be called "qualitative" social research had caused lasting harm to its further development.[27]

---

22. Blumer 1969.
23. Anderson 1923.
24. Shaw 1930.
25. Gottschalk, Kluckhohn, and Angell 1945.
26. Under the pseudonym Hinrichs 1936.
27. Paul 1979; Platt 1996.

Neurath's interpretations of his experiences in the camps fully satisfy the criterion of communicative validation, which was only later to be formulated as such. What is even more astonishing is the fact that in the original text of the dissertation, there is absolutely no explanation of the methodology. This lack would later oblige him, after the official submission of the manuscript as a dissertation, to write an addendum, which is the text printed here. In this appendix, Neurath counters all of the objections that he might well have foreseen, had he studied the methodological publications of the time.

The members of the Sociology Department at Columbia University, where Neurath finally submitted the report on his life as an inmate of two German concentration camps, were nonetheless friendly and obliging to the newcomer; several seem to have been interested in his report. An intellectually nurturing micro environment, however, in which his work on the dissertation might have enjoyed specific stimuli, was not offered to Neurath. The faculty was too much interested in other topics and concerned with studies to which Neurath's project bore little resemblance. But even he himself was not exclusively interested in the topic of his dissertation. Neurath had very quickly developed a liking for statistics, where he soon made his name as an expert and from which he was increasingly able to make his living. This aspect of his abilities no doubt met with unanimous approval and open acceptance; the work on the dissertation certainly aroused less interest.

Of the two senior members of the department, Robert MacIver and Robert Lynd—who were indeed continually at loggerheads—it was MacIver who, for reasons now unknown, took Neurath on. This alone may well have been sufficient to motivate MacIver's antipode Lynd to cast a particularly critical eye on the work of the other's pupil. In terms of length of tenure, third place among the faculty was held by Theodore Abel, but he was being increasingly pushed aside by the newcomers Paul F. Lazarsfeld and Robert K. Merton, both hired in 1940, and Abel eventually decided to leave Columbia.[28] The Polish-born Abel, however, was the researcher whose work on the early following of the Nazis, published in 1938 under the title, *Why Hitler Came Into Power: An Answer Based on the Original Life Stories of Six Hundred of His Followers,* showed the strongest affinity to Neurath's project in terms of content.[29] Abel's multi-volume diary, to which he gave the title *Journal of*

28. Abel 2001.
29. Abel 1938.

Thoughts and Events,[30] showed that as the war in Europe wore on, his interest in esoteric sociological questions receded into the background. From 1940 on, sociological questions were only occasionally discussed in the diary, while Abel tormented himself for months with thoughts of how he himself could contribute to the defeat of the Nazis. On the other hand, during the time when Neurath was at work on his dissertation, the future titans of the Columbia sociological tradition, Lazarsfeld and Merton, were likely too occupied with their own work to offer further support to someone who was somewhat older than the usual students.

In March 1942 Neurath finished a provisional chapter, which he submitted to his supervisor MacIver to determine whether he could be accepted as a doctoral candidate. In addition to this chapter, he had already written two more. At the same time, he began to discuss these texts with former camp prisoners, as well as with others from outside this group. From the beginning, Neurath wanted to be certain of two things—the precision of his description and the acceptance of his explanations and elucidations by a wider, not necessarily scientific, audience.[31] To this end, he imposed upon himself the criterion of general comprehensibility (possibly a legacy of the educational politics in Red Vienna). "I write as 'simple' [in English in the original] and straightforwardly as possible, and express all of the sociological considerations in completely nonacademic language, for the very purpose of possibly bringing the topic to a larger readership."[32]

In early 1943, in addition to his studies and his job, Neurath had completed a first draft of his thesis. But even before he submitted this to his dissertation supervisor, he sought to make systematic contact with people who had been incarcerated in the camps with him and who were available in the United States. Among the first of these was Felix Reichmann, an art historian and bookseller from Vienna, like Neurath a prisoner in Dachau and Buchenwald, and after 1945 professor and library director at Cornell University. Reichmann treated Neurath with a mixture of benevolence and skepticism; he indeed considered the work to be important, but did not think it was a sociological study. In his formulations, Reichmann addressed the most basic dilemma of Neurath's thesis—the attempt to strike a balance between personal analysis and the desired academic acknowledgement. "From a sober and pedantic standpoint,

30. Excerpted in Abel 2001.
31. Neurath to Whiteman, 1942.
32. Neurath to Willy Ernst, Jan. 23, 1943.

your thesis has one major flaw, though an inevitable one. It is based on personal experience (including some personal experiences of your companions). Even if hundreds of former Dachau prisoners were to offer you critical material, it would never become reliable sociological data. The patient can never describe his condition as well as the physician. Not merely because he fails to see the connections, which wouldn't be true in your case, but rather simply because the physician suffers no pain."[33] The possibility that a patient could become a physician seems never to have occurred to Reichmann.

At about the same time, Neurath made contact with Willy Ernst, who was then living in San Francisco. Ernst, like Neurath, had been a member of the Red Falcons. In Ernst, Paul Neurath found approbation for his project, and on a factual level, Ernst was able to contribute corroborative details and correct minor errors. Moreover, he was in a position to provide the addresses of other former prisoners then living in the United States. Ernst read Neurath's first draft exactly from the standpoint of a representative of the prisoners' community. "For *us* [emphasis added] it is extremely important to have such a strictly scientific, almost dispassionate factual report."[34]

Paul Neurath also found an 'editor' for his text, with whom he carried on an intense correspondence. With great precision, Vienna-born Trautl Aull, who lived outside of New York, not only reviewed the work's content, but also corrected all kinds of linguistic lapses and errors. Neurath repeatedly demanded sharp criticism from Aull, specifically in written form. "If someone attacks me in conversation, I defend *myself*, if he attacks me with the written word, I defend the *topic*." On this psychologically very interesting premise, an involved debate over the text ensued. A close and trusting relationship developed between Neurath and Aull, and the correspondence increasingly developed into a kind of background conversation about his text. He disclosed his main intentions; he wanted to give the political prisoners priority over the others, to give the Austrians priority over the Prussians, and to ascribe a special, positive role to the Viennese Jews (in Dachau). For example, in his portrayal of the Austrians saying, "*Bittschön Herr Kapo: A leicht's Tragerl*" ("Please, Herr Kapo, give me a light little handbarrow"), he shows how, by means of such unreasonable requests, the Austrians/Viennese/Jews were able to demoralize the "*Piefkes*"—the German senior prisoner functionaries who were accustomed to the camps—at every turn.

---

33. Felix Reichmann to Neurath, Apr. 12, 1943.
34. Willy Ernst to Neurath, Feb. 12, 1943.

In this correspondence we find reflected a central problem of many immigrant intellectuals—the necessity of expressing oneself adequately in a still unfamiliar language. Neurath described this as follows: "My command of the German language is not bad for a layman's use, by which I mean I can handle it, play with it, speak in nuances, draw allegories, construct complicated phrases, and nonetheless keep it clear. A German sentence that I've stretched out over ten lines can still easily be read, simply because it's built so that the three different clauses hidden in it can still be distinguished from each other. In English, I can't do all that. In English, for the time being, I've let every imaginable cook spoil the broth and force a curt, clipped style on me that principally consists of primitive, uncomplicated direct sentences, without the slightest intellectual demands on the reader." Neurath's way out of the dilemma of having attained only a low level of complexity in the new language consisted of "making these clipped sentences into something like a personal style."[35]

These discussions of the text took place while Neurath was under a great deal of pressure to complete the work. On April 15, 1943, he wrote that he had finished 270 pages, with about 150 more pages to come; but the thesis would soon be due.

While Neurath's informal supervisors were either acclaiming or criticizing his thesis, however, there arose problems with the gatekeepers of academia shortly before the completion of his Ph.D. studies. On May 3, 1943, Lynd sent a memorandum to MacIver, beginning with the sentence, "I do not think Neurath's dissertation should be accepted in its present form." For a doctoral student in the last stages of his studies, and shortly before the final examinations, there can hardly have been a worse judgment. Lynd had no difficulty with the text itself: "It is a fascinating book for *popular* consumption." That, however, was exactly what gave rise to the reproach that the work was unscientific and lacked systematic analysis. Lynd stressed twice in his memorandum that it would not suffice, as far as he was concerned, merely to add a further chapter to the text; rather, he insistently demanded that the text be rewritten in its entirety in order to be acceptable as a dissertation. In four pages, Lynd set out a detailed structure for the new version of the thesis that he envisioned. Since it was impossible to provide an overview of the entire camp, he demanded that the dissertation writer—following the sociometry of Jacob L. Moreno—describe and analyze group processes as exemplified by his barracks, or a portion of his barracks. The tone in

---

35. Neurath to Trautl Aull, Apr. 19, 1943.

which the memorandum is couched seems perfectly benevolent; Lynd evidently wanted to help, even if his suggestions were by no means appropriate. Although some of his criticisms seem to be based on a misunderstanding—a later handwritten comment of Neurath's explains that Lynd knew only the first part of the manuscript, not the second, "The Society"—he raised a point that Neurath had already discussed previously with several of his correspondents. The thesis was not a sociological study in the academic sense, and Neurath knew this, in any case. As late as 1946 he wrote to Rudolf Pass, "Actually it can't be called a sociological report at all; it is simply a report on certain phenomena that someone with sociological interests sees better and describes better than someone without them."

There was one further irritation, however. Neurath felt that his work would satisfy the demands of scientific originality. In late October 1942 he reported of his dissertation project: "It is meeting with uncommonly good support, it seems that something like this has never been attempted."[36] In October 1943, Bruno Bettelheim's study, "Individual and Mass Behavior in Extreme Situations," completed a year previously, was published in the *Journal of Abnormal and Social Psychology*.[37] Bettelheim was a former camp prisoner whose life had been extremely similar to Neurath's. A native of Vienna, he was first transported to Dachau and later transferred to Buchenwald. Bettelheim's publication seemed to encroach upon the exclusivity of Neurath's dissertation topic. In Neurath's circle, some believed that he himself had submitted an article on Dachau and Buchenwald under the pseudonym Bruno Bettelheim. Neurath much later reported, "I was working on my doctoral dissertation on the concentration camps at Columbia, and one evening I came to an event put on by the Graduate Sociology Club. Professor Abel was there, and as I come in the door he calls to me across the whole, quite large, room: 'Hello Mister Bettelheim, hello Mister Bettelheim!' and I look at him stupidly, no idea what he's talking about.... Yes, I say, I really don't understand—until it finally comes out that this article of Bettelheim's ... had appeared.... [They] thought, because it was well known that I was writing my dissertation on the concentration camp and that chiefly on Abel's orders, ... that it was an article I had written under the pseudonym Bettelheim. [I just said,] listen, that's kind of a funny pseudonym in America, if I was looking to use one."[38] Bettelheim's and Neurath's

36. Neurath to Rudolf Pass, Oct. 30, 1942.
37. Bettelheim 1943.
38. Neurath 1989.

interpretations, however, were markedly different. While Neurath attempted throughout to describe the differentiation between patterns of behavior and to explain significant differences simply by means of group membership and group background, Bettelheim aimed at psychoanalytically inspired generalizations and assumed that there was an identification with the aggressor. Neurath noticed these differences immediately. However, as he explained in retrospect, he was still too little socialized in the academic system to compose an appropriate rejoinder. Moreover, he wanted to avoid a situation in which two former concentration camp prisoners came to trading verbal blows in public.[39]

Because American universities keep only rudimentary notes on the dissertation process, Neurath's difficulties in having the report of his experiences accepted as a thesis for a sociological degree can only be approximately reconstructed. In the unpublished records left behind by Abel, Lazarsfeld, Lynd, MacIver, and Merton, there is as little information to be found on this point as in Abel's diaries and MacIver's autobiography.[40] However, Neurath's "Addendum" to the dissertation, his "Statement on the Validity of the Observations that Form the Basis of the Dissertation," discusses the points that were raised in criticism of his thesis—and what points could have been raised, purely in the interest of maintaining the disciplinary identity of the still young field of "sociology."

Neurath's explanation that it was impossible to smuggle notes of any kind out of the camp, though it may sound strange today, was no doubt in response to a criticism in just this regard—a criticism that he indeed was not alone in facing. Bruno Bettelheim reported that he, too, had been confronted with such objections.[41]

In the Dissertation and Defense and Deposit Office of Columbia University, there remains a register of names of those who belonged to Neurath's examination committee. Unusually, this board comprised ten examiners; the normal number was three to five. The list of examiners included practically the entire sociology department, with the exception of Paul Lazarsfeld. Under the chairmanship of Lynd, the examination committee included, among others, the sociologists Abel, MacIver, Merton, and Associate Professor Willard W. Waller, as well as William S. Robinson (lecturer in statistics and sociology), Nathaniel Peffer (professor

39. Cf. Fleck and Müller 1997.
40. MacIver 1968.
41. Bettelheim 1960, p. 118; Bettelheim 1979, pp. 14f.

in international relations) and Abraham Wald (assistant professor in economics).[42]

The size of the examination committee could well be explained by the fact that the final oral examination and the dissertation defense took place simultaneously. However, it could also indicate a rather conflict-laden event. In any case, Neurath later described his final examination as follows: "And one fine day in the month of May 1943, between 9:00 and 11:00, I passed my 'orals,' immediately afterward defended my dissertation before the same committee, and at 12:00 noon I was finished with my doctorate—not quite two years after I had arrived in New York."[43]

Thus Paul Neurath had indeed completed his higher studies in only two years; but he as yet had no right to the title of Ph.D. At that time, the Faculty of Political Science of Columbia University demanded of every candidate the submission of seventy-five copies of his thesis.[44] At a time when photocopiers were a thing of the future, this meant either having the dissertation accepted by a publisher who would print the thesis as a regular book—and as late as January, Neurath still had hopes of an acceptance from Columbia University Press—or paying the high cost of printing the copies out of one's own pocket.

In a letter, Neurath summarized, in ironic fashion, the enormous workload of completing his thesis: "I'll put some statistics on the record. On about March 15 I began the present version of the book. It has 465 pages (without the foreword, which I've got in the typewriter just now). That means that in fifty-five days, rain or shine, I've produced eight pages a day. This is a distorted picture, however, since at the beginning I frittered a way a lot of the time. The second part, that is, the sociological part, has 190 pages.... These 190 pages I produced in the period from April 28 to May 9, that is, in twelve days. That's about sixteen pages a day, rain or shine. And that's not quite right either. Because the truth is that I frittered away those first few days as well. Of this second part, at least one hundred pages are first draft, which means never previously written. And they're still the best thing in the whole book."[45]

As the work was taking shape, it was not easy for Neurath to situate his dissertation project unequivocally. It had at least four dimensions—as a political project; as a project of assimilating both a group history

---

42. The names of two further examiners could not be deciphered.
43. Neurath 1987, p. 524.
44. In his correspondence, Neurath repeatedly gives the number erroneously as 125.
45. Neurath to Aull, May 20, 1943.

and Neurath's own; as a project with which he desired to become famous as an author; and finally as a project meant to satisfy the standards of the academic culture of which he had become a member. This tetralemma, with its divergent demands, was beyond Neurath's ability to solve. He himself was in any case well aware of the inconsistencies of his project, for he began to develop strategies to justify them. Thus he explained to his former fellow prisoner Willy Ernst the book project's distance from politics: "I'd like to forestall criticism of a couple of things. When you read the thing, please don't forget that it's a doctoral dissertation planned for Columbia University, which certainly isn't one of the most reactionary American universities, but one of the most distinguished, and so has to be somewhat cautious with political statements coming out in print under its name. What's more, it seems to me that there's little gained if the thing is written with more political bite and then nobody reads it because it's classified as 'red stuff.'"[46] Neurath also expressed himself in similar terms to his former fellow prisoner Ponger. After listing "a couple of main theses" of his study, he gave the following hint: "Besides, the whole thing is written in thoroughly nonacademic language, because I want it to be read. I consider it a political responsibility to write the book so that the reader clearly understands the attitude and function of the political prisoners. To be sure, this has to be done in as general a form as possible, so it can be widely accepted and not immediately taken for red propaganda."[47] Not being considered "red stuff" and "red propaganda" had to be associated with a political goal, the representation of Neurath's own group. This problem was also raised, at least indirectly, to the dissertation's supervisor, MacIver, as Neurath reported on his reading of Georg Karst's book: "Karst, for example, writes that he as a Catholic is a sworn enemy of the Communists, but still has to admit that they were the most comrade-like and helpful men he met in the camps. I think it might be worthwhile to bring in a few quotations like that in order to prove that my high esteem for the political prisoners is not an unjustified bias. Because I am expecting criticism in that direction."[48]

A further problem was the sociological status of the study. Neurath went into particular detail on this matter to Reichmann, who had repeatedly referred to the dissertation's lack of sociological character, for in-

---

46. Neurath to Ernst, Jan. 23, 1943.
47. Neurath to Ponger, Mar. 2, 1943.
48. Neurath to MacIver, Jan. 15, 1943.

stance, "Repeating 'society' ten times over and saying 'rule of the game' once doesn't yet make you a sociologist. You'll forgive me for being malicious."[49] Neurath gave reasons for not having written his thesis on the basis of sociological literature: "I had ... very much disregarded the sociological side, that is to say, I wrote a book from sociological viewpoints without laying stress on the method. Just as I've always hesitated to recommend books on the materialist view of history to people, because I've always thought that instead they should just read historical works written from that viewpoint ([e.g.,] Franz Mehring).[50] ... I not only promise to derive the behavior of people and groups of people in the new society from their earlier milieu, background etc., as for example, Donal[d] Clemmer in *Prison Community*,[51] promises. Rather, I carry it through, quite consistently, as far as I can judge. This seems to be rare. I'd be happy if I could find out where I've got this from. I'm afraid I can't quote any great sociologist who said it should be done this way, or did it this way himself—and I can't quote any minor one from whom I might have stolen it behind his back.... The reason I can't cite any of the patriarchs I've robbed, plundered, or observed or followed seems to me to be that the great masters, including the anthropologists, concern themselves with original cultures, while I concern myself with a derivative culture. Apparently there aren't many reports, maybe even almost none, on derivative cultures written by sociologists. Children's homes, boarding schools, monasteries, army units, would likely offer a rich field, but apparently the sociologists who write books are neither children nor students nor nuns nor soldiers. At the moment there must surely be a couple of sociologists serving as soldiers, and I hope that the books that come out of that will show how the soldiers' society functions. I'd probably write something like that, but I'm not a soldier either—for the time being, at least not yet."[52]

The passage cited is very revealing, insofar as Neurath here displays a general skepticism toward sociological research, a skepticism toward the sociological tradition and its "classics," and a skepticism toward its methods. At the same time, he nonetheless insists that he has written an original sociological study, which indeed can have as its only basis the fact that he had "been there"—just as, in his opinion, any good study

---

49. Reichmann to Neurath, Apr. 21, 1942.

50. Editors note: Franz Mehring (1846–1919) was a leading German Marxist historian.

51. Clemmer 1940.

52. Neurath to Reichmann, Mar. 22, 1943.

could only take as its basis the fact that someone had "been there." Sociologists would literally have to become nuns—this is one ironic inference from Neurath's explanation.

In the discussions with his "editor," his distance from sociology became even more apparent. "At the moment I'm working on the foreword. At first I thought of writing only a very short one for the department, but somehow that won't work. Twice already all my rage from ten years of political silence has spilled forth, and there's nothing left for it but either not to submit a foreword for the examination ... or else to write the actual foreword that goes with the book. And you can count on it, if the actual foreword is there, then the afterword will have to be there too, the one that's been stuck in my throat for years. I already knew why I threw myself into statistics and didn't want to teach sociology. I myself often find it disturbing how much social satire I've smuggled into the book.... But how I'm supposed to teach sociology at an American college with this lack of political self-control is an utter riddle to me. It will be a catastrophe."[53]

Nonetheless, Paul Neurath remained unsatisfied with the results of all the effort he had put into the writing. For the summer of 1943 he planned further revisions and abridgements, which, due to his professional career, were only partially completed. In 1946, Neurath finally summed up, "I'm afraid I'm bogged down with the dissertation. I should have had it published in '43, after its acceptance by the faculty. But I'd got it into my head to rewrite it one more time for literary reasons, and that wasn't done until spring 1945. By then it was already too late for commercial publication. Publishers didn't want to print any more about concentration camps without gas chambers. Who wants to hear that? The audience is spoiled. The fact that our people were hanged by their wrists from the trees during a snowstorm, crying for their fathers and mothers, who cares about that in the age of crematorium ovens and millions murdered.... Yes, yes, 'we greatly appreciate your objectivity and the clarity of your analysis, but the readers want to have more sensational accounts.'"[54]

Neurath's self-diagnosis carries some plausibility. Certainly, the development of the camps itself had to some extent "outpaced" his description. The establishment of the extermination camps did not occur until after Neurath's release. By the end of the war, however, the main

---

53. Neurath to Aull, May 10, 1943.
54. Neurath to Pass, Sept. 26, 1946.

impression received by the public was of gas chambers and crematorium chimneys, based on images of the mountains of victims' corpses, eyeglasses, suitcases, and meager possessions. The version of the dissertation that finally bore the date 1951 does indeed refer at some points to the Shoah; these additions, however, seem oddly extraneous and artificial. Neurath did succeed in describing, analyzing, and assimilating his own experiences, and those of his reference group; the other, later developments elude description. This is not very surprising, however. Other authors as well, such as Benedikt Kautsky, for example, who experienced all the phases of the camps' development—including the mass annihilation by means of poison gas—had great difficulties integrating these various phases into one description.

The ambivalent feelings to which Neurath was subject during the composition of his dissertation have already been pointed out; so, too, the difficulties he encountered in terms of the work's linguistic realization. These difficulties must be seen in the context of Neurath's high expectations for the linguistic presentation of his observations. Contemporary dissertations were usually not particularly demanding in this regard. The description and rationale of a research problem would be given, followed by the empirical investigation of the topic at hand, concluding with a brief summary. Neurath's thesis differed profoundly from this simple model; it followed another dramaturgy altogether, consistently marked by something like creative deviance. A reader who looks at no more than the table of contents outlining the architecture of the work will notice the clear division into two sections. In the first part the author introduces his actors—the prisoners and their oppressors—on the forestage (the title "The Scene" is significant here). In the second, he illuminates the backstage of functioning methods, balances and imbalances in the social life ("The Society") of the camps.[55] The actual arrangement of the text itself, however, goes well beyond this basic architecture.

Let us begin with the "paratexts," a term that has become current since the work of Gérard Genette,[56] for the description of a book's literary "accessories" or liminal features, with whose aid an author explicitly or implicitly labels the intentions of his or her work and "situates" it in various regards. The introductory quotation of Neurath's book di-

---

55. Cf. the original title of Neurath's dissertation: *Social Life in the German Concentration Camps Dachau and Buchenwald.*
56. Genette 1997.

rectly addresses the object—the concentration camps. The quoted speaker, the former commandant of Dachau, refers to the difference between prison and penitentiary on the one hand and concentration camp on the other. "There is a difference. You will soon see what the difference is." This information is not only for the prisoners arriving in the camp, but also for the intended readers of Neurath's text. With this quotation, the author emphasizes not only the peculiarity of the camps and of his experiences as their inmate, but also the peculiarity of the text. The structural analysis of the text reveals a semantic homology; with these sentences the prisoners are initiated into the camp, the readers into the book.

The dedication page also emphasizes the text's peculiarity. The author dedicates his work to three people. The first person is a woman, Lucie; her family name goes unmentioned. The author thanks Lucie for his release from the camp and describes her as accompanying him "through and out of hell." He probably owes her his life. Lucie was Neurath's girlfriend; their relationship, however, fell apart after his release, and they broke off contact due to a quarrel. Neurath mentioned in his letters that he intended this dedication not only to express his debt of gratitude, but also to re-establish communication.

Both of the other dedicatees are men; they are given their family names and they are both already dead. The attorney Oswald Richter, a friend of the Neurath family, could not take living in the camp and died; the author wanted to clear Richter's name. Franz Steinberg was a camp acquaintance of Neurath's. The dialogue reproduced in the dedication, from the day before Steinberg's death, speaks to the author's intentions: justice, remembrance, and—vengeance.

Neurath's text itself by no means begins with the usual academic rationale for his topic. His "Prelude" is rather the dramatic story of his arrest. Although the actors are described—the Gestapo men, the neighbors in the Vienna municipal apartment block, the treacherous farmers at the border, the author himself as antifascist—the situation into which the reader is immediately plunged nonetheless remains virtually unexplained. No motivation is offered for the situation, even though the course of the action seems to possess a plausibility all its own. The situation at hand is one that might well be described as "Kafkaesque."

The section entitled "The Scene" begins (as do many other depictions of the camps) by portraying "standard situations" in the concentration camps. To this end, Neurath's text makes use of a rhetoric of description. To be sure, here too the narrator remains part of the narrated events, part of the situations presented; the characteristic style, however, moves within the territory of conventional eyewitness testimony, meant to signal "objectivity" above all. The direct speech woven into the depiction here emphasizes the element of authenticity, often additionally stressed in the English original by the use of the German language. In the final section of "The Scene," which bears the heading "Kaleidoscope," the dramaturgy of the text changes. With the aid of a technique of "montage" borrowed from cinématography, scenes of completely different significance are strung together. The individual "cuts" are each introduced by a heading giving the location and date: "Buchenwald, Winter 1938," "Buchenwald, January 4, 1939," "Dachau, Summer 1938," "Buchenwald, Spring 1939," "Buchenwald, April 20, 1939," "Dachau, April 1938" ... the series goes on. It is clear that neither a chronological principle nor a principle of spatial or thematic unity is being maintained here. What matters are the brief "flashes." The last entry under "Kaleidoscope" bears the title "Buchenwald, December 21, 1938," and offers something like a climactic intensification of what has gone before. Here Neurath describes the execution of Peter Forster, an event that numbers among the *lieux de mémoire* of the historiography of the camps. Forster had fled from the camp and fallen again into the Nazis' hands. He was hanged in front of 20,000 Buchenwald prisoners. With this episode, Part One, "The Scene," abruptly ends. The function of this last section obviously consists of a kind of counterpoint to the previous sections containing typology and structural analysis. The reader should not fall victim to the illusion that the topic presented here deals with an object that can be grasped by means of simple, disciplined description.

Part Two, "The Society," returns again to the text's characteristic descriptive style. But here, too, the narrator once again takes up his testimony. With the sentence, "In the winter of 1938–39 my hand was frostbitten," Neurath introduces the story of the legendary Buchenwald prisoner Rudi Arndt. In the second section, the sociological analyses already implemented in the first section are intensified. Under headings such as "Power," "Cooperation," or "Conflict," central social "elements" are analyzed. The section on the "Moor Express," with its social peculiarities and its significance for the formation of an elite, becomes a "classic" case study involving the interpreting observer himself.

Many reports on concentration camps written by prisoners end with the camp being liberated or the narrator released, and the description of the concentration camps usually ends there as well. As a result, reports on the concentration camps become part of the tradition of the "descent into hell," a central literary genre in the West, exemplified by such representatives as the Orpheus myth or Dante's *Divina Comedia.*

Neurath's text refuses to adapt itself to this literary tradition, a fact that can be interpreted to mean that the author considered the discussion of the concentration camps unfinished, or unfinishable. At the end of the text, the question is posed, "Why don't they hit back?"—notice the use of the present tense. The text explores this question, which is both politically and morally explosive, in minute detail. It is here—not in questions of the camps' immeasurable anti-humanity or in the supposedly concomitant "breakdown of civilization"—that the text's central research interest lies. And the attempt is made to answer this question. During their transport into the camps, as a kind of "proto-initiation," the future prisoners are "broken," as it were, by means of methods of absolute terror. To bolster this argument, the text returns to an episode that was not described earlier in the transition from "The Prelude," the story of the arrest, to "The Scene," the structural description of the camp as such—whose absence at first formed an empty slot, a "minus device." Now Neurath describes the episode of the transport in all its drama. Completely without any claim to analysis or any attempt at sociological classification, what befell Neurath and his companions on April 1, 1938, and the following night is recounted with extreme urgency. Immediately after the description of what the author himself experienced, we are told that other groups and individuals suffered directly comparable experiences. The coda, which echoes the section's title ("Why Don't They Hit Back?"), yet again highlights the central (and unsolved) problem: "Why They Don't Hit Back." The text summarizes the arguments already put forward—and adds a new one: In those (rare) cases where the prisoners succeeded to some degree in making the conflict between themselves and the SS guards a personal conflict, there was some possibility of defense and resistance. The SS guards knew this as well, and therefore they systematically resisted personal involvement: "Don't you dare look at me!" (*"Schau mich ja nicht an!"*) The text posits this imperative as the general maxim of the SS.

* * *

The offer of a temporary position as a statistics lecturer at the Business School of the City College of New York finally decided Neurath's further career—but also, however, the fate of his book. Anyone whose intellectual portfolio demonstrates more than one specialty is in a fortunate position; for a long time, he does not have to decide what he would actually like to do. When someone like this is offered a job, other interests retreat into the background. Something similar may have taken place with Neurath in the years after 1943. While he probably continued to work on his book in the beginning, during the following years he seems to have become less and less interested in it. In 1946, when he was offered a position at Queens College, he accepted it, and for the next three decades, he taught statistics and sociology there. After Columbia University changed its requirements for submitting author's copies, Neurath officially handed in his dissertation once more in 1951 and received his Ph.D. He abandoned his plans to make his name as an author and sociologist with a book on his experiences in the camps. In later years he repeatedly and steadfastly declined all offers to publish his dissertation; he did so, however, in a laconic fashion that was otherwise untypical of him. During Neurath's lifetime, only Jack Kamerman succeeded in gaining permission to publish the dissertation's concluding chapter, which had been so important to Neurath himself, in an anthology of criminological studies.[57]

* * *

This is also an opportunity to offer a brief sketch of Neurath's further career as a sociologist. In 1946 Neurath was granted American citizenship, and in that same year, as mentioned above, he became a professor at Queens College, New York. In 1949 his position became a tenured one, and he carried out his duties until he became professor emeritus in 1977. During this period, Neurath also worked for a decade carrying out statistical analyses for an economic consulting firm. In addition, from 1949 until the end of the 1960s, he held the position of visiting professor in the Graduate Faculty of the New School for Social Research; here, too, he taught statistics and social scientific methods.

In spring 1946, Neurath succeeded in re-establishing contact with his uncle, who had survived the Nazi era in Graz. After his uncle's death, he maintained contact with his uncle's daughter, to whom he regularly sent reports on his life in the United States. A visit to Austria which Neurath had planned for 1947 had to be postponed briefly, but in the summer of 1949, he returned to Austria for the first time.

Neurath used his first sabbatical in 1955 to travel to India, not only to teach there as a Fulbright Professor, but also to carry out a large-scale

---

57. Kamerman 1998.

radio study in Bombay on behalf of UNESCO, which he then reported on in American journals. In the 1960s, he worked on two similar media research projects in India. In 1959 Neurath was given the opportunity to study for a year as a Fulbright Professor in Cologne, where he made the acquaintance of René König, who was working persistently to establish empirical social research in the Federal Republic of Germany. König invited Neurath to write an article for a handbook of empirical social research that he was editing. This article, which first appeared in 1962, was to make Neurath's name a lasting influence in German-language sociology. A short time later, Neurath brought out an expanded version as a book, which was published only in German. In 1961 he taught in Vienna for the first time, and he was of considerable help in establishing empirical social research and statistics there. At the same time, the foundation was laid for a long-term collaboration with Viennese sociology. During the 1960s, Neurath taught during several one- to two-month visiting professorships at the University of Vienna, and also at the newly founded Institute for Advanced Studies in 1965. In 1971–72 he took up another visiting professorship, and a decree of April 13, 1973 named him Honorary Professor of Sociology at the University of Vienna. In that same year Neurath was also negotiating for a regular professorship in Vienna. The negotiations, which had been going positively, "finally ran aground on a complication that lay beyond the influence of all of us [i.e., the faculty, the ministry, and Neurath]."[58] It has been impossible to trace exactly what these complications, which Neurath does not describe in more detail, might have been. His typically reserved description of his failure to obtain a regular appointment at Vienna, however, did nothing to hinder all manner of interpretations of the reasons and causes from circulating later on, although most of these do not stand up to closer scrutiny. The main topics of Neurath's lectures during his series of visiting professorships, which continued without a break into the 1990s, were statistical methods and problems in demographics. From 1978 on, Neurath set up the Paul Lazarsfeld Archive at the Department of Sociology at the University of Vienna, with which he not only honored this pioneer of social scientific methods—to whom he had also devoted a biographical study—but also raised the profile of the history of the social sciences in general.

Paul Neurath died on Sept. 3, 2001. To the end of his life he remained associated with the University of Vienna Department of

58. Neurath 1987, p. 536.

Sociology, maintaining his New York contacts at the same time. He left his papers to the Vienna Department.

* * *

The history of the examination of the German concentration camp system began even before the end of the Nazi system. Reports appeared before 1945, written above all by individual prisoners who had been released, offering eyewitness testimony.[59] Immediately after the end of the Nazi dictatorship, the documentary films of the camps' liberation shocked the audiences of the victorious nations; they probably also shocked those in the successor states of the German Reich.[60] In Vienna, an exhibition mounted in the city hall at the behest of former Dachau prisoner Viktor Matejka drew an immense number of visitors. Around the world, journalists reported on the camps, newspapers printed reports of survivors' experiences, and immediately the first analytical investigations of the Nazi terror appeared—for example, from the pen of Neurath's dissertation supervisor Theodore Abel.[61] In the journal *Jewish Social Studies* there appeared a series of articles on the concentration camps and the Shoah, among them Hannah Arendt's methodological article, "Social Science Techniques and the Study of Concentration Camps."[62] Jewish groups such as the Conference on Jewish Relations financed mass screenings of camp prisoners, although their results would be published only much later.[63] Among the early authors who wrote about the camps not merely as eyewitnesses, but also as researchers, there were a remarkably large number of Austrians. Eugen Kogon, who had been active in Vienna until his internment, undertook the first attempt to portray the camps immediately after his liberation from Buchenwald, doing so on behalf of the American occupation forces. His *Der SS-Staat (The Theory and Practice of Hell)*[64] quickly became a standard work. Kogon's report was based on his own experiences in Dachau and Buchenwald, and on reports from approximately 150 fellow prisoners who had been questioned after the liberation in 1945.[65] From his own experience, Viktor

---

59. See, however, Koestler ([1945] 1985).
60. *Die Todesmühlen/Death Mills,* Dir. Hanuš Burger, Germany/USA, 1945.
61. Abel 1945 and Abel 1951.
62. Arendt 1950.
63. Goldstein, Lukoff and Strauss 1991.
64. Kogon ([1946] 1950).
65. Hackett 1995.

Frankl attempted to write as a psychologist about his internment in Auschwitz.[66] Benedikt Kautsky, who had survived Dachau, Buchenwald, and Auschwitz, wrote his sociological study *Teufel und Verdammte* (*Devils and Damned*) during his recuperation in Switzerland.[67] In the first trials of war criminals, eyewitness statements regarding the camps played a prominent role. Very soon, however, interest in the camps was to subside; the new geopolitical configuration of the Cold War was not least responsible for this development.[68] From the end of the 1940s until the prosecution of Adolf Eichmann in Jerusalem and the German Auschwitz trials of the early 1960s, it seemed that reports and descriptions from the concentration camps provoked the German public to deliberate obliviousness, skepticism, incredulous head-shaking, relativizing calculations of other alleged victims, and even determined resistance. People wanted to be left in peace, and policy and public opinion did nothing to oppose this. Reinforced and underpinned by the Cold War, in subsequent years hardly any aspect of these attitudes changed.[69]

On the other hand, as a locus of oppression, tragedy, forced labor, and annihilation from the very beginning of the Nazi system of rule, the concentration camps were not only a consistent component of the exercise of power, but they were also in many respects completely visible to the public.[70] The borders of the terror society did not end at the gates and barbed-wire barriers of the concentration camps.[71] As Hannah Arendt emphasized in an early essay on the terror society, however, "there are no parallels to life *in* concentration camps."[72]

Just as the regimes, the structures, and the functions of the individual camps changed in the course of the Nazi government, so too the historical analysis of the camps has gone through cycles of varying interest. This development, and the forms of remembering the concentration camps, will be briefly sketched in the following section. This description can by no means replace a systematic, detailed, and theoretically comprehensive definition of the preliminary stages, the history, the various time periods, and the variations in the willingness to reflect on the

---

66. Frankl ([1946] 1959).
67. Kautsky 1946, cf. also: Poller ([1946] 1961); Rousset 1946.
68. Cf. Novick 1999.
69. Klüger ([1992] 2001).
70. Milton 1998.
71. Sofsky 1996, p. 7.
72. Arendt 1948, p. 314.

Nazi concentration camps.[73] The references given to the still growing literature can only indicate a general direction.

Neurath's insider views of Dachau and Buchenwald in the years 1938 and 1939 make the social reality of the camps comprehensible to us from the prisoners' perspective. The *Society of Terror* allows us a look into the suffering of the prisoners, into their reduced social cosmos, into the social stratification of the prisoners' society, and also into the brutal behavior of the culprits and their apparatus of power and oppression.

Neurath's dissertation was written before the gruesome photos taken during the liberation of the camps in 1945, for example in Bergen-Belsen, had become public knowledge. Neurath's view is therefore not yet marked by those images that later established the apparently immutable structures of memories of fellow prisoners and of historians. The images of the Nazi regime's concentration camps in the consciousness of those who have come after are strongly stylized; they are particularly and quite rightly permeated by the horror of the extermination camps.[74]

There are remarkable differences, however, in the work of remembrance.[75] Thus, in the German Democratic Republic there was less interest in mountains of corpses than there was in (Communist) resistance. The subjective experiences of the camps' inmates were disregarded. Their place was taken by the "antifascist legend [of resistance], which [in contradistinction to the Federal Republic] became the founding myth of the GDR."[76] Buchenwald became in the GDR a central locus and symbolic nucleus of the heroizing strategy for coming to terms with the past.[77]

The concentration camp system developed through a series of intermediate steps to the extermination camps. The prisoners' camp experiences were formed and decisively molded by the time and the circumstances of their arrest, by their own personalities, by the various prisoner groups to which they belonged, by the conditions in the respective camps, by the functions of the various camps, and by the political developments outside, to which the prisoners could react, and had to react, differently each time. For example in the beginning, Dachau was above all a place for the internment of political opponents, whom the Nazis attempted to debilitate and then annihilate by means of pointless work. Later prisoners were annihilated, for instance in Mauthausen or Mittelbau-Dora, by

---

73. Cf. e.g., Pollak 1988; Pollak 1990; Novick 1999.
74. Brink 1998; Knoch 2001.
75. See Herf 1997.
76. Niethammer 1994, p. 16.
77. See also Apitz ([1958] 1960).

means of "productive" labor. Both forms of camp, however, had in common the fact that work was a crucial instrument of the society of terror.

The first camps were established in March 1933, immediately after the Reichstag fire; they formed part of a brutal terrorizing strategy for seizing and maintaining power. At first it was almost exclusively political opponents who were incarcerated. The years 1936 and 1937 were a turning point in the development of the concentration camps. The Nuremberg race laws came into effect in mid-September 1935. In addition to the terrorizing strategy aimed at opponents, there was now a strategy of racial terror. New enemies were identified, for example the Jehovah's Witnesses. Even more momentous were the *categorical* classifications, which from this point on were systematically enforced. In this development, one can read the transition from a political preventive measure to a racist "general preventive measure" by the Nazi regime.[78] This period also saw the decision to implement a camp system ruled by the SS alone.[79] In 1938 and 1939 additional political prisoners from Austria and the Sudetenland arrived. In November 1938, immediately following the pogrom, 30,000 Jews were taken into the concentration camps. Neurath handles this phase of the concentration camps' development with a keen eye for detail. At the beginning of the war, there were 21,000 prisoners in the newly established and/or expanded concentration camps Dachau, Buchenwald, Sachsenhausen, Flossenbürg, Mauthausen, and Ravensbrück. In 1941 and 1942 came the establishment of the actual death camps, particularly Birkenau, Majdanek, and Auschwitz; several of these camps "functioned" until they were liberated by the Red Army.

Despite the development of the concentration camps as outlined here, it is possible to presume a certain continuity in the camps' structure that justifies speaking generally of a system of terror in the camps. The precursors of the concentration camps Dachau and Buchenwald were camps for prisoners under "preventive detention," a concept that appears for the first time in Germany in a Prussian law of 1848. Thus, one could say that the Nazis could "fall back on the considerable experience that previous governments had accumulated with preventive detention and concentration camps."[80]

---

78. Herbert 1998.

79. See Tuchel 1998; Orth 1999.

80. Drobisch and Weiland 1993, p. 21. See also Tuchel 1991, Tuchel 1998, and Drobisch 1996.

Roughly subdivided, two *written* genres of concentration camp descriptions can be distinguished: the pure memoirs of former prisoners, and observations on a scientific basis of the system of terror in the camps. This categorical division, however, does not rule out the existence of especially valuable, sensitive, and harrowing observations, that unite the elements of both memoirs and scientifically oriented perspectives. Among these above all are Paul Neurath's study presented here, along with Kogon's *SS-Staat,* Ernst Federn's essay "Terror as a System," Viktor Frankl's *Ein Psychologe erlebt das Konzentrationslager (A Psychologist Survives the Concentration Camp)*, Bettelheim's above-mentioned study, "Individual and Mass Behavior in Extreme Situations," and *Prisoners of Fear* by the Viennese physician Ella Lingens, who had been educated in the social sciences.[81] The survivors' memoirs are among the most important testimonies.[82]

In the last few decades, the scope of all sorts of written memoirs of concentration camp internment during the various phases of development of the Nazi terror has continued to grow. Kogon calls his work not a history of the German concentration camps, but rather "mainly a sociological work."[83] Thus it is justifiable to understand Kogon's and Neurath's work as both eyewitness reports and "factual reports," taking no notice of the boundaries between memoir and scientifically oriented description.

A further phase in the memoir literature began around the time of the Eichmann trial, with the notes of Primo Levi, Jean Améry, and later the memoirs—particularly significant as regards Buchenwald—of Jorge Semprun.[84] The scientific investigation of the concentration camps made little progress over decades. The "Dilemma of Emotionality and Objectivity" in dealing with the Nazi past, and particularly the Holocaust,[85] is also a feature of the scientific studies of the concentration camps in the postwar period, which will be discussed briefly here. Only in the most recent period is it no longer a question of researchers whose foreknowledge and scientific attitude are decisively marked by immediate experiences with and involvement in the Nazi regime.

Among the most influential of the scientifically oriented memoirs of the Nazis' exercise of power are those of Bruno Bettelheim. Bettelheim

---

81. Kogon 1946; Federn 1946; Frankl ([1946] 1959); Bettelheim 1943; Lingens 1948.
82. See also Levi ([1986] 1989); Young 1988; however, cf. also Hilberg 2001.
83. Kogon ([1946] 1950).
84. Levi ([1958] 1959); Améry ([1980] 1966); Semprun 1982 and 1997.
85. See Arendt 1948.

justifies his approach and perspective for explicating his own experiences of concentration camp internment by emphasizing that the camps' total "order" cannot be understood if one only reports on the atrocities and the fate of individual prisoners. "It is the sociological significance of the camps that makes them an important example of the essence of the despotic and mass state."[86] Bettelheim's general conclusions about the prisoners' way of life in concentration camps was particularly poignantly expressed in his formulation that the prisoners' adjustment to the exceptional situation of the camp frequently created a personality structure that "was ready and willing to assimilate the values and behavior of the SS."[87] This interpretation found a wide audience.[88]

The scientifically oriented perspective makes the atrocities' and the terror's uniqueness an exemplar of the function and consequences of the rule of oppressive mass society by means of a massive intervention in the personality of the individual. The prisoners themselves were to become part of an obedient mass. To the outside world, the prisoners' humiliation was meant to serve as a deterrent and suppress any resistance. The camps themselves, from this viewpoint, became a kind of experimental apparatus, a laboratory "in which one researched by what means the . . . specified goals could best be reached."[89] Or more generally formulated, the camp system is treated as a scientific investigation of how to organize a politically successful regime by altering the personalities of individuals so that they become "useful subjects of the total state."[90]

The fate of the prisoners thus becomes raw data.[91] The force of the terror fades, as does the suffering occasioned by the extreme exceptional situation. Statistics regarding the number of prisoners, or of the dead, tell us little about the practice of everyday terror, suffering, humiliation, and torment, or about the manner of killing and dying in the concentration camps. To be sure, Bettelheim self-reflexively tells us that it was not distanced curiosity that induced him to observe and question his fellow prisoners, but rather his instinct for self-preservation.[92] Among the early scientific studies on the society of terror must also be counted

---

86. Bettelheim 1960, p. 119. Cf. Bettelheim 1943 and 1979.
87. Bettelheim 1960, p. 186.
88. See Fleck and Müller 1997, pp. 22–28.
89. Bettelheim 1960, p. 121.
90. Bettelheim 1960, p. 122; cf. Sutton 1996, pp. 133–182.
91. See Klüger 1996, pp. 35–36.
92. Bettelheim 1960, p. 123.

the American researchers who, as soldiers, had experience with the concentration camp prisoners in the immediate post-war period.[93]

Among the first important systematic scientific studies to deal with the Nazi reign of terror from a biographical distance, apart from contemporary essays and books, were the research studies of the sociologist Wolfgang Sofsky in the 1990s, as well as the more recent work of the historian Karin Orth on the political history of the concentration camps' organization. An anthology by Ulrich Herbert, Karin Orth, and Christoph Dieckmann contains studies by a large number of German researchers who concern themselves with various problems in concentration camp research.[94]

* * *

Paul Neurath's dissertation remained unpublished, was long unknown to researchers, and was rediscovered only recently.[95] Since then, however, it has been cited with increasing frequency,[96] and lately it has been utilized extensively.[97] With the present belated publication, we hope to make Neurath's significant contribution to the history of the camps even more widely known.

In conclusion, we would like to draw attention to the principles of this edition. The basis of the text is the 1943 dissertation, in the version submitted in 1951 (to which Neurath had made minor corrections up to at least 1945). We added the "Addendum" prepared by Neurath in the course of his examinations in 1943; this was not originally a part of the dissertation. The text was essentially left unaltered, except for errors regarding minor details such as isolated misspellings of names, which, if we were able to recognize them, were silently corrected.

Our particular gratitude goes to Margarete Neurath, Paul Neurath's widow, in Vienna. She made the publication of the thesis possible. We thank Hans Benninghaus, Bernd Florath, Albert Knoll, Reinhold Knoll, Volker Meja, Irene Müller, Birgitta Nedelmann, Reinhard Rürup, Harry Stein, and Hermann Strasser for their friendly advice and critical reading of earlier versions of this Afterword. Both editors particularly wish to express their gratitude to Albert Müller for the part he played in the

93. E.g., Bloch 1947.
94. Sofsky 1990, 1993, and 1997; Orth 1999; Herbert, Orth, and Dieckmann 1998.
95. Pingel 1978; Fleck and Müller 1997.
96. E.g., Daxelmüller 1998.
97. Kuschey 2003.

genesis of the present volume. Without his help the present Afterword would have been somewhat poorer in content, since it is due to him that documents hidden among Paul Neurath's personal effects were found and files in the possession of the University of Vienna were brought to light. We wish to thank Anton Amann of the Department of Sociology at the University of Vienna for generously granting us access to Paul Neurath's still unorganized unpublished documents; Thomas Maisel for his support of our research in the Archives of the University of Vienna; and Heinz Achtsnit, Director of the Dean's Office of the Faculty of Economics and Computer Science of the university, for his support in finding Paul Neurath's personnel file and other materials. Our further thanks to Harriet Zuckerman for access to the unpublished documents of Robert K. Merton, Jack Kamerman for his assistance with the research in New York, Bernard R. Crystal of the Rare Book and Manuscript Libary at Columbia University, and Abby M. Lester of the Columbia University Archives-Columbiana Library.

The publication was kindly supported by the Paul Lazarsfeld Society (Germany) and the National Fund of the Republic of Austria for Victims of National Socialism. We thank these organizations for their assistance.

Bibliography

Abel, Theodore F. (1938), *Why Hitler Came into Power: An Answer Based on the Original Life Stories of Six Hundred of His Followers*. New York: Prentice-Hall.

Abel, Theodore F. (1945), "Is a Psychiatric Interpretation of the German Enigma Necessary?" *American Sociological Review* 10 (4): 457–464.

Abel, Theodore F. (1951), "The Sociology of Concentration Camps," *Social Forces* 30 (2): 150–155.

Abel, Theodore F. (2001), *The Columbia Circle of Scholars: Selections from the Journal (1830–1957)*, ed. Elzbieta Halas. Frankfurt am Main, New York: P. Lang.

Améry, Jean ([1966] 1980), *At the Mind's Limits: Contemplations by a Survivor on Auschwitz and Its Realities*, trans. Sidney Rosenfeld and Stella P. Rosenfeld. Bloomington: Indiana University Press.

Anderson, Nels (1923), *The Hobo: The Sociology of the Homeless Man*. Chicago: University of Chicago Press.

Apitz, Bruno ([1958] 1960), *Naked among Wolves*, trans. Edith Anderson. Berlin: Seven Seas Publishers.

Arendt, Hannah (1948), "Konzentrationslager," *Die Wandlung* 3: 309–330.

Arendt, Hannah (1950), "Social Science Techniques and the Study of Concentration Camps," *Jewish Social Studies* 12 (1): 49–64.

Bettelheim, Bruno (1943), "Individual and Mass Behavior in Extreme Situations," *Journal of Abnormal and Social Psychology* 38: 417–452.

Bettelheim, Bruno (1960), *The Informed Heart: Autonomy in a Mass Age*. Glencoe, IL: Free Press.

Bettelheim, Bruno (1979), *Surviving, and Other Essays*. New York: Knopf.

Bloch, Herbert A. (1947), "The Personality of Inmates of Concentration Camps," *American Journal of Sociology* 52: 335–341.

Blumer, Herbert (1969), *Symbolic Interactionism: Perspective and Method.* Englewood Cliffs, NJ: Prentice-Hall.

Brink, Cornelia (1998), *Ikonen der Vernichtung. Öffentlicher Gebrauch von Fotografien aus nationalsozialistischen Konzentrationslagern nach 1945.* Berlin: Akademie Verlag.

Cartwright, Nancy, Jordi Cat, Lola Fleck, and Thomas E. Uebel (1996), *Otto Neurath: Philosophy between Science and Politics.* Cambridge: Cambridge University Press.

Clemmer, Donald (1940), *The Prison Community.* Boston: Christopher Publishing House.

Daxelmüller, Christoph (1998), "Kulturelle Formen und Aktivitäten als Teil der Überlebens- und Vernichtungsstrategie in den Konzentrationslagern," in Ulrich Herbert, Karin Orth, and Christoph Dieckmann, eds., *Die nationalsozialistischen Konzentrationslager.* Göttingen: Wallstein, 983–1005.

Dollard, John (1935), *Criteria for the Life History.* New Haven: Yale University Press (published for the Institute of Human Relations).

Drobisch, Klaus (1996), "Frühe Konzentrationslager," in Karl Giebeler, Thomas Lutz, and Silvester Lechner, eds., *Die frühen Konzentrationslager in Deutschland. Austausch zum Forschungsgegenstand und zur pädagogischen Praxis in Gedenkstätten.* Bad Boll, 41–60.

Drobisch, Klaus, and Günther Wieland (1993), *System der NS-Konzentrationslager 1933–1939.* Berlin: Akademie Verlag.

Federn, Ernst (1948), "Terror as a System: The Concentration Camps," *Psychiatric Quarterly Supplements* 22: 52–58.

Fleck, Christian, and Albert Müller (1997), "Bruno Bettelheim and the Concentration Camps," *Journal of the History of the Behavioral Sciences* 33: 1–37.

Frankl, Victor E. ([1946] 1959), *From Death-camp to Existentialism: A Psychiatrist's Path to a New Therapy,* trans. Ilse Lasch. Boston: Beacon Press.

Genette, Gérard (1997), *Paratexts: Thresholds of Interpretation,* trans. Jane E. Lewin. Cambridge: Cambridge University Press.

Goldstein, Jacob, Irving F. Lukoff, and Herbert A. Strauss (1991), *Individuelles und kollektives Verhalten in Nazi-Konzentrationslagern.* Frankfurt am Main: Campus.

Gottschalk, Louis R., Clyde Kluckhohn, and Robert C. Angell (1945), *The Use of Personal Documents in History, Anthropology, and Sociology.* New York: Social Science Research Council.

Hackett, David A. (1995), *The Buchenwald Report,* translated, edited, and with an introduction by David A. Hackett. Boulder: Westview Press.

Haller, Rudolf (1985), "Der erste Wiener Kreis," *Erkenntnis: An International Journal of Analytic Philosophy* 22: 341–58.

Haller, Rudolf (1993), *Neopositivismus*. Darmstadt: Wissenschaftliche Buchgesellschaft.

Hartmann, Frank, and Erwin K. Bauer (2002), *Bildersprache. Otto Neurath Visualisierungen*. Vienna: WUV.

Heilig, Bruno (1941), *Men Crucified*. London: Eyre & Spottiswoode.

Herbert, Ulrich (1998), "Von der Gegnerbekämpfung zur 'rassistischen Generalprävention'. 'Schutzhaft' und Konzentrationslager in der Konzeption der Gestapo-Führung 1933–1939," in Ulrich Herbert, Karin Orth, and Christoph Dieckmann, eds., *Die nationalsozialistischen Konzentrationslager*. Göttingen: Wallstein, 60–86.

Herbert, Ulrich, Karin Orth, and Christoph Dieckmann, eds. (1998), *Die nationalsozialistischen Konzentrationslager. Zwei Bände*. Göttingen: Wallstein.

Herf, Jeffrey (1997), *Divided Memory: The Nazi Past in the Two Germanys*. Cambridge, MA: Harvard University Press.

Hinrichs, Klaus (pseud. Karl August Wittfogel) (1936), *Staatliches Konzentrationslager VII. Eine "Erziehungsanstalt" im Dritten Reich*. London: Malik-Verlag.

Hilberg, Raul (2001), *Sources of Holocaust Research: An Analysis*. Chicago: Ivan R. Dee.

Kamerman, Jack B., ed. (1998), *Negotiating Responsibility in the Criminal Justice System*. Carbondale, IL: Southern Illinois University Press.

Karst, Georg M. (pseud.) (1942), *The Beasts of the Earth*, trans. Emil Lengyel. New York: A. Unger.

Kautsky, Benedikt (1946), *Teufel und Verdammte. Erfahrungen und Erkenntnisse aus sieben Jahren in deutschen Konzentrationslagern*. Zürich: Büchergilde Gutenberg.

Klüger, Ruth ([1992] 2001), *Still Alive: A Holocaust Girlhood Remembered*. New York: Feminist Press at the City University of New York.

Klüger, Ruth (1996), *Von hoher und niedriger Literatur*. Göttingen: Wallstein.

Knoch, Habbo (2001), *Die Tat als Bild. Fotografien des Holocaust in der deutschen Erinnerungskultur*. Hamburg: Hamburger Edition.

Koestler, Arthur (1945), "On Disbelieving Atrocities," in *The Yogi and the Commissar and Other Essays*. New York: MacMillan Company, 88–93.

Kogon, Eugen ([1946] 1950) *The Theory and Practice of Hell: The German Concentration Camps and the System Behind Them*, trans. Heinz Norden. New York: Farrar, Straus.

Kuschey, Bernhard (2003), *Die Ausnahme des Überlebens. Ernst und Hilde Federn. Zwei Bände*. Giessen: Psychosozial-Verlag.

Levi, Primo ([1958] 1959), *If This Is a Man*, trans. Stuart Woolf. New York: Orion Press.

Levi, Primo ([1986] 1989), *The Drowned and the Saved*, trans. Raymond Rosenthal. London: Abacus.

Lingens, Ella (1948), *Prisoners of Fear.* London: Gollancz.

MacIver, Robert M. (1968), *As a Tale That Is Told: The Autobiography of R. M. MacIver.* Chicago: University of Chicago Press.

Marcuse, Harold (2001), *Legacies of Dachau: The Uses and Abuses of a Concentration Camp, 1933–2001.* Cambridge: Cambridge University Press.

Milton, Sybil (1998), "Die Konzentrationslager der dreissiger Jahre im Bild der in- und ausländischen Presse," in Ulrich Herbert, Karin Orth, and Christoph Dieckmann, eds., *Die nationalsozialistischen Konzentrationslager.* Zwei Bände. Göttingen: Wallstein, 111–134.

Neurath, Paul (1982), "Otto Neurath und die Soziologie," *Grazer Philosophische Studien* 16/17: 223–40.

Neurath, Paul (1987), "Wissenschaftliche Emigration und Remigration," in Friedrich Stadler, ed., *Vertriebene Vernunft I: Emigration und Exil österreichischer Wissenschaft 1930–1940.* Vienna: Jugend & Volk, 513–37.

Neurath, Paul (1989), *Interview of July 12, 1989 in Vienna,* interviewers: Christian Fleck and Albert Müller. Recording and transcript in the Archive for the History of Sociology in Austria, Graz.

Niethammer, Lutz, ed. (1994), *Der 'gesäuberte' Antifaschismus. Die SED und die roten Kapos von Buchenwald. Dokumente.* Berlin: Akademie Verlag.

Novick, Peter (1999), *The Holocaust in American Life.* Boston: Houghton Mifflin.

Orth, Karin (1999), *Das System der nationalsozialistischen Konzentrationslager. Eine politische Organisationsgeschichte.* Hamburg: Hamburger Edition.

Paul, Sigrid (1979), *Begegnungen. Zur Geschichte persönlicher Dokumente in Ethnologie, Soziologie und Psychologie.* Hohenschäftlarn: Renner.

Platt, Jennifer (1996), *A History of Sociological Research Methods in America 1920–1960.* Cambridge: Cambridge University Press.

Pingel, Falk (1978), *Häftlinge unter SS-Herrschaft. Widerstand, Selbstbehauptung und Vernichtung im Konzentrationslager.* Hamburg: Hoffmann und Campe.

Pollak, Michael ([1985] 1988), *Die Grenzen des Sagbaren. Lebensgeschichten von KZ-Überlebenden als Augenzeugenberichte und als Identitätsarbeit,* trans. Hella Beister. Frankfurt am Main: Campus.

Pollak, Michael (1990), *L'Expérience concentrationnaire. Essais sur le maintien de l'identité sociale.* Paris: Métailié.

Poller, Walter ([1946] 1961), *Medical Block, Buchenwald: The Personal Testimony of Inmate 996, Block 36.* London: Souvenir Press.

Rousset, David (1946), *L'univers concentrationnaire.* Paris: Éditions du Pavois.

Schapire, Anna (1902), "Eine Antwort von Anna Schapire," *Dokumente der Frauen,* 40–45.

Scheu, Friedrich (1985), *Ein Band der Freundschaft: Schwarzwald-Kreis und die Entstehung der Vereinigung Sozialistischer Mittelschüler.* Vienna: Böhlau.

Schwarz, Gudrun (1990), *Die nationalsozialistischen Lager*. Frankfurt am Main: Campus.

Semprun, Jorge (1982), *What a Beautiful Sunday!* trans. Alan Sheridan. San Diego: Harcourt Brace Jovanovich.

Semprun, Jorge (1997), *Literature or Life,* trans. Linda Coverdale. New York: Viking.

Shaw, Clifford R. (1930), *The Jack-Roller: A Delinquent Boy's Own Story*. Chicago: University of Chicago Press.

Sofsky, Wolfgang (1990), "Absolute Macht. Zur Soziologie des Konzentrationslagers," *Leviathan* 18: 518–535.

Sofsky, Wolfgang (1993), "Die Perfektion der Vernichtung," *Neue Rundschau* 104: 152–158.

Sofsky, Wolfgang (1996), "Eugen Kogons 'SS-Staat' und die Perspektive der KZ-Forschung," *Polis* 15: 2–8.

Sofsky, Wolfgang ([1993] 1997), *The Order of Terror: The Concentration Camp,* trans. William Templer. Princeton: Princeton University Press.

Stadler, Friedrich, ed. (1982), *Arbeiterbildung in der Zwischenkriegszeit Otto Neurath, Gerd Arntz*. Vienna: Löcker.

Stein, Harry (1998), "Funktionswandel des Konzentrationslagers Buchenwald im Spiegel der Lagerstatistiken," in Ulrich Herbert, Karin Orth, and Christoph Dieckmann, eds., *Die nationalsozialistischen Konzentrationslager*. Göttingen: Wallstein, 167–192.

Sutton, Nina (1996), *Bettelheim: A Life and a Legacy*. Boulder, CO: Westview Press.

Tuchel, Johannes (1998), "Planung und Realität des Systems der Konzentrationslager 1934–1938, in Ulrich Herbert, Karin Orth, and Christoph Dieckmann, eds., *Die nationalsozialistischen Konzentrationslager*. Zwei Bände. Göttingen: Wallstein, 43–59.

Tuchel, Johannes (1991), *Konzentrationslager: Organisationsgeschichte und Funktion der 'Inspektion der Konzentrationslager' 1934–1938*. Boppard: Boldt.

Tuchel, Johannes (1994), "Die Kommandanten des Konzentrationslagers Dachau," *Dachauer Hefte* 10: 69–90.

Wallner, Peter (1941), *By Order of the Gestapo: A Record of Life in Dachau and Buchenwald Concentration Camps,* trans. Lawrence Wolfe. London: J. Murray.

Whyte, William Foote (1943), *Street Corner Society: The Social Structure of an Italian Slum*. Chicago: University of Chicago Press.

Winkler, Ernst (pseud.) (1942), *Four Years of Nazi Torture*. New York: D. Appleton-Century.

Young, James E. (1988), *Writing and Rewriting the Holocaust: Narrative and the Consequences of Interpretation*. Bloomington: Indiana University Press.

About the Author and Editors

Paul Martin Neurath had just completed his doctorate in law at the University of Vienna when Austria was taken over by Nazi Germany in 1938. Shortly afterwards, Neurath was arrested, and from April 1, 1938, to May 27, 1939, he was a Jewish political prisoner in the concentration camps Dachau and Buchenwald. He owed his survival to a temporary Nazi policy allowing the release of prisoners who were willing to go into exile, and to the help of friends on the outside who helped him obtain a visa. He fled to Sweden before coming to the United States in 1941. By 1943, he had completed *The Society of Terror,* based on his experiences in Dachau and Buchenwald, and submitted it as a dissertation at Columbia University. After graduation, he embarked on a long career teaching sociology and statistics at universities in the United States and later in Vienna, until his death in September 2001.

Christian Fleck is Professor of Sociology at the University of Graz in Austria, where he is also director of the Archive for the History of Sociology in Austria. He has published on the history and sociology of the social sciences, especially about refugee scholars of the Nazi era. In addition he is the series editor of the Library of Emigre Social Scientists.

Nico Stehr is Karl Mannheim Professor of Cultural Studies at the Zeppelin University, Friedrichshafen, Germany, and Fellow of the Center for Advanced Cultural Studies, Essen, Germany. He is the editor of the *Canadian Journal of Sociology.* His recent books include *Biotechnology: Between Commerce and Civil Society* (Transaction Books, 2004),

Knowledge (with Reiner Grundmann) (Routledge, 2005), and *Knowledge Politics: Governing the Consequences of Science and Technology* (Paradigm Publishers, 2005).